Praise and Influential Messages...

For *Meaning-Centered Therapy Manual: Logotherapy & Existential Analysis Brief Therapy Protocol for Group & Individual Sessions ~ 8 Session Format ~*

"What is Logotherapy, and what relevance does it have for psychotherapy and everyday life? In this compact and yet surprisingly comprehensive manual, Dezelic and Ghanoum address this question in a manner that is at the same time elegantly theoretical and strikingly practical, translating abstract principles into "news you can use" as a meaning-oriented psychotherapist— or, for that matter, as a potential reader seeking to live more deeply and authentically. Verbal learners will find in these pages a lucid summary of the key concepts and methods of Frankl's approach and its contemporary extensions, and visual learners will find original conceptual pictographs that relate these same concepts graphically in a way that promotes their integration. Part primer, part lesson plan, and part slide show, this well-organized manual of existential precepts and practices delivers."

Robert A. Neimeyer, PhD
Professor, Department of Psychology, *University of Memphis, TN*
Editor, ***Death Studies***
Editor, ***Journal of Constructivist Psychology***
Author of ***Grief and the Expressive Arts: Practices for Creating Meaning; Meaning Reconstruction & the Experience of Loss; Lessons of Loss: A Guide to Coping; Techniques of Grief Therapy: Creative Practices for Counseling the Bereaved;*** and several other titles

"This is a timely, important and welcomed addition to the growing literature on the application and clinical practice of Logotherapy and Existential Analysis – a book which, no doubt, will be especially useful for practitioners in their everyday dealings with patients and clients across clinical settings. This manual and toolbox is a treasure-house of life-changing, comforting and activating methods for the helping professions."

Alexander Batthyany, PhD
Professor, *University of Vienna,* and Dept. of Psychiatry, *Vienna Medical School*
Chair, Science and Research Department, *Viktor Frankl Institute, Vienna, Austria*
Principle Editor, ***Collected Works of Viktor Frankl***
Author of ***Viktor E. Frankl, The Feeling of Meaninglessness: A Challenge to Psychotherapy and Philosophy;***
Co-Author of ***Empirical Research on Logotherapy and Meaning-Oriented Psychotherapy: An Annotated Bibliography; Existential Psychotherapy of Meaning: Handbook of Logotherapy and Existential Analysis;*** and several other titles

"Everything can be manualized. Even a 'search for meaning.' But not meaning itself, of course! Meaning – as a freely chosen expression of our cosmic tri-partite essence – is a moment-specific existential accomplishment available to each and every one of us. The two Floridian-based psychotherapists, Marie Dezelic and Gabriel Ghanoum, with their 8-session Logotherapy protocol, have created the equivalent of the Cape Canaveral launching pad into the orbit of meaning – a manualized clinical path for breaking away from the gravity pull of circumstance and meaninglessness."

Pavel Somov, PhD
Licensed Psychologist
Author of ***Choice Awareness Training: Logotherapy and Mindfulness Training for Treatment of Addictions***; ***The Lotus Effect: Shedding Suffering and Rediscovering Your Essential Self; Eating the Moment;*** and several other titles
www.eatingthemoment.com

"The universe does not provide a formula for living the gift of a deep and meaningful life, but it does present spiritual landmarks. Drs. Dezelic and Ghanoum alchemize biological inclinations, existential and spiritual concepts, within the realities of lives being lived in our personal-social worlds of vulnerabilities, exploration and potential for transformation. *Meaning-Centered Therapy Manual: Logotherapy & Existential Analysis Brief Therapy Protocol for Group & Individual Sessions* is one of very few practical, therapeutic bridges that actively engages all of the senses, along with rational and irrational thought, toward an integration of body and soul that would make Viktor Frankl proud to see his concepts of love, healing and redemption realized. The 8 outlined sessions activate creative processes that make the information accessible to both novice and experienced clinicians in individual and group therapeutic settings. The strategic use of Conceptual Pictographs is especially innovative, powerful, engaging, and is evidence-based. Although the experience Drs. Dezelic and Ghanoum offer is especially relevant to people confronting life-crises, their message of courage and hope is a gift to all of us."

Matthew J. Loscalzo, LCSW
Liliane Elkins Professor in Supportive Care Programs,
Administrative Director, Sheri & Les Biller Patient and Family Resource Center,
Executive Director, Department of Supportive Care Medicine,
Professor, Department of Population Sciences,
City of Hope, Duarte, CA
Co-Author of ***Psycho-Oncology, 3rd Ed.;*** and ***For the Women We Love: A Breast Cancer Action Plan and Caregiver's Guide for Men***

"Marie Dezelic and Gabriel Ghanoum are two of the greatest expositors of Viktor Frankl's work. Their *Meaning-Centered Therapy Manual: Logotherapy & Existential Analysis Brief Therapy Protocol for Group & Individual Sessions* represents a remarkably clear, concise, and comprehensive view of Logotherapy. Not only do they accomplish the herculean feat of such an overview, but go farther to delineate an eight-session protocol that is quite easy to understand.

The application of this manual is far-reaching, as all forms of psychological distress essentially arise out of crises of personal meaning, purpose, and direction. Viktor Frankl's work taps into, among other things, the ancient Greek wisdom tradition, which held that every individual has a unique character (*ethos*) and calling, logic, purpose (*logos*). Within these pages lie the keys for clinicians to aid clients in unlocking the porthole, not only overcoming distressing states of mind, but to gain entry into their unique purpose in life."

Brent Potter, PhD
Author of ***Elements of Self-Destruction;***
Elements of Reparation: Truth, Faith, & Transformation
in the Works of Heidegger, Bion & Beyond; and
Co-Author of ***Borderline Personality Disorder:***
New Perspectives on a Stigmatizing and Overused Diagnosis

"This highly creative ***Meaning-Centered Therapy Manual*** by Marie S. Dezelic, PhD, and Gabriel Ghanoum, PsyD, is an extraordinary way to present Logotherapy & Existential Analysis for group and individual sessions. A *Foreword* by Dr. William Breitbart, Psychiatrist and Chairman of the Department of Psychiatry and Behavioral Science at Memorial Sloan Kettering Cancer Center in New York City, introduces the manual, along with an Editor's Note from Dr. Ann-Marie Neale, Education Consultant & Faculty Member at the Viktor Frankl Institute of Logotherapy in Abilene, Texas, and Karen Horney Professor of Counseling and Psychology at the Graduate Theological Foundation.

This *Meaning-Centered Therapy Manual* has a well-organized and easy to follow format divided into the following sections:

I: Gives a Logotherapy overview of the philosophy, theory & clinical applications.

II: Features a "Brief Therapy Protocol" in an 8 session format, summarized by Conceptual Pictographs—Client Handouts.

III: Conclusion, activates possibilities through Logotherapy.

An *Epilogue* by Lexie Brockway Potamkin, author of *What is Death; What is Love; What is Peace; What is Spirit;* and *What is Laughter* book series, addresses the concluding benefits of this manual. An Appendix is also featured, Conceptual Pictographs—Client Handouts in black-and-white for photocopying are provided, as well as a *Glossary* to make it easy to follow and understand the nomenclature of Logotherapy and Existential Analysis.

It can readily be seen that this ***Meaning-Centered Therapy Manual*** is a gem that will be helpful to all who are looking for comprehensible tools and handouts to use in diverse settings, such as: Existential Exploration and Personal Growth, Therapeutic Clinical Settings, as well as Spiritual Growth groups. Congratulations!"

Ann V. Graber, PhD, DMin
Diplomate in Logotherapy
Director of the Graduate Center for Pastoral Logotherapy,
Graduate Theological Foundation
Author of ***Viktor Frankl's Logotherapy: Meaning-Centered Counseling;*** and
The Journey Home: Preparing for Life's Ultimate Adventure

"Dezelic and Ghanoum have made a creative leap by blending Viktor Frankl's comprehensive psychological method with other thoughtful clinical approaches to produce a contemporary psychoeducational tool. As Frankl's Logotherapy moves into the future, it is encouraging to see it engage, inform, and enhance the growing body of practical, clinical tools designed to help in the search for and discovery of meaning. As meaning becomes increasingly recognized as a vital factor in well-being and recovery, Dezelic and Ghanoum's new book makes a significant contribution to this much needed practice."

Marshall H. Lewis, PhD
Diplomate in Logotherapy
Co-Editor, ***International Forum for Logotherapy***
Faculty Member and Member of the International Board of Directors,
Viktor Frankl Institute of Logotherapy, Abilene, TX
Accredited Member and Science Committee Member,
International Association of Logotherapy and Existential Analysis,
Viktor Frankl Institute Vienna

"Drs. Dezelic and Ghanoum provide a practical, step-by-step guide for Logotherapy and Existential Analysis (LTEA) group and individual sessions. Based and expanded on Dr. Viktor Frankl's work, this manual guides the therapist with the knowledge and skills needed for effective discussions and interventions throughout the eight sessions. By providing clear guidelines and informative conceptual pictographs, the therapist is equipped with well-defined instructions to guide clients through creative and insightful sessions that provide them with the opportunity to discover their individual meaning in life. I highly recommend this manual for all therapists."

Cynthia Wimberly, PhD
NCC, NCSC, LPC-S, Diplomate in Logotherapy
Chair of the Viktor Frankl Education and Credentialing Committee,
Viktor Frankl Institute of Logotherapy, Abilene, TX
Associate Professor, Dept. of Counseling & Guidance,
University of Texas, Rio Grande Valley
Accredited Member
International Association of Logotherapy and Existential Analysis,
Viktor Frankl Institute Vienna

About the Artwork

"I grew up with the perspective that 'Ugly does not exist.' Today, rather than ugly, I think about it in this way: It is about what I like and what I don't like. It can be a huge dilemma to grapple with the beauty in something. If you like something, you often see or feel it as beautiful; if you don't like it, you often see or feel it as ugly or off-putting. The question is: What if we see something as beautiful and then see something that we think is more beautiful? Do we still see the first one as beautiful?- or has our initial perspective changed?

When I was creating this piece, I was contemplating and applying the same principle about beauty to my current moment of existence and wondering about my emotions; whether I was aware of each one, and how to guide myself from one emotional state to another.

My answer was: There is no right or wrong way, but there is a 'what, why, how, who and when.' Also, in the end, I realized that what we might see as 'mistakes' actually helps us to grow and learn. We can become wiser through our 'mistakes.' In fact, if we do nothing in an effort to avoid making mistakes, we limit our experiences of and in the world. In those moments of clarity, the colors guided me, guided my brush, from corner to corner, with rage and calmness, from sadness to happiness, from stuck-ness to living and being alive! I started with an empty white space; I discovered beauty, my beauty, and uncovered happiness and grace.

I just needed to start! I needed to embark on a new adventure, as part of a longer journey!
Now, it is your turn: Start something today, and let the colors and energy of life guide you to finish one of your new adventures.

Drs. Dezelic and Ghanoum: Thank you both for dedicating your lives to helping and guiding others. I am honored to have my artwork on the cover of this book, knowing that this manual will help guide many people to discover the meaning of their existence!"

Cover Artwork: "Existence" by Artist, **Chady Elias**
www.ChadyArt.com

MEANING-CENTERED THERAPY MANUAL

LOGOTHERAPY & EXISTENTIAL ANALYSIS BRIEF THERAPY PROTOCOL FOR GROUP & INDIVIDUAL SESSIONS

8 Session Format

~ Applicable Across Clinical Therapeutic and Spiritual Settings ~

MARIE S. DEZELIC, PHD
Diplomate in Logotherapy

GABRIEL GHANOUM, PSYD
Diplomate in Logotherapy

Meaning-Centered Therapy Manual:
Logotherapy & Existential Analysis Brief Therapy Protocol for Group & Individual Sessions

Edited by Ann-Marie Neale, PhD

For more information, contact Chady Elias at www.CHADYART.com

Library of Congress Cataloging-in Publication Data
Includes bibliographical references and glossary
ISBN 978-0-9846408-5-0 (Paperback)
ISBN 978-0-9846408-4-3 (Electronic edition)

Presence Press International
Miami, FL
Printed 2015

Through Meaning-Centered Logotherapy & Existential Analysis, both the therapist and the patient/client make a difference and brighten each other's lives, discovering and activating meaning, creativity, healing, and growth through the therapeutic-Nöetic encounter.

This Book is dedicated to:

Javier Bleichner, Lukas Bleichner, &
Katarina Bleichner

For bringing immense love, joy, peace, fun, and spiritual enlightenment
to all of us who love you and know your unique essences.
The world and this life are yours to explore and discover!

And to our Patients

For the gift of allowing us to help make a difference in your lives,
in your different struggles, your different circumstances throughout life,
and in some cases, facing your own deaths or of those you love;
you have imprinted on our hearts and spirits
through our journeys of discovery together.

Special Recognition...

We want to immensely thank all those that contributed to this manual, whether in thoughts, ideas, reading, collaborations, spirit, or supportive energy. We truly appreciate you all.

Thank you Robert Neimeyer, Alexander Battyhany, Pavel Somov, Matthew LoScalzo, Brent Potter, Ann Graber, Marshall Lewis, and Cynthia Wimberly, for your influential and important roles in the field, for your tremendously needed work and projects, for taking time to review the manuscript, and lastly for offering your comments, critiques and generous words of support.

Thank you Bill Breitbart, Julius Rogina, and Lexie Brockway Potamkin, for being key contributors to this project, and for sharing your energy, work, expertise, and wisdom in these pages.

Thank you Ann Graber, for your amazing mentorship and friendship throughout the years, and for supporting our efforts directly, in spirit, and behind the scenes.

Thank you Chady Elias, for your beautiful, unique artwork exhibited on the cover, your message within the art, and for allowing your creative gift to be a focal point for the starting of this existential exploration.

And last, but certainly not least, we want to thank our Editor, Ann-Marie Neale. Thank you for your tireless efforts, dedication, and friendship in shaping this manuscript to be the best it could be. Your unique spirit, love, and commitment to Logotherapy and Existential Analysis (LTEA), psychology, and education are infused in these pages.

Table of Contents

I. LOGOTHERAPY OVERVIEW: PHILOSOPHY, THEORY & CLINICAL APPLICATIONS

II. LOGOTHERAPY BRIEF THERAPY PROTOCOL: 8 SESSION FORMAT GROUP & INDIVIDUAL SESSIONS

III. CONCLUSION

Foreword ….. *By Dr. William Breitbart*

"Meaning, Creativity, Attitude: Creating Your Soul in Every Moment"

Drs. Dezelic and Ghanoum are long time collaborators who have dedicated much of their work, as Logotherapists and mental health practitioners, to the advancement of the practice of Logotherapy and Existential Analysis, and what many of us now refer to as "Meaning-Centered" psychotherapy and counseling approaches, applied to a wide range of patient problems and populations. This latest manual collaboration represents the ever–evolving creative processes of Marie and Gabriel, as they both integrate and innovate the newest concepts of existential and meaning-centered approaches that are now enriching the field of Logotherapy. It will be clear and obvious to clinicians who utilize this manual in their practice that creativity is at the heart of this intense and authentic project. The concepts and illustrations are bursts of imaginative new perspectives on a field that is now more than 60 years old. Creativity is at the heart and soul of this project and the meaning-centered approach to counseling that it presents.

"Creative" sources of meaning are especially important resources for patients in despair; my understanding of Creative sources of meaning has evolved over time and is reflected in not only the content of this manual, but in the process of creating this manualized approach in Logotherapy and Existential Analysis. For much of the last 10 years spent in the development of "Meaning-Centered Psychotherapy" for Advanced Cancer Patients in the Psychotherapy Laboratory I lead at Memorial Sloan Kettering Cancer Center, I had thought of Creative sources of meaning as including the aspects, values, efforts, creative processes, etc., that go into the process of discovering your life. Viktor Frankl would often refer to "work" as one of the central creative sources of meaning. But with attending to advanced cancer patients, for whom work was no longer an available expression or source of meaning, I realized that work itself could not possibly be the sole element of this source of meaning. It soon became evident that "Creative" sources of meaning also referred to what we really cared about in the world, and the process of fostering, creating, and discovering that entity, value, virtue, person (self) into being. Upon further reflection, I began to see that we begin to discover and create not only "What" we are, and "What" we care about in the world, but also "Who" we are, and "Who" we care about and love in this world.

Over the past 30 years I have been involved in the fellowship training of over 300 psychologists and psychiatrists working in the psycho-oncology field, as well as numerous palliative medicine physicians. Recently, I began to meet regularly with our palliative medicine fellows in order to help "debrief" them after the first 6 months of fellowship. The presumption was that by the half-year point, these physicians in training had encountered an overwhelming amount of pain, suffering and death in their patients. The discussions we shared were astounding, but not for the reasons I had expected. What was striking to me was that none of these extraordinarily bright and motivated young physicians could answer the following question: "Who do you want to 'become' in this world?" The answer was always "I want to be a good palliative care doctor." The answer was continuously an answer to "What" they wanted to be in the world, in terms of a role. This made me realize that enacting one's responsibility to discover and create a life of meaning and authenticity, of growth, transformation, self actualization, and self-transcendence, certainly involved the process of discovering and creating "Who" we become in the world, as well as the "What" (or work) that allows us to express who we are.

So the process of becoming a "Who" in order to discover the "What" in our lives took on greater significance for me as an element of a meaning-centered psychotherapy. What comprises the "Who" of a human being, and how does one create who one becomes? There are values, virtues, emotions, cognitions, behaviors, and physical functions that all seemed like reasonable candidates in some combination or perturbation. Ultimately, I believe it is "Attitude" that is at the core of "Who" we are. The process of discovering and creating ourselves, at its essence, involves the formation of the attitude we take toward and in life, love and suffering. "Choosing" our attitude is essentially creating our soul (our mind and spirit integration). Suddenly, it became clear to me why being loving, empathic, generous, and caring to others brought so much personal reward. It was because this is how we create our Attitude in the world, and this gives birth to and nurtures our souls.

Marie and Gabriel have given us a gift generated by their attitudes of generosity, love, hope, healing and spirit, which can assist all of us and those we help in discovering our deeper selves and meaning in life. They have my love and gratitude for this work of art.

William Breitbart, MD, FAPA, FAPM, FAPOS
Chairman, Jimmie C. Holland Chair in Psychiatric Oncology
Chairman and Chief, Psychiatry Service, & Department of Psychiatry and Behavioral Sciences
Memorial Sloan Kettering Cancer Center, NYC, USA
Professor of Clinical Psychiatry
Weill Medical College of Cornell University
Founding Member, *American Psycho-Oncology Society (APOS)*
Former President, *International Psycho-Oncology Society (IPOS)*
Former President, *Academy of Psychosomatic Medicine*
Editor-in-Chief, ***Palliative and Supportive Care***
Author of ***Meaning-Centered Group Psychotherapy for Patients with Advanced Cancer: A Treatment Manual; Individual Meaning-Centered Psychotherapy for Patients with Advanced Cancer: A Treatment Manual; Psychosocial Palliative Care; Handbook of Psychiatry in Palliative Medicine;*** and several other titles

Editor's Note ..... *By Dr. Ann-Marie Neale*

It is my honor and privilege to be the Editor of Drs. Marie Dezelic and Gabriel Ghanoum's *Meaning-Centered Therapy Manual* with its focus on a Brief Therapy Protocol for Group and Individual Sessions. This Manual is based on Viktor Frankl's Logotherapy and Existential Analysis (LTEA) and stays true to his teachings and philosophy; however, the authors have utilized their own creative talents in the development of innovative, colorful and informative Figures and Conceptual Pictographs—Client Handouts, as well as individual and group exercises. This manual will be helpful in many diverse settings, such as clinical groups, hospital inpatient therapy, outpatient programs, support groups and spiritual retreats, in addition to individual counseling and self-exploration. Having the unique perspective of editing Dr. Dezelic's highly acclaimed *Meaning-Centered Therapy Workbook* (2014), which is also based on the teachings of Viktor Frankl, I am delighted that this new Manual has added another significant contribution to the clinical literature, as well as the ever-important and increasing demand for "hands-on" manuals designed to assist therapists, clients and other seekers in the quest to discover meaning in their lives.

In deciding what was important to share in this Editor's Note, I concluded that the overview of Logotherapy and Existential Analysis, which I wrote for Marie Dezelic's Meaning-*Centered Therapy Workbook* (2014), would prove beneficial to the reader of this new Manual. With this in mind, the following is a brief synopsis of the philosophy, theory of therapy, and personality theory of Viktor E. Frankl:

Viktor Frankl's Logotherapy and Existential Analysis is based on three tenets: Life has meaning under all circumstances; the motivating force of life is the will to discover meaning; and we have the freedom of will not only to seek meaning, but to embrace that meaning by living in its service. Frankl believed that we discover meaning through self-transcendence; that is, the giving of ourselves to others and the world. We do this in three possible ways: Through our creative gifts – such as our career and work, or by raising children; through our experience of the love for or from someone else, as well as our appreciation of nature and artistic expression; and most importantly, through our attitude in the face of unavoidable pain, guilt and death. When we cannot change a situation (such as the loss of a loved one, a diagnosis of cancer, the devastation of a terrorist attack); we can change our attitude and turn suffering into triumph over tragedy. Frankl called this attitude shift "Tragic Optimism."

In addition, Viktor Frankl introduced the concept of our Nöetic (the Greek word for Spirit) Dimension or Spiritual Core—that which makes us distinctly human and separates us from the animal kingdom. According to Frankl, we have a Psyche (Mind) and a Soma (Body), but we ARE Spiritual Beings. He was not referring to spirit in a religious sense; rather, he was referring to that which makes us distinctly human. Furthermore, Frankl suggests that our Spiritual (Nöetic) Dimension is incapable of becoming sick. No matter how psychologically, emotionally or physically ill or disturbed we are, our Nöetic or Spiritual Core remains healthy. It contains our "Defiant Power of the Human Spirit" through which we are able to overcome unavoidable pain or tragedy. The Nöetic-Spiritual Core also contains our creativity, our sense of humor, our ability to forgive and our personal conscience. It is by accessing these gifts—what Dr. Dezelic calls the "jewels" of our Spiritual Core—that we are able to discover our true meaning and purpose in life.

The task of Logotherapists is to help patients or clients discover their own unique gifts and ways to find meaning through self-transcendence. Frankl suggests that each of us is being called by Life to be response-able; that is, to respond to life's challenges and fulfill our own unique purpose. Furthermore, the direct pursuit of happiness is always bound to fail and seldom brings satisfaction. According to Viktor Frankl, true happiness occurs when we fulfill our unique purpose and meaning in life.

There are so many aspects of this Manual that are worth mentioning; however, I would like to comment on the innovative *Meaning Construct Model* found in Section One, which examines the bio-psycho-social-spiritual context of discovering meaning in our lives. The information found in Figure 2—Meaning Construct Model, as well as the written explanation, describes the process we all go through when determining our inner and outer appraisals of situations and events. We then examine our appraisals and assimilate this information in order to discover the unique meaning inherently present for each of us. Section One also includes an excellent overview of the history and principles of Logotherapy and Existential Analysis (LTEA). Section Two contains the practical methods for utilizing Logotherapy through the eight-session protocol, including Conceptual Pictographs—Client Handouts and specific exercises for facilitators, individuals and group participants. There are also black-and-white copies of the conceptual pictographs to be utilized as client handouts along with each session in the appendix.

I would like to leave you with a sense of the passion and commitment that flows through every page of this manual. Both Marie Dezelic and Gabriel Ghanoum are dedicated professionals who each bring their unique personalities and strengths to every aspect of their careers and personal lives. Whether finding meaning through their creative gifts, such as in this current Manual with its innovative exercises and conceptual pictographs, by offering meaning-centered workshops, providing psychological counseling, developing their research projects, giving presentations and lectures on their therapeutic models and mental health topics worldwide, or by being fully present to family, colleagues and friends, they are both truly outstanding examples of Logotherapy Lived! Welcome to the journey of discovery present in their newest creative addition to the field of Logotherapy and Existential Analysis.

Ann-Marie Neale, PhD
Diplomate in Logotherapy
Education Consultant & Faculty Member
Viktor Frankl Institute of Logotherapy, Abilene, TX
Karen Horney Professor of Counseling and Psychology
Graduate Theological Foundation, Mishawaka, Indiana
Accredited Member
International Association of Logotherapy and Existential Analysis,
Viktor Frankl Institute Vienna

How To Use This Manual

This workbook is based on Viktor Frankl's *Meaning-Centered* and *Spiritual-Ontological, Existential* theory of personality, philosophy of life and psychotherapy known as Logotherapy & Existential Analysis (LTEA). Although it is not the official terminology utilized by Viktor Frankl, "Meaning-Centered" has been added before "Logotherapy" and throughout this manual. Since the Greek word "Logos" can be translated as "Meaning," Frankl named his existential theory and therapy "Logotherapy." Logotherapy focuses on the concept of "Meaning" in its many forms and constructs, and can be thought of as a Meaning-Centered existential approach. The authors have added "Meaning-Centered" to emphasis that Frankl's theory is about discovering meaning in our lives; and have also expanded on Frankl's original theory of personality and psychotherapy while remaining true to its basic concepts.

Clinician/ Facilitator Manual:

Throughout the specific sessions in this manual, clinicians function mainly as facilitators, group leaders, and guides for clients who are seeking meaning in life and who will use the specific exercises to work through their existential concerns. The clinician's primary purpose is to address the existential frustrations and despair encountered in life by utilizing a mind-body-spirit integrative approach. The 8-session protocol is applicable for **diverse clinical populations,** (i.e. particular mental illness diagnoses, co-occurring disorders, personality disorders, addiction and recovery, medical illness diagnoses, palliative care, grief), for group or individual therapy, growth and exploration.

This manual contains an **8-session protocol,** including reproducible client handouts and specific exercises to be followed in each session. Clinicians should familiarize themselves with the manual before conducting individual or group therapy sessions. Each Session usually lasts between 1.5 to 2 hours.

Black-and-White copies of the color Conceptual Pictographs are found in the Appendix. These duplicates, along with the copyright notice, are suitable for printing and can be used as handouts.

Support Group Manual:

This 8-session protocol is designed for support groups of various types and spiritual settings, for self-exploration, existential awareness and growth. **Examples of group types** include but are not limited to: clinical staff support groups for inpatient hospital and outpatient clinical settings, non-therapy grief support groups, spiritual center support groups for adults and adolescents.

Group leaders follow the 8-session protocol functioning as facilitators of the information presented. If any member of a group displays extreme discomfort, the group leader should recommend the member seek outside psychological or medical assistance. The authors suggest that group leaders should function as professional therapists, pastoral counselors, social workers or clinicians only if they hold licensure or credentials from a licensing or credentialing agency in their particular area(s) of expertise. Group leaders should inform members of their professional background and licensure or credentials. This disclosure serves as a protection for both the group leader and the members.

Self-Help and Self-Exploration:

When using this manual in a *self-help* and *self-exploration* manner, individuals can follow the 8-session protocol in a workbook fashion, follow the order of exercises, and choose the specific exercises they find most useful and helpful. It is our experience; however, that it is often helpful to have a therapist, counselor, or spiritual mentor/ advisor/ director to turn to for guidance and assistance.

Creativity is Key:

This brief 8-session workbook is a manualized approach based on the *Meaning-Centered Therapy Workbook* by Marie Dezelic, PhD (Dezelic, 2014b). Each of the 8 sessions described in Section II presents ideas on how to best utilize the *"Conceptual Pictographs" — Client Handouts* in group or individual therapy, as well as for self-exploration and growth. Information on various applications, all of which have shown positive results in formal research conducted by Logotherapists, as well as from the authors' personal clinical experience, is also included.

Any exercise can be adapted and tailored specifically to the type of population being treated and can be modified for individual, family and group exercises as well as psycho-educational lectures, etc. Suggestions are given for altering or adjusting exercises in individual and group therapy and for in-therapy sessions. Exercises can also be offered as "take home" assignments for further exploration. Everyone is encouraged to adjust or enhance exercises according to their own unique and personal experiences as well as for the specific needs of clients or their own situations. **Make this work your own, allow your essence to shine through your personal creativity, and let your talents and experience be your guiding force.**

"Logo-Journey Journal"
Paper Exercises, Projects, Electronic-Based Adaptations:

It is suggested that individuals create a **"Logo-Journey Journal"**: a folder or notebook that can contain the *"Conceptual Pictographs"—Client Handouts,* specific exercises and notes or material collected during the entire therapeutic process. In addition to a traditional handwritten folder and journal, this can be done using "apps" (applications) or the "notes" section on Smart Phones, iPads/tablets, or computers. Collages or creative projects can be designed on poster boards, or can be developed using the computer graphics in design programs. Films, music, digital photo books, and other multimedia platforms can be utilized for the suggested exercises. The possibilities will continue to increase because the beauty of these "Conceptual Pictographs" and exercises is that they can easily be adapted to new options in our ever-evolving technological world.

Information about "Therapist" and "Client":

Throughout this workbook, the words "therapist(s)" and "client(s)" are used. Feel free to substitute clinician, counselor, chaplain, facilitator, or leader, for "therapist"; and patient, individual, member, self, for "client," or whatever terms work best for your particular situation or setting. The term "man" refers to all human beings and is not gender specific.

The ***Conceptual Pictographs—Client Handouts*** included in this workbook provide a new visual way for understanding and applying ***Meaning-Centered Logotherapy & Existential Analysis***. They each address existential issues, including suffering and growth, as well as the notion of existence itself. The Conceptual Pictographs will not only improve interaction with clients, but also offer techniques to help motivate therapists as well as clients to discover ***Meaning*** through ***Creativity, Experiences, Attitudes,*** and ***Self-Transcendence.***

I.
LOGOTHERAPY OVERVIEW

PHILOSOPHY, THEORY & CLINICAL APPLICATIONS

Final Analysis:
On the 'Meaning' of Meaning-Centered Logotherapy & Existential Analysis

We live in a world where suffering, tragedy and despair may be waiting around every corner and upon every step we take; yet at the same time, it is a world full of wonder, precious moments, extraordinary experiences, and astonishing triumphs that are filling our hearts and souls with ultimate excitement, knowledge, courage, resilience and strength. Meaning-Centered Logotherapy & Existential Analysis is the unique, dynamic, experiential therapy of the spirit and psyche; the metaphorical midwife, birthing the inner wisdom held deep within the tapestry of our fabric and design. It reaches and touches our spiritual wells, which contain the wealth and purity of all the distinctive capacities of our spirits. It is not a redemptive, but rather an evolutionary approach, toward celebrating the possibilities and potentialities of the ongoing transformation and transcendence of human beings through the existence we call "Life."

Meaning-Centered Logotherapy & Existential Analysis passionately ignites and empowers the creativity central to our essence and being, while viewing our unbroken wholeness as our simple strength in creating a life worth living—one we will be both grateful and happy to fully experience each and every day, and will be grateful to have lived. Meaning-Centered Logotherapy & Existential Analysis celebrates life, existence, possibilities, growth, and new beginnings, through a multi-perspective attitude and multi-dimensional methodology. Logotherapists join clients on their path, willing to journey with them in their fully experiential existence, empowering them through the interconnectedness of the artful Logotherapeutic-Nöetic encounter. The gift that Meaning-Centered Logotherapy & Existential Analysis brings to the world is its subtle yet distinctly crafted existential approach, which gently guides us to an awareness of our unique essence as well as our unique purpose and meaning in life.

-M. Dezelic

Introduction

"Along the journey, all paths lead toward meaning and a meaningful existence."
-M. Dezelic

"Meaningful living is the essence of a life well-lived."
-G. Ghanoum

Section I, Logotherapy Overview, is designed to give sufficient, general background information on the theory, philosophy and therapy of Logotherapy & Existential Analysis. This will ensure that clinicians, counselors and others who use this manual will have sufficient background in its general ideas, therapeutic methods, and existential concepts, thus enabling them to facilitate individual and group therapy within the framework of this clinical approach.

Section II, Logotherapy Brief Therapy Protocol, is an 8-session manualized format, *(adapted from Dezelic, 2014b)* and expanded with specific *"Conceptual Pictographs"— Client Handouts,* followed by clinical exercises for 8 separate 1.5 to 2 hours sessions. When exploring existential concepts, specific questions may arise that are not covered within the 8 sessions; therefore, Section I and the Glossary of Terms can serve as clinical information to inform therapy and address these issues.

Section III, Conclusion, includes an epilogue written by author, spiritual leader and human rights activist, Lexie Brockway Potamkin who discusses the existential questions of life. The extensive **Glossary of Terms** can be used as a reference for the various Logotherapy and existential concepts covered throughout this manual.

1. Integrative Therapeutic Treatment: The Foundational Aspects of Logotherapy & Existential Analysis

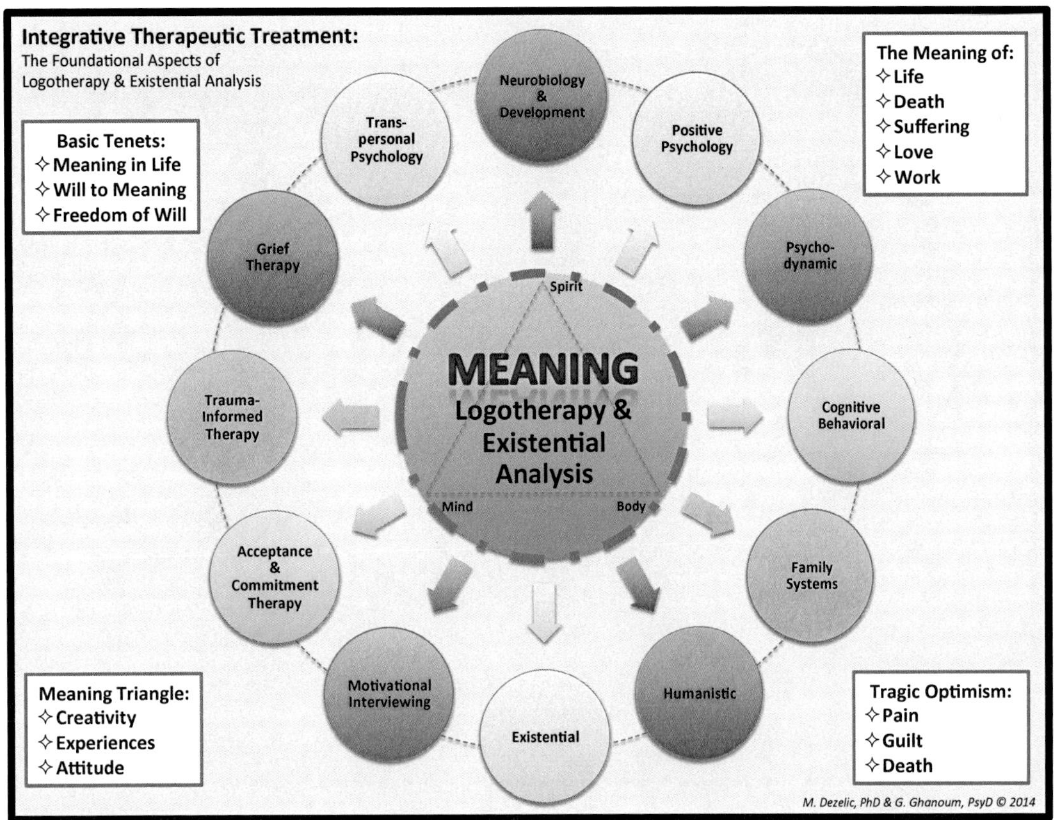

Figure 1

Meaning is at the core of all human existence and human experience. We are meaning-seeking beings, discovering meaning and significance in all of our life experiences, and searching for meaning and purpose throughout our lifecycle. Current therapeutic practice in the behavioral sciences encompasses Meaning in various ways. While most therapeutic modalities address the question of Meaning in relation to self and one's life throughout the course of therapy, therapists from diverse theoretical backgrounds would benefit from gaining knowledge and understanding of Logotherapy & Existential Analysis (LTEA), a clinical approach that is centrally focused on Meaning, as well as the existential aspects of the human condition. LTEA can be readily and easily integrated with other therapeutic approaches and models of treatment **(Figure 1).**

2. Meaning Construct Model: Through a Bio-Psycho-Social-Spiritual Context

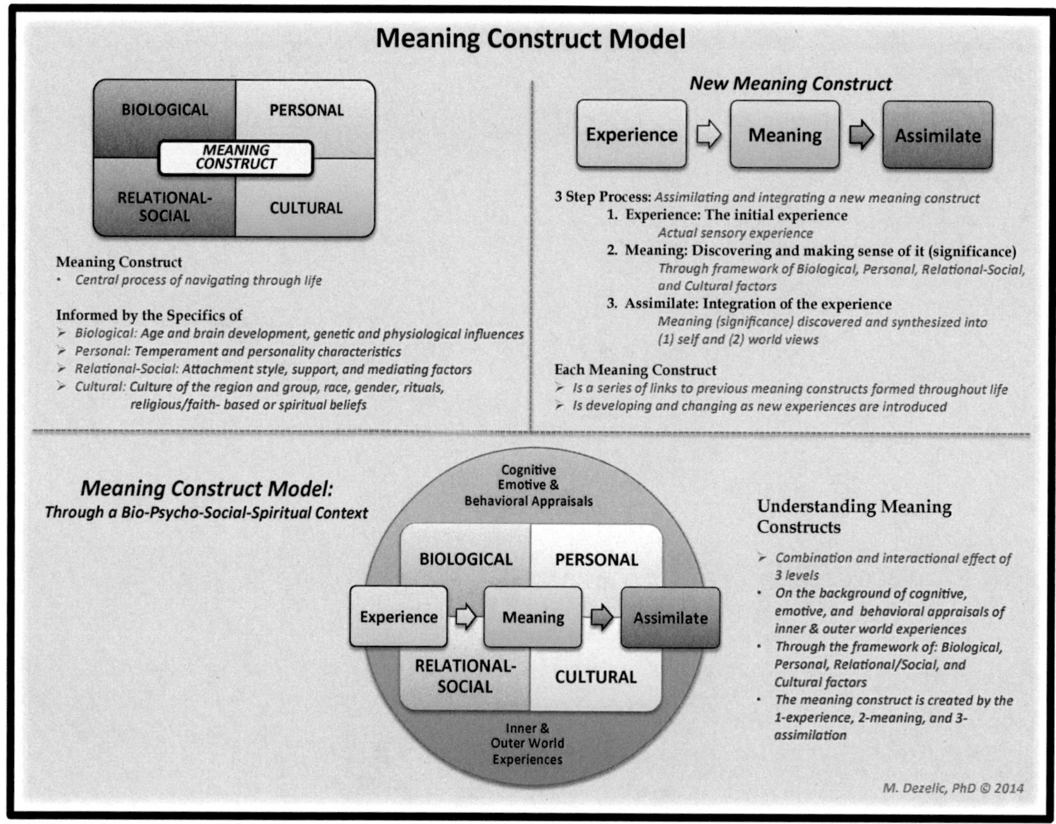

Figure 2 - (Dezelic, 2014c)

It seems that most if not all human beings have a desire to uncover, discover, maintain and even embrace meaning in life. This desire is present despite the inevitable challenges, pain, suffering and discomfort that can result from conflict, loss, traumas, tragedies, setbacks and limitations. Since it is unavoidable that all of us will face these difficult situations at one point or another during the course of our lifetime, we may experience despair, hopelessness or meaninglessness—what Viktor Frankl termed the existential vacuum (Dezelic, 2014a; Dezelic, 2014b; Frankl, 1986; Frankl, 2004; Frankl, 2006; Graber, 2004; Lukas, 2000; Rice et al., 2004).

One of the difficulties we encounter when faced with the challenge of uncovering, discovering, maintaining, and embracing meaning, is the lack of a universal definition of Meaning itself. While most would agree that Meaning is a universal concept, there is no operational definition that has been agreed upon by researchers, personality theorists and other professionals. This is likely due to the many and varied biological, personal, social-relational and cultural differences in individuals, groups and societies as a whole.

In addition, the word Meaning is referenced from two different perspectives. One aspect of Meaning refers to the "understanding" or "making sense" of a concept or situation, (i.e. when something happens, it "means"...); Meaning can also refer to a "greater purpose" or "significance" (i.e. the "meaning of life," "meaning in the moment" or "discovering meaning within the suffering"). What often happens is that each of us defines meaning according to our own inner and outer worldviews, within our unique cognitive, behavioral and emotive appraisals of experiences. We often base our understanding on current biological, personal, relational-social, and cultural aspects of our lives. Thus "Meaning" can be viewed as an ongoing creative and dynamic process (Dezelic, 2014c).

Merriam-Webster's Collegiate Dictionary (2005) has several **"definitions" of Meaning:**

1) *a: the thing one intends to convey especially by language; (purport)*
   b: the thing that is conveyed especially by language; (import)
2) *something meant or intended; (aim)*
3) *significant quality; (implication of a hidden or special significance)*
4) *a: the logical connotation of a word or phrase*
   b: the logical denotation or extension of a word or phrase

Throughout this workbook and the 8-session therapy protocol, **Meaning refers to a "significance" or "greater purpose";** such as the "meaning of life," or "discovering meaning within the suffering or situation," as this is the most compatible with Meaning-Centered Logotherapy and Existential Analysis.

"Meaning Construct Model" (Figure 2)

A *Construct* is a theoretical description of several factors or complex ideas that are not necessarily directly observable, such as self-esteem, self-confidence, or Ultimate Meaning. The ***"Meaning Construct Model: Through a Bio-Psycho-Social-Spiritual Context,"*** (Figure 2) lists the factors that influence or impact the discovery of our own unique and individual Meaning in Life. These factors are based on theoretical concepts that are found in Developmental Psychology, Cognitive-Learning Theory, Constructivist Psychology, Neurobiology, Attachment Theory, Family Systems Theory, Multicultural Psychology, Trauma-Informed Treatment, and Grief Therapies, along with Logotherapy & Existential Analysis, and inform the developmental and navigating process of discovering Meaning throughout the course of our lives (Dezelic, 2014c). The prototype of this model was first introduced in the *Meaning-Centered Therapy Workshop,* and the Panel presentation on *Meaning-Oriented Interventions, and Social and Cultural Impacts on Meaning* at the *International Network on Personal Meaning's Meaning Conference* in Vancouver, Canada, July 24-27, 2014.

A Meaning Construct for each unique individual is established through:

- ***Biological Influences:*** Age and brain development, genetic and physiological influences.
- ***Personal Influences:*** Temperament and personality styles.
- ***Relational-Social Influences:*** Attachment style (i.e. secure, anxious-ambivalent, avoidant, disorganized), support network, and mediating factors. Mediating factors include situations that create a positive or negative impact, such as a safe and secure environment during developmental years, caregiver support and connection, caregiver neglect and disconnection, peer support or disengagement, mental illness within the family, traumatic and tragic situations, grief, poverty, education.
- ***Cultural Influences:*** Family, geographic region, race, gender, rituals and religious, spiritual/existential or faith-based beliefs.

The Meaning Construct Model shows that discovering Meaning is a three-step process of assimilating and integrating new and novel experiences as they unfold throughout our lifetime:

1) ***Experience:*** the initial event occurs.
2) ***Meaning:*** the appraisal and "significance" of the experience discovered and informed through Biological, Personal, Relational-Social, and Cultural factors.
3) ***Assimilation:*** the integration of the Experience and Meaning (or significance) into our understanding of ourselves (self-view), and our world views (others-view).

We are continually discovering new Meaning constructs and appraisals often through the process of refining or adapting previous understandings of Meaning in our lives. We may even choose to disregard or abandon some of our older Meaning constructs as new ones are learned and assimilated. And likewise, when we look back on our lives, we may discover Meaning in past moments, happenings or events. For as we know, there are many changes in the Biological, Personal, Relational-Social, or Cultural domains throughout our lives. There are also times when we may actually feel stuck in step 2, the "Meaning" stage. It can sometimes be difficult to make sense of a situation, especially if we are feeling overwhelmed or influenced in any of the Biological, Personal, Relational-Social, or Cultural domains; thus making it challenging to discover "Meaning" within the experience. Likewise, we may experience difficulty moving from the "Meaning" stage to the "Assimilation" stage, where we can make sense of the new experience. Sometimes we may even be confused and have trouble finding adaptive ways of integrating difficult yet potentially meaningful experiences into the context of our lives. Should this pattern become extreme or maladaptive, we might see the immergence of PTSD (Posttraumatic Stress Disorder) symptoms or symptoms of other diagnoses such as in Depression or Anxiety disorders (Dezelic, 2014c).

As therapists and facilitators, we may think we understand the Meaning others experience in a particular circumstance; however, it is always wise and necessary to explore our clients' own unique understanding and appraisal of the situation. This assures that we are not projecting our own life circumstances and Meanings onto others, and that we are instead assisting them in discovering and uncovering their own unique, personal Meanings. The three-step process (1-Experience, 2-Meaning, 3-Assimilation) is incorporated and integrated into our lives through the ongoing and ever changing framework of Biological, Personal, Relational-Social, and Cultural influences. The process is always based on the background of cognitive, behavioral and emotive appraisals of self and world views. For example, when greeting someone, do we make eye contact? Do we stand near or far away when speaking with someone? Do we embrace or offer a handshake when saying hello? All of these behaviors and gestures are interpreted differently based on our Biological, Personal, Relational-Social, and Cultural experiences and upbringing. We need to be sensitive to these idiosyncratic differences, especially in therapeutic and medical environments.

As mentioned above, Meaning, significance and purpose in life, a central concept in Meaning-Centered therapies (Batthyany & Levinson, 2009, Dezelic 2014b) can have different interpretations across cultures. One person's "meaning in the moment" or "ultimate meaning in life" will be completely unique to that individual through the framework of the four domains. It is important to remember that the search for "meaning in life" is an innate and inherent pulling force within human beings (Dezelic, 2014a; Dezelic, 2014b; Frankl, 1986; Frankl, 2004; Frankl, 2006; Graber, 2004; Lukas, 2000), yet what is discovered and interpreted as meaningful and significant varies across the globe.

3. General Existential Therapeutic Process

As you begin this Meaning Centered Therapy Manual, it would be helpful to have an understanding and **general definition of Existential Therapy** and the Existential therapeutic process before exploring the unique aspects and modality of Logotherapy & Existential Analysis (LTEA) as a specific existential therapeutic approach. ***Existential*** refers to existence, the experience of existence, and the human condition. An ***Existential Therapy*** focuses on the human condition; that is, our existence and the conditions of being human.

"Existential Therapy" Definition: (M. Dezelic, PhD)

A **growth process experience and encounter** between a therapist/clinician/counselor or other professional **guide** and a **seeker** (patient, client, individual, consumer, family members, or group members), where these guides provide **existential psycho-education,** focusing on the **human condition and "existence,"** and through the encounter in the here-and-now, offer an open invitation to **explore and discover** one's **ontological being** (mind, body, and spirit-unique essence) by examining:
(1) The inner world—how one can learn to "be" in oneself, by connecting to one's own existence, and understanding one's sense of self in the world;
(2) The outer world—how one can learn to "be" in oneself in relation to other human beings, animals, nature, creations, and processes.

The existential therapeutic encounter is an **unfolding, creative, and dynamic process** that focuses on:
* **Self-Awareness**
* **Freedom, Choice** and **Responsibility** for one's unique existence
* **Meaning in Life**
* **Meaning Constructs** (through Biological, Personal, Relational-Social, and Cultural aspects)
* **Meaningful Relationships**
* **Living in the face of inevitable Death, and Death Anxiety**
* **The areas of Freedom and Choice, within the Limitations and/or Tragic Aspects of life**
* **Experiences, Creativity, and Attitudes**
* **Discovering** one's own unique life
* Exploring the human condition—**"being"** human
* Exploring and creating a balance between **dialectical experiences, thoughts, behaviors, and views.**

(www.DrMarieDezelic.com)

4. Existential Therapeutic Process: Logotherapy & Existential Analysis (LTEA)

Logotherapy & Existential Analysis (LTEA) falls under the larger umbrella of Existential Psychotherapies. LTEA is a *specific existential therapeutic approach,* developed by Viktor Frankl in the 1920's, although it was not until the 1970's that it was widely recognized in the United States.

A general definition, overview and understanding of the unique aspects and modality of **Logotherapy & Existential Analysis (LTEA),** as a specific existential therapeutic approach, will help guide the process and protocol depicted in this manual. Further in-depth explanations of the theory and methods are found in the following chapters of Section I.

Logotherapy & Existential Analysis (LTEA) Definition:
(M. Dezelic, PhD and G. Ghanoum, PsyD)

Logotherapy & Existential Analysis (LTEA), widely known as the 'Third Viennese School of Psychotherapy,' is a **meaning-centered psychotherapy, theory of personality,** and **philosophy of human existence** developed in the 1920s by the psychiatrist and neurologist, **Viktor Emil Frankl. LTEA** centers on **"Logos"—denoted as Meaning,** as the primary motivational and striving force in human beings; and focuses on the **meaning of human existence,** one's **search for the unique Meaning of the Moment,** the **Overall Meaning in Life,** as well as **Ultimate Meaning.** Frankl viewed humans as **ontological beings,** comprised of three interconnected and in-extractible dimensions—mind (psyche), body (soma), and spirit (existential, non-religious context).

The three **Primary Tenets of LTEA:**

* Freedom of Will
* Will to Meaning
* Meaning in Life

The **Main Methodologies of LTEA:**

* Existential Analysis—analysis of one's existence and meaning in life.
* Socratic Dialogue—open-ended dialogue to promote discovery of meaning.
* Paradoxical Intention—intending with humorous exaggeration an over-amplification of a behavior in order to eliminate it .
* Dereflection—shifting focus from symptoms to other meaningful encounters or activities in order to reduce hyper-intention or hyper-reflection, and increase self-distancing.
* Modification of Attitudes—the ability to change, or alter thoughts or mindsets in the face of unavoidable difficult, limiting, traumatic or tragic situations.
* Medicine Chest—located in the Nöetic (Spiritual) Dimension, the unique, internal personal resources of the human being, (such as personal conscience, creativity, love, forgiveness, and intuition).

With the Primary Tenets of Logotherapy & Existential Analysis as the starting point, and through the use of its main methodologies and many complementary methods, LTEA therapists assist clients in utilizing their own **Personal Freedom, Choice** and **Responsibility,** and also in developing an awareness of **Inner Strengths and Resources.** Ultimately, Logotherapists practice the principles and techniques of LTEA and guide individuals to recognize and respond to their unique meaning in life, uniqueness as human beings, and responsibility to and for their existence.

LTEA is the only existential therapy that stresses the importance of **Self-Transcendence** as a way to discover and fulfill our unique meaning and purpose in life.
By a process of discovering and activating individuals' **Meaning Triangle:**

* Creativity
* Experiences
* Attitude

LTEA addresses the **Existential Realities of Life, Existential Frustration** and the **Existential Vacuum,** which are often byproducts of:
The Tragic Triad:

* Unavoidable Suffering
* Inescapable Guilt
* Death;

The Neurotic Triad:

* Aggression
* Depression
* Addiction;

Finally, LTEA rejects the view that human beings are pre-determined or fated by drives, instincts, or solely by genetic endowment, and instead, sees humans as ontological, self-determining individuals with **Free Will** and the capacity for change, empowered by their **Unique Existence** and **Search for Meaning.**

(Batthyany & Levinson, 2009; Batthyany, 2010; Dezelic, 2014a; Dezelic, 2014b; Frankl, 1978; Frankl, 1986; Frankl, 1988; Frankl, 2006; Graber, 2004; www.logotherapyinstitute.org, *Official Viktor Frankl Institute of Logotherapy, TX, United States;* www.viktorfrankl.org, *Official Viktor Frankl Institute, Vienna, Austria).*

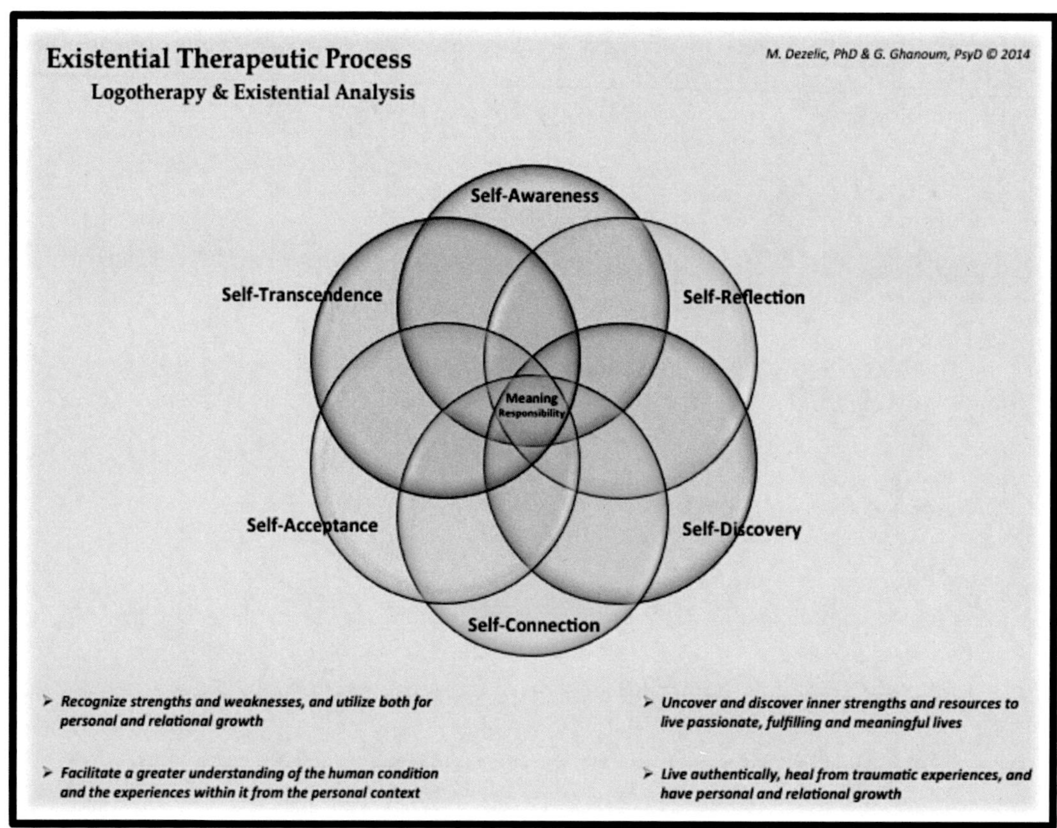

Figure 3

Logotherapy & Existential Analysis (LTEA) falls into the category of Existential, Humanistic Psychology and philosophy.

LTEA assists individuals to: **(Figure 3)**

- Recognize strengths and weaknesses, and utilize both for personal and relational growth.
- Facilitate a greater understanding of the human condition and the experiences within it from the personal context.
- Uncover and discover inner strengths and resources to live passionate, fulfilling and meaningful lives.
- Live authentically, heal from traumatic experiences, and have personal and relational growth.

This process facilitates accessing and **Discovering Meaning,** and fulfilling our **Existential Responsibility** to life through:

- Self-Awareness
- Self-Reflection
- Self-Discovery
- Self-Connection
- Self-Acceptance
- Self-Transcendence

The therapeutic work that develops from this modality increases a sense of Self-Compassion by increasing inner awareness and deeper existential connection, as well as compassion toward others through transcendence—going beyond the self to connect with others, important endeavors and causes.

5. Historical Overview of Schools/Theories of Psychotherapy

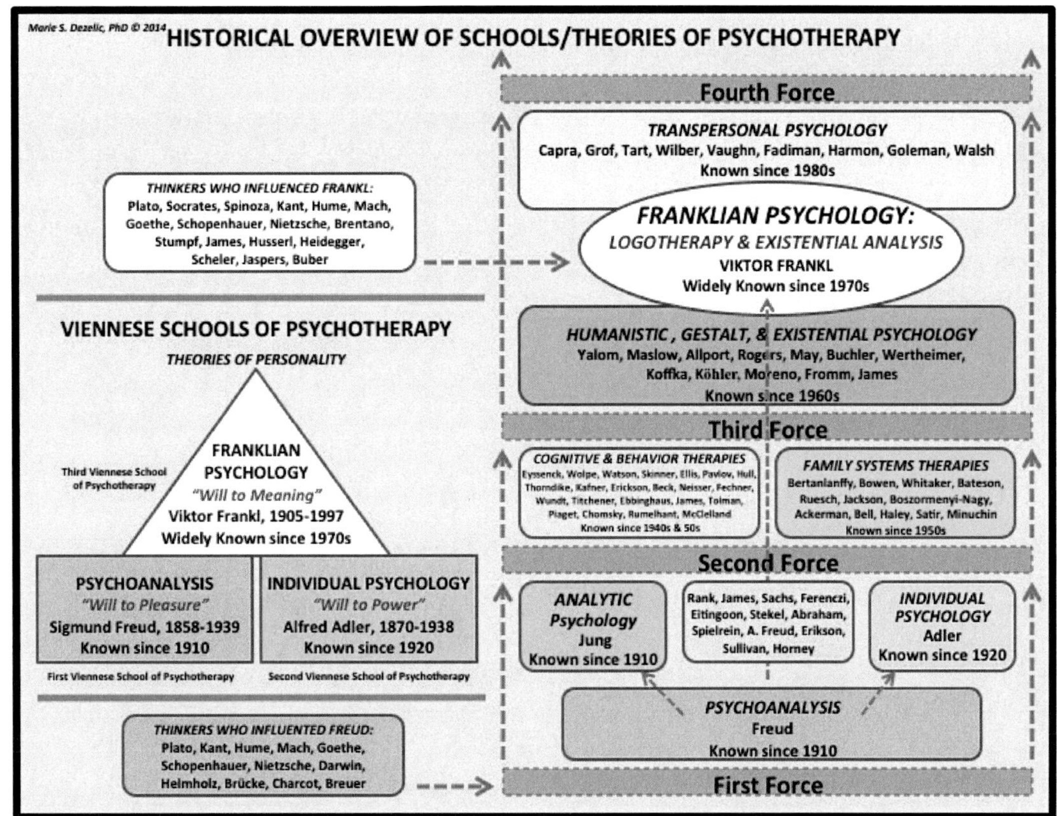

Figure 4 - (Dezelic, 2014b)

This **Historical Overview of Schools/Theories of Psychotherapy** *Conceptual Pictograph* **(Figure 4),** illustrates how **Meaning-Centered Logotherapy & Existential Analysis** (LTEA) fits into a general timeline of the **Main Schools of Psychotherapy**, as well as within the **Three Viennese Schools of Psychotherapy** (Rice et al., 2004; Graber, 2004).

It is important to note that only the main theories and important historical figures are represented by this *Conceptual Pictograph*. It does not include all of the many different psychological approaches, schools, and theories. We recognize that many other schools of psychotherapy not only exist, but also play an integral role in our understanding and treatment of the human condition. We certainly encourage readers to look beyond the general approaches, and examine how Meaning-Centered Logotherapy & Existential Analysis can become a specific or complementary addition to your chosen orientation.

Viktor Frankl believed that the *Will to Pleasure* (Freud's theory) and the *Will to Power* (Adler's theory) can be obstacles to discovering meaning in life (Frankl, 1986). To summarize:

- ***The Will to Pleasure***: Sigmund Freud's psychoanalytic personality theory suggests that all humans have innate drives for pleasure, with the sexual or sensual drive being primary. Within the framework of the psychic energy of the mind (Id, Ego, and Superego), these drives are found in the Id. Beginning in the earliest stages of childhood, humans develop defense mechanisms in the Ego and Superego to mediate these unconscious impulses and desires that continue throughout the lifespan. This theory denies the existence of Free Will.

- ***The Will to Power***: Alfred Adler's Individual Psychology, while acknowledging the existence of Free Will, assumes that our inferiority complexes drive us toward striving for power, and toward becoming successful through overcoming our inferiority complexes and adversities. One area that has some commonality with Logotherapy is Adler's recognition of the importance of our family relationships and our interaction in society. For example, he maintained that in order for adults to be fully mature, they need to develop Social Interest—a concern for their community.
- ***The Will to Meaning***: Meaning-Centered Logotherapy & Existential Analysis, moves away from drives and deterministic approaches to a non-deterministic, future-oriented approach, looking toward the meanings to be discovered and fulfilled in the present and the future. Its founder, Viktor Frankl, suggests that individuals are pushed by their past, yet pulled by their future that has not yet been determined, while having the freedom of will in the present to choose their attitude and stance in life.

6. "Logotherapy & Existential Analysis: A Meaning-Centered & Spiritually Integrated Psychotherapy, Applicable Across Clinical Settings" (Dezelic, 2014a)

(Modified and adapted, published in Foundation Theology 2014, 30th Anniversary Edition)

Viktor E. Frankl's *Logotherapy & Existential Analysis* is a Meaning-Centered and Spiritually Integrated Psychotherapeutic approach. It is applicable for clinicians who provide psychotherapy to diverse populations: individuals, couples, families, group settings, and pastoral counseling, addressing the needs of varied psychiatric diagnoses, as well as everyday psychosocial-spiritual and existential issues. ***One cannot remove the human experience from a human being, nor dismiss the unique essence of each individual.*** Consequently, regardless of the theoretical approach one utilizes, or the particular techniques one finds necessary for dealing with specific diagnoses, a therapy addressing existential concerns will be appropriate in most cases. Viktor Frankl revolutionized psychotherapy by addressing the ***spiritual component of the human being's existence***—one's unique essence. Logotherapy & Existential Analysis can provide clinicians with a theoretical base and practical therapeutic techniques to guide clients toward ***meaningful and purposeful living!*** It is a ***specific*** as well as an ***adjunctive therapy;*** Frankl emphasized that Logotherapy is not only open toward cooperation with other schools of thought, but that collaboration with other techniques should be encouraged and welcomed (Frankl, 1988).

I. OVERVIEW OF LOGOTHERAPY & EXISTENTIAL ANALYSIS

What is Viktor Frankl's Logotherapy?

Frankl suggests that we are NOT the ones who should pose the question: What is the meaning of Life, rather, it is Life itself that asks each of us to respond to its ultimate challenge. And this challenge is: What will each of us do to fulfill our own unique responsibilities in our lifetime? (Frankl, 2000). Viktor E. Frankl's *Logotherapy & Existential Analysis*, also known as *Franklian Psychology*, is a philosophical, anthropological, and phenomenological approach to an understanding of the human being. Viktor Frankl, *(1905-1997)*, born in Vienna, Austria, was a neurologist and psychiatrist who earned his M.D. and Ph.D. from the University of Vienna. Imprisoned in four different Nazi concentration camps including Auschwitz between 1942 and 1945, where his entire family (except for his sister who had fled to Australia) perished, Frankl lived to further develop his theory and therapy of Meaning and to write about his horrific experiences, including his perspective regarding why some prisoners were able to survive the concentration camps.

Frankl is best known for addressing the existential themes of *meaning, human freedom, responsibility, values, spirituality,* and *death,* founding what has become known as the ***Third Viennese School of Psychotherapy*** (Frankl, 1986). Frankl's Meaning-Centered Logotherapy and Existential Analysis (LTEA), which followed in part and extended from his original Existential Analysis work, was a novel therapeutic approach, one that is a philosophy of human existence, an anthropological theory of personality, and a therapy which addresses the question—*What is the meaning of life?* Frankl chose the Greek word *"Logos"* because it denotes *Meaning*, and expresses that Logos is deeper than logic and explanation. Frankl sought to convey that *Meaning* opens an entirely new dimension, as if peering through the looking glass: looking through the *Pathos*—the pathology, into the *Spirit*—the unique essence of the human being, to and into the *Logos*—the Meaning. He explained that ***Meaning*** is the primary motivational force activated in our lives, and that potential *Meaning* is inherent and dormant in every situation we face or encounter.

Frankl's theory deals specifically with the ***Will to Meaning,*** and can be used as a specific therapy in particular cases and as an adjunctive therapy in most cases. Frankl believed that the *Will to Pleasure*

(Freud's Psychoanalysis) and the *Will to Power* (Adler's Individual Psychology) holds us back from *"being free"* to focus on our *Will to Meaning* in life (Frankl, 1986). As Logotherapy's primary focus is on the meaning of human existence and our search for meaning, we are confronted with and reoriented toward our meaning in life. Becoming aware of this meaning possibility enhances our ability to overcome the difficulties we face in life (Frankl, 2006).

Philosophy of Logotherapy: The Basic Assumptions

The philosophy of Logotherapy contains ***Basic Assumptions*** about human beings and their existential qualities. Therapists can utilize these Basic Assumptions, also known as the innate capacities of human beings, along with the therapeutic encounter to address the difficulties that involve emotions, cognitions and behaviors that are found in all *Situations of Life*.

The Basic Assumptions of Logotherapy (Barnes, 2005, p.20-29):

- *Defiant Power of the Human Spirit*
- *Uniqueness of the Individual*
- *Demand Quality of Life*
- *Capacity for Choice*
- *Freedom to Find Meaning or New Attitudes*
- *Responsibility to (Not from)*
- *Life has Meaning Under All Circumstances, Even the Most Miserable Ones*
- *Will to Meaning*
- *Importance of the Therapeutic Relationship*
- *Human Being is Comprised of Mind, Body and Spirit*
- *Spiritual Dimension is the Healthy Core*
- *Dignity of the Human Being*

Frankl often quoted Nietzsche: ***He who has a why to live can bear with almost any how.*** Therapists use the principles of Meaning-Centered Logotherapy to assist individuals in becoming aware of their spiritual readiness—that is, their innate capacity found in their healthy spiritual core to transcend; thus, enabling them to become conscious of these resources, and to access their ***Defiant Power of the Human Spirit,*** which allows them to stand up against adversity, trials and tribulations. Through these actions, therapists assist clients to transform suffering into human achievement.

The 3 Primary Tenets of Logotherapy

The 3 Primary Tenets of Logotherapy are the central concepts on which the theory is based. *Meaning*, often influenced by cultural values, societal descriptions, familial purposes, and shaped by experiences in the world, is entirely personal. Although human beings may have similar concepts, definitions and understandings, *Meaning* is, by its fundamental nature and virtue, a unique, experiential, multi-dimensional, non-linear, abstract, and exclusively human concept. Frankl also asserted that meaning is not created but rather it already exists and is to be discovered by each individual in every moment of their lives.

The Three Tenets of Logotherapy (Frankl, 1988; Frankl, 2000; Frankl, 2006):

- ***Freedom of Will***: The ability to take a stand toward conditions, and change attitudes in the face of life's difficulties; not freedom FROM the conditions of life such as situations happening to us and around us.
- ***Will to Meaning***: The basic striving to discover meaning and purpose in life; not as a drive or pursuit, but as a choice of direction in life.
- ***Meaning of Life***: Meaning (a unique significance and purpose) is always available for us to discover and uncover; we are free to search for and fulfill our unique meaning as we "walk toward" ultimate meaning.

The Situations of Life:

- ***Unique Conditions of Life***: All of the conditions we each experiences in life, regardless of whether or not they are freely chosen.
- ***Unavoidable Suffering***: The suffering we experience when a situation occurs outside of our direct control, (i.e. Nazi concentration camps, traumatic childhood events, rape, abuse, cancer diagnosis, natural disasters, acts of terror,...).
- ***Unfortunate Blows of Fate***: Life's difficult and unavoidable past or present situations and circumstances, (i.e. a tragic accident with damaging repercussions to self or loved ones, loss of job, loss of house, breakup of marriage/relationship, death of a loved one,...).

Dimensional Ontology: The Multidimensional Aspects of Human Beings: Body (Soma), Mind (Psyche), & Spirit (Noös)

Viktor Frankl used the term ***Dimensional Ontology*** to describe the inseparable dimensions of the human being: the ***Soma***—Body, ***Psyche***—Mind, and ***Noös***—Spirit. We can visualize these areas as three separate yet interconnecting parts, each containing a specific area of functioning. *"Human spirit is not a substance, it is pure dynamic (dynamic=movement). Logotherapy would not say 'Man has a spirit.' Instead,* ***man is spirit.*** *We have a body (soma) and a mind (psyche), but* ***we are a spirit"*** (Barnes, 2005, p.37).

Frankl chose the German word "Geist" for "Spirit" because this word is secular and lacks religious overtones and simply refers to the dimension of the human being that is ***"free, responsible, and directed toward finding meaning"*** (Frankl, 2004). Unfortunately there is no secular word for spirit in the English language so it is even more important to understand this distinction.

According to Logotherapy, this distinctly human dimension—the ***Nöetic (Spiritual) Dimension***—houses the following resources:

- ***Choice***: Freedom to look at available options including modifying attitudes when options are limited.
- ***Humor***: The capability of distancing from the situation so as to feel less disturbed and/or to derive a delightful or pleasurable moment.
- ***Creativity***: Our unique capabilities of being original, inspired, imaginative, artistic, resourceful, ingenious, and innovative.
- ***Conscience***: Our unique and authentic ideals and values that may or may not be in agreement with our upbringing, culture, societal norms; includes how we choose to actualize our values in thought or action.
- ***Decision Making***: The ability to and process involved in making choices despite limitations and constraints; to choose a possible new action; to modify attitudes in dealing with a situation.

- ***Taking a Stand Toward Somatic and Psychic Limitations***: Not allowing the limitations of body and/or mind to hinder or diminish our essence and very personhood; making choices when we still has the capability and capacity to do so.

Logotherapists help orient clients to discover their innate *Meaning*, which will allow them to achieve ***Self-Transcendence***—the human capacity to be directed/pulled toward something or someone, other than oneself, whether a meaning to fulfill or another human being to encounter. Frankl believed that *self-actualization is possible only as a result of self-transcendence* (Frankl, 2006).

II. APPLYING LOGOTHERAPY & EXISTENTIAL ANALYSIS IN CLINICAL SETTINGS

Role of Logotherapists

Clinicians should never assume the responsibility of determining what is meaningful for their clients; rather, through the use of Socratic or Maieutic Dialogue, they assist clients to be responsible and accountable for practicing self-transcendence and discovering the meaning present in every moment of their lives (Frankl, 1986).

Logotherapists are interactive members of the therapeutic encounter. Therapists and clients are unique individuals; each will alter the encounter and leave an impact on the other. In this way, the ***Logotherapeutic encounter*** is a unique set of circumstances that requires therapists to be completely present to the situation, and tailor the therapy to each client. As a result, Logotherapy becomes a uniquely designed experiential, existential (here-and-now) therapy, utilizing primary methodologies as well as many complementary methods.

Logotherapists are responsible for:

- ***Building Trust:*** Trust is the initial building block in creating any meaningful therapeutic work.
- ***Upholding Ethical Standards:*** The responsibility to maintain and protect the mental health and well-being of clients. This includes being aware of such aspects of therapy as *autonomy, nonmaleficence, beneficence, justice,* and *informed consent.*
- ***Preventing of Iatrogenic Damage:*** Prevent damage resulting from a medical/ psychological diagnosis or treatment interventions on the part of the therapist.
- ***Providing Medical Ministry:*** Provide treatment to help clients cope with and endure suffering that is necessitated by fate; i.e. when the client has to face an inoperable disease or medical condition.
- ***Utilizing the Therapeutic Relationship:*** Use the therapeutic encounter to assist clients in their personal *search for meaning* and *finding meaning potentials* in life.
- ***Engaging Humor:*** Engage the ability of humor to distance clients from the situation, as well as within specific therapeutic methods—(i.e. *Paradoxical Intention).*
- ***Maintaining Human Dignity:*** Always maintain the dignity of the human being, and one's unique essence and presence in the world, regardless of the medical illness, psychological diagnosis, or *noölogical* (spiritual) frustration.
- ***Viewing each Individual as a Unique Being:*** Treat each person as a unique being, and use wisdom in tailoring treatment according to the specific needs of the client.
- ***Activating Will to Meaning and Attitudinal Change:*** Help clients uncover and activate their innate *Will to Meaning* and examine possible *Attitudinal Change.*

General Existential Analysis Exploration

Another goal of Logotherapy is to assist clients in becoming aware and conscious of ***their responsibility to life.*** This awareness will help them discover their own unique, meaningful existence. Through exploring ***the meaning of life, the meaning of death, the meaning of suffering, the meaning of love,*** and ***the meaning of work*** (Frankl, 1986), clients are hopefully able to get in touch with their own existence and meaning inherent within it.

Exploration topics:

- ***Meaning of Life***: Exploring the search for *Ultimate Meaning* and *Meaning in the Moment* throughout existence; experiencing *meaning and purpose* in life which offers a reason for existence and leads to feelings of fulfillment and satisfaction; saying *yes to life* despite any and all inherent difficulties.
- ***Meaning of Death***: In that death marks the end of our temporal existence, we can acknowledge this reality and finds ways to activate our sense of *meaning and purpose* in life; we can create a meaningful existence because of the *transitoriness of life;* we can realize the opportunity to make a difference in our life and that of others within our limited time on earth.
- ***Meaning of Suffering***: Throughout life, we experience suffering on a multitude of levels; it is how we *respond to the suffering* that ultimately impacts our experience with this reality; examining how suffering influences our existence facilitates growth possibilities.
- ***Meaning of Love***: The uniqueness of one person's essence meets the uniqueness of another's essence. It is at this spiritual level that we truly encounter another person and transcend beyond a purely physiological love; where we see the potentials not yet realized and actualized in our beloved; and where we experience *meaning, purpose* and *self-transcendence*.
- ***Meaning of Work***: Our work and profession can be what activates *meaning in life*. We can manifest creative values and our contribution to others through our attitudes about the work we choose, especially if we give of ourselves to others and the world through this experience—what Frankl called *"self-transcendence."*

Methodology of Logotherapy: Eliciting and Discovering Wisdom and Meaning Inherent Within the Spirit of Each Seeker

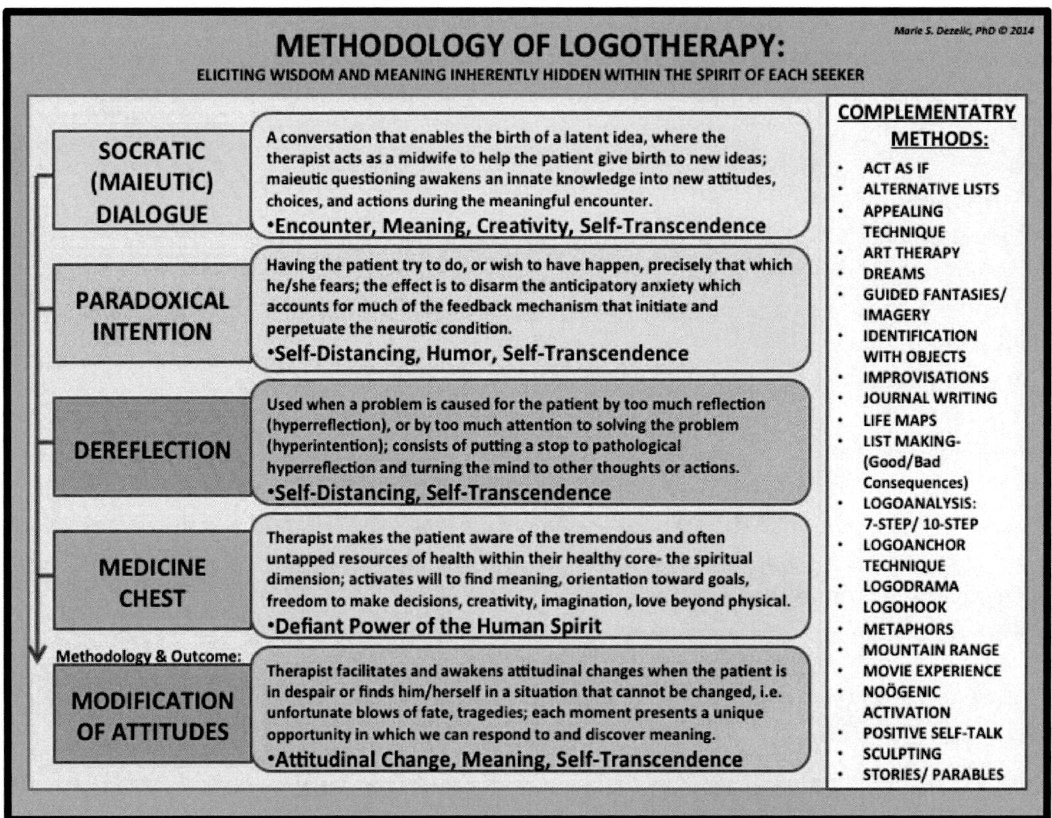

Figure 5 - (Dezelic, 2014b)

Methodology—Primary Methods of Logotherapy: (Figure 5)
(Barnes, 2005; Dezelic, 2014a; Dezelic, 2014b; Fabry, 1988; Frankl, 1978; Frankl, 1986; Frankl, 1988; Frankl, 2004; Frankl, 2006; Graber, 2004; Lukas, 2000; Rice et al., 2004; Welter, 2005)

- ***Socratic (Maieutic) Dialogue***: A conversation that enables the birth of latent ideas. Therapists act as "midwives" assisting clients to birth new ideas; maieutic questioning awakens innate knowledge so that new attitudes, choices, and actions are revealed during the meaningful encounter.
  Produces: **Positive Therapeutic Encounter, Self-Transcendence, Activation of Meaning, & Creativity**
- ***Paradoxical Intention***: Directs or suggests that clients try to do, or wish to have happen, precisely what they fear; the effect is to disarm the anticipatory anxiety, which accounts for much of the feedback mechanism that initiates and perpetuates the neurotic or anxiety producing condition.
  Produces: **Self-Distancing, Self-Transcendence, & Humor**
- ***Dereflection***: Used when too much reflection *(hyperreflection)* on a problem or when too much attention to solving a problem *(hyperintention)* causes discomfort; consists of putting a stop to pathological *hyperreflection* and turning the mind to other thoughts or actions; reflecting away from self-focus and towards another interest, person or task.
  Produces: **Self-Distancing & Self-Transcendence**

- ***Medicine Chest***: The gifts contained within our *Nöetic Dimension* such as creativity, sense of humor, personal conscience and forgiveness. Assist clients to become aware of the tremendous and often untapped resources of health within their healthy core—the *Nöetic Dimension*—the spiritual dimension; activates will to find meaning, orientation toward goals, freedom to make decisions, creativity, imagination, and love beyond the physical.
  Produces: **Engagement with the Defiant Power of the Human Spirit**

Method and Outcome of Treatment:

- **Modification of Attitudes:** Facilitating and awakening attitudinal changes when clients are in despair or find themselves in a situation that cannot be changed (i.e. unfortunate blows of fate, tragedies); each moment presents a unique opportunity that clients can respond to and discover meaning.
  Produces: **Attitudinal Change, Meaning, & Self-Transcendence**

Complementary Methods of Logotherapy: (Figure 5)
(Barnes, 2005; Dezelic, 2014a; Dezelic, 2014b; Fabry, 1988; Frankl, 1978; Frankl, 1986; Frankl, 1988; Frankl, 2004; Frankl, 2006; Graber, 2004; Lukas, 2000; Rice et al., 2004; Welter, 2005)

- ***Act As If***: Ask clients to *act as if* they have already accomplished their goal or achieved their meaningful task, and describe what it feels like to have done this; roll play can assist in connecting to these feelings.
- ***Alternative Lists***: Ask clients to make a list of desirable activities that would provide meaning, as well as alternative things they can still do despite their current situation/ diagnosis.
- ***Appealing Technique***: Use this Autogenic training combined with positive affirmations and guided imagery to strengthen the client's *Nöetic*—spiritual resources.
- ***Art Therapy***: Ask clients to use artistic expression as a means to illustrate a meaningful experience; clients can give the art to someone significant as a gift, or keep as a legacy-building piece. This can be accomplished through writing, painting/ drawing/ sculpture/ woodworking/ any artistic medium, photography, videography, or creating something unique such as a scrapbook, cookbook, photo book, short story, poetry, knitting, etc.
- ***Dream Analysis***: Identify the dream content which is giving a voice and vision to the client's unconscious— *Nöetic*—spiritual dimension; free association is used to connect to meaningful cues and new meaning possibilities.
- ***Guided Fantasies/ Imagery***: Take clients on a journey through guided fantasies and imagery toward achieving meaningful tasks; meditational and mindfulness based.
- ***Identification with Objects***: Ask clients to share stories related to significant objects that they have collected over the years. They can bring in the actual object or, if this is not possible, they can take a photograph of it instead; identify ways clients can continue to use the object as a means of activating *will to meaning.*
- ***Improvisations***: Create "On the spot," techniques that focus on clients' uniqueness and assist in activating their *Meaning Triangle.*
- ***Journal Writing***: Ask clients to write about particular topics in order to look for meaningful cues that will enhance their search for meaning.
- ***Life Maps***: Ask clients to map out their lifetime impactful experiences, both positive and negative; have them map out where they would like to see themselves in one, five, ten and fifteen years.
- ***List Making—(Good/Bad Consequences)***: Ask clients to make lists of good and bad consequences, as well as meaning interpretations of each.

- ***Logoanalysis-7 Steps***: Utilize this modality developed for the treatment of addictions; The 7-step process consists of: (1) Identifying one's belief system; (2) Experiencing loss of value; (3) Develop self-confidence through meditations, relaxation, exercise, and using the *Power of Freedom*; (4) Learning to cope with future problems; (5) Exploring Relationships; (6) Administering the *MILE (Meaning in Life Evaluation Scale)*; (7) Committing to daily work on activating their *will to meaning* to reinforce their uniqueness as human beings.
- ***Logoanchor Technique***: Ask clients to recall and share impactful experiences, events and images that previously filled them with wonder and a sense of uniqueness. This will enable them to use these past meaningful moments as meaning-anchors for the present.
- ***Logodrama***: Ask clients to imagine a future time when they are close to death, and to reflect back on their major accomplishments and meaningful moments, in order to ignite possible goals and plans.
- ***Logohook***: Make use of a meaningful experience expressed or object the client has shown, and use it to activate and ignite meaning in the present moment.
- ***Metaphors***: Use metaphors of ideas or goals that interest clients, in order to impart helpful information that will connect them to meaningful concepts in their lives.
- ***Mountain Range***: Ask clients to draw a mountain range, and place significant people/situations who touched their lives on the distant peaks; meaningful individuals/ encounters can be discussed or written about.
- ***Movie Experience***: Have clients create a movie of their life. The Movie has three parts: (1) Life In Review, (2) Life in Preview, (3) Fast-Forward Experience. Ask them to choose which actors or historical/current figures would play them and other key members in each part, describe the setting, the budget, and the story lines.
- ***Noögenic Activation Method:*** Utilize this seven stage method for Logotherapeutic change which consists of: (1) Pre-contemplation; (2) Contemplation; (3) Preparation/ Determination/ Freedom of Will; (4) Action/ Will to Meaning; (5) Maintenance/ Living Meaningfully; (6) Relapse/ Existential Distress & Frustration; (7) Noö-dynamics and Self-Transcendence. There is also a seven-step protocol to be explored within each stage of change: (1) Access to the Nöetic Dimension; (2) Recognize the Uniqueness of the individual; (3) Examine choices; (4) Be aware of responsibility to... not from; (5) Activate the Will to Meaning; (6) Recognize Freedom of Will; (7) Examine Meaning in Life, Meaning in the Moment, Ultimate Meaning.
- ***Positive Self-Talk***: Assist clients in strengthening and building internal resources and strengths, and accessing their *Nöetic Dimension.*
- ***Sculpting***: Assist clients as they sculpt, shape and adapt a story or experience into something that provides meaning.
- ***Stories/Parables***: Use stories/parables to illustrate a point that or idea that will help clients discover meaning in their lives.

Discovering Meaning in Life

Frankl believed that meanings are always present, are unique, and are ever changing; in other words, life is never lacking a meaning (Frankl, 1978). Logotherapists consistently assist clients in reorienting toward and activating *Meaning* in life. Clients can be taught the difference between:

Meaning of the Moment—which can be found and fulfilled, and where clients have the opportunity to act with purposeful living, and to be aware of the meaning possibilities of each moment; and

Ultimate Meaning—which can be defined in terms of an existing order in the Universe or by one's concept of God and that can basically never be fully attained during our lifetime on earth, for like the horizon, no matter how close we seem to approach it, we are far away from Ultimate Meaning's unreachable and elusive reality until the moment of death or beyond.

One of the major principles of Logotherapy is described by Dr. Ann Graber, Director of the Pastoral Logotherapy & Existential Analysis Program at the Graduate Theological Foundation:

Each person is a unique individual, going from birth to death through a string of unique life situations. Every situation, every unrepeatable moment, offers a specific meaning potential. To respond to these meaning offerings of the moment is to lead a meaningful life (Graber, 2004, p.87).

The Meaning Triangle, comprised of Creativity, Experiences, and Attitudes allows us the opportunity to discover meaning in the moment and in life.

The Meaning Triangle (Frankl, 2006):

- ***Creativity:*** Our innate talents that we give the world and others through our endeavors, work, deeds done, and goals accomplished; also includes creating a family, and raising children.
- ***Experiences:*** The experiences we engage in through encountering others in relationships of all kinds, and from our appreciation or encounter with nature, culture or religion.
- ***Attitudes:*** The courageous and self-transcending values we realize by taking a stance toward and changing our perspective about unavoidable pain, guilt or death.

Dr. Ann Graber's ***Reflections on the Meaning Triangle*** depicted in her book: *Viktor Frankl's Logotherapy: Method of Choice in Ecumenical Pastoral Psychology,* suggests that reflecting on these three areas is in keeping *"with Logotherapy's emphasis on 'what's right about you,' and [that] by deemphasizing 'what's wrong with you,' it can serve as a starting point for the therapeutic process"* (Graber, 2004, p.195).

In Graber's ***Strengths Awareness Instrument,*** each angle of ***The Meaning Triangle*** represents an avenue toward finding meaning:

1. "What I give to life through my ***creativity.***
2. What I receive from life through ***experiences.***
3. The stance I take toward life through my ***attitude."***

According to Graber, ***reflections*** upon the following questions aid in the ***discovery of meaning*** during a previous time in life:

1. "What ***creative*** gifts have I offered to others through my talents, my work, deeds done, goals achieved that held meaning for me?
2. What ***experiences*** have I received from encountering others in relationship of all kinds, from nature, culture or religion that were deeply meaningful?
3. What ***attitudinal*** values have I realized by taking a stance toward situations or blows of fate that was courageous or self-transcending?" (Graber, 2004, p.94, Figure 6).

Tragic Optimism of Logotherapy: Optimism In The Face of Tragedy

Another specific goal of Logotherapy is to contend with what Frankl calls ***"the case for Tragic Optimism"*** (Frankl, 2006, p.137). Specifically, to remain or become optimistic in the face of tragedy requires a modification of attitude, where one becomes optimistic or positive when it appears one could become discouraged or lose hope.

Tragic Optimism (Frankl, 2006):

- Turning suffering and pain into a human achievement and accomplishment
- Extracting from existential guilt the opportunity to change ourselves for the better
- Extracting from the awareness of life's transitoriness an incentive and the possibility to take responsible action

Dr. Elisabeth Lukas describes four hints from Frankl's *Medical Ministry,* which can assist in the process of attitude modification (Lukas, 2000, p.158-159):

1. ***Pointing Out Value***
2. ***Pointing Out Meaning***
3. ***Pointing Out What Remained Intact***
4. ***Pointing Out Perspectives***

Logotherapists assist clients in answering the question: How can we move beyond the ***suffering, guilt,*** and ***transitory aspect of life*** so as to derive meaning from the tragic situations and unfortunate blows of fate in life? The trajectory can ultimately be an upward and outward movement from life-limiting circumstances.

Challenges of Human Suffering: The Tragic Triad and The Neurotic Triad

The challenges of human suffering often lead to the ***Existential Vacuum***—an internal pulling force, of inner void, emptiness, boredom, apathy, struggle, and meaningless existence. Logotherapists look at the possibilities of the *human existence,* which can lead to the *Existential Vacuum*, thus blocking access to the *Nöetic (Spiritual) Dimension*, and possibly affecting our mental and physical health. These challenges are divided into the Tragic Triad and the Neurotic Triad (Barnes, 2005; Graber, 2004).

One of the main goals of ***Logotherapy & Existential Analysis*** is to address the challenges of human suffering—experiences of ***The Tragic Triad*** and ***The Neurotic Triad,*** which often bring clients into therapy in the first place. Within the *Nöetic* encounter between the therapist and client, and through Logotherapy's specific and complementary methods, therapists assist clients in activating and re-orienting themselves towards their ***Meaning Triangle,*** which can ultimately lead toward ***Self-Transcendence,*** a meaningful existence, adaptive behavioral functioning, and a sense of healing.

The Tragic Triad—people in ***despondency*** experience:

- ***Unavoidable Suffering***: Pain experienced from suffering that is caused by situations that could not be prevented or escaped or arises from acts of fate or situations over which we have no control.
- ***Guilt***: Responsibility, fault, or self blame we experience due to a situation we have caused, been a part or sometimes have been affected by, for example, when we wanted to do something that for whatever reason was not possible; the self-blame we feel when reflecting back on missed opportunities with people or situations.
- ***Death***: The deep sadness and/or questioning we experience upon the realization of the transitoriness of life after the death of someone or the realization of our own mortality.

The Neurotic Triad—people in ***despair*** turn toward or experience:

- ***Depression***: The feelings we experience in our inner world when we have had a significant tragedy or loss, or have given up our will toward life; feelings of hopelessness or helplessness.
- ***Aggression***: An outward expression of violence perhaps caused by the anger and rage experienced internally. Often a means of controlling others; or it could be aggression turned

inward—the attempt to harm oneself through self-mutilation or, at the extreme end, a suicide attempt—to extinguish one's existence from this world completely.

- ***Addiction***: The attempt to numb or dull pain and despair through substance abuse or a particular behavior. This can also be exhibited as thrill-seeking behavior in order to feel a bodily sensation, experience invincibility and appear larger-than-life, without regard to consequences.

The Existential Triangle: From Meaningless To Meaningful Existence

In assessing clients' current situation and difficulties, Marie Dezelic, has coined a term that helps us visualize Frankl's three basic triangles—***The Tragic Triad, The Neurotic Triad,*** and ***The Meaning Triangle*** as parts of one larger Triangle, naming this larger triangle—"***The Existential Triangle: From Meaningless to Meaningful Existence***" (Dezelic, 2014b). Conceptualizing a client's movement through ***The Existential Triangle*** offers therapists a holistic view of inherent possibilities within the difficulties experienced. Therapists can use this tool to help their clients create awareness of and responsibility for the *meaning potentials,* which are always possible regardless of *The Tragic Triad, The Neurotic Triad, Existential Frustration* and the *Existential Vacuum.*

At the base, in the two lower angles of the main triangle *(The Existential Triangle),* are ***The Tragic Triad*** (Unavoidable Suffering, Guilt, and Death) and ***The Neurotic Triad*** (Depression, Aggression, and Addiction). ***Existential Frustration***—fed by the inner pain and outer despair experienced from the two triads, respectively—exists in this area.

When clients experience inner emptiness and despair, they feel the force of the ***Existential Vacuum*** pulling them down, maintaining desperation, and ultimately blocking access to the *Nöetic Dimension.* ***"The Existential Vacuum is in itself not a pathological state. It should be seen as a sign, calling to our attention that access to the Nöetic Dimension is blocked"*** (Graber, 2004, p.143).

The main triangle *(The Existential Triangle)* leads toward a peak, where we cross an invisible barrier into the positive areas of growth, possibilities and meaningfulness. In this upper area of the main triangle, we become engaged in ***The Meaning Triangle*** through *Creativity, Experiences,* and *Attitudes,* culminating in ***Self-Transcendence*** and ***meaningful living.*** Utilizing the methods and tools of Logotherapy, therapists assist clients who are experiencing the lower aspects of this *Existential Triangle,* namely the thoughts, emotions and behaviors of *The Tragic Triad* and *The Neurotic Triad,* to cross the invisible barrier into the realm of *Meaning,* through *The Meaning Triangle* and beyond—toward *Self-Transcendence.* It is important to recognize that due to the unpredictability of life, human beings will always fluctuate throughout ***The Existential Triangle.*** It is precisely for this reason that therapists who practice the principles of Logotherapy & Existential Analysis (LTEA) meet clients exactly where they are at any given point in time, and do their best to assist these clients in their quest to discover their own unique ultimate goals and possibilities.

Post-Traumatic Growth and Possibilities Activated in Logotherapy

Logotherapy addresses our ***Post-Traumatic Growth and Possibilities*** rather than our Post-Traumatic behavioral difficulties and stress. Logotherapists look past the ***Pathos*** **(Pathology)** to the ***Logos*** **(Meaning)** within each unique individual.

Logotherapy explores:

- ***"How"*** we have grown from the experience.
- ***"What"*** we have taken away from the difficulty.
- ***"Where"*** we see new possibilities in the face of setbacks.
- ***"When"*** we will actualize the new possibilities.
- ***"Who"*** is making a difference in our own life and whose life/lives we are influencing.

Logotherapy emphasizes that humans are not pre-determined beings, reduced and fated by intrinsic drives; rather, we have inherent ***Choices, Freedom, Meaning*** and ***Responsibility.*** We are to some extent ***Pushed by our Past*** while simultaneously being ***Pulled by our Future,*** concurrently fully existing and living in the ***Present Moment.***

III. CONCLUSION

Frankl's existential work is perfectly described by one statement: ***"'Logos' means the humanness of the human being—plus the meaning of being human!"*** (Frankl, 1988, p.18).

Logotherapy & Existential Analysis (LTEA), a therapeutic approach conceptualized, designed and intended for addressing the difficulties of life humans experience on the existential realm, ultimately aims to assist clients to reorient themselves toward meaningful and purposeful living. *"Logotherapy, with its meaning-seeking motivation—its spiritually based psychotherapy—can help clients find their nöetic goals and build a meaning-filled future"* (Graber, 2004, p.186).

Frankl always believed that life is potentially meaningful in any condition, whether pleasurable or painful (Frankl, 1986).

The Logotherapeutic encounter is where therapists experience the fragility of human beings, yet simultaneously, meet their ***defiant power of the human spirit.*** The Logotherapeutic encounter and methods used in Logotherapy provide the resources for encouraging our creativity and interaction with others as we search for the unique meaning of the moment and examine our day to day life. As Socrates once said, ***"An unexamined life is not worth living."*** To be alive is to be creative, and likewise to be creative is to be alive. When we wake up to and become conscious of this aliveness, we can realize and actualize the many possibilities of our lives, and discover the inherent *Meaning* held within it!

7. Synopsis of Meaning-Centered Logotherapy & Existential Analysis (LTEA)

(Meaning-Centered Therapy Workbook: Based on Viktor Frankl's Logotherapy & Existential Analysis, Dezelic, 2014b, p.4-5)

Meaning Centered Logotherapy & Existential Analysis:

- Is a ***non-deterministic, non-reductionistic, self-transcending*** and ***holistic psychological therapy*** and theory addressing the human existence, and ***being in the world.***
- Is a psychological theory of great depth in terms of understanding the human being and great height in terms of the process by which we live and encounter life.
- Has ***Logos—Meaning*** as its core philosophy.
- Uses our ***Search for Meaning*** as it primary therapeutic approach.
- Relies heavily on the ***therapist-client relationship*** and *encounter.*
- Helps individuals discover and uncover their ***meaning and purpose in life.***
- Utilizes both a directive and reflective approach; thus therapists, with wisdom, intuition, and skillful artistry, individualize each session based on clients' needs.
- Goes beyond merely addressing and analyzing disorders and pathology by recognizing and validating the individual's full human capacities and capabilities.
- Incorporates ***spirituality in therapy*** without the connotation of religiosity or theology.
- Recognizes that human beings are comprised of three inseparable and integrated parts, ***Body (Soma), Mind (Psyche),*** and ***Spirit (Noös),*** where the whole is greater than the sum of its parts.
- Describes Spirit (Noös) as the unique essence of human beings; that which sets them apart from all others, as well as the key difference between human beings and animals.
- Emphasizes that, while the soma and psyche can become damaged, ill, or function pathologically, the **spiritual core—the *Nöetic Dimension,*** is the source of health in all human beings.
- Suggests that the ***Will to Meaning*** exists at the core of the human being, specifically in the *Nöetic*—spiritual dimension.
- States that the *Nöetic Dimension* contains all of the necessary tools to help individuals activate their resources for a healthy lifestyle.
- Recognizes the ***Defiant Power of the Human Spirit*** as the motivator of change and the initiator of health.
- Is not a deterministic or fatalistic theory of therapy; but rather, is a future-oriented therapy, whereby as human beings we have the capacity for ***Self-Distancing***—removing focus off the self and detaching from the situation, and through ***Self-Transcendence***—going beyond ourselves to discover meaning.
- Fosters the discovery of meaning in life through examining our (1) ***Experiences*** and encounters in the world and with others, (2) expression and use of ***Creativity,*** and (3) modification of ***Attitudes*** toward self and others in unalterable situations and unavoidable suffering.
- Affirms that humans are unique beings with the capacity to ***act in freedom*** and ***with freedom,*** toward their central purpose—***Search for Meaning*** through their *Will to find Meaning* and purpose in their lives.
- Explains that ***Existential Frustration*** and the ***Existential Vacuum*** develop when we are stuck in the ***Tragic Triad***—dealing with ***Unavoidable Suffering, Guilt,*** and ***Death,*** and/or the ***Neurotic Triad***—dealing with ***Aggression, Depression,*** and ***Addiction,*** and/or from ***Noögenic Neurosis***—neurosis originating specifically in our spiritual dimension because our *Will to Meaning* has become difficult to see or seems blocked in some way.

- Seeks to activate the *Will to Meaning*, addresses *Existential Frustration*, and the *Existential Vacuum*, through its techniques and methodologies.
- Addresses the existential exploration of the ***Meaning of Life, Meaning of Death, Meaning of Suffering, Meaning of Love***, and ***Meaning of Work.***
- Uses ***Socratic (Maieutic) Dialogue, Paradoxical Intention, Dereflection,*** *the* ***Medicine Chest—Nöetic Dimension,*** and ***Modification of Attitudes,*** as its primary methodologies, in addition to many complementary therapeutic methods.
- Is a therapy that can be used for specific mental illnesses and psychological functioning, as well as an adjunctive therapy to various theories and therapies.
- Has a behavioral and experiential quality to its eclectic and unique, existential therapy.
- Is founded on the belief that ***Freedom of Will, Will to Meaning,*** and ***Meaning in Life*** are the primary motivators of human beings, and are essentially what differentiates human beings from animals.
- Suggests that when we discover *meaning* in any situation, whether perceived as good or bad, it becomes not only tolerable, but it can motivate us toward a meaningful life; also maintains that meaning and hope can be found in even in the face of tragedy once we are willing to modify our attitude.

II.
LOGOTHERAPY
BRIEF THERAPY PROTOCOL

8-SESSION FORMAT
GROUP & INDIVIDUAL THERAPY

OUTLINE
SESSIONS 1 – 8 PROTOCOL

Session 1: Introduction: Concepts of Logotherapy & Existential Analysis (LTEA)
(1) What is Viktor Frankl's Logotherapy?
(2) Philosophy of Logotherapy: The Basic Assumptions
(3) Basic Concepts of Logotherapy: The 3 Primary Tenets

Session 2: Exploring Meaning
(4) Discovering Meaning in Life
(5) Identity: Doing vs. Being

Session 3: The Human Ontology of Body, Mind, Spirit (Essence)
(6) The Human Being's Multidimensional Aspects: Body (Soma), Mind (Psyche), Spirit (Noös)
(7) The Human Being's Unique Aspect: Spiritual (Nöetic) Dimension

Session 4: Inner Resources and Strengths
(8) Nöetic Dimension: The Medicine Chest of Logotherapy
(9) Mind-Body-Spirit: Simple Techniques for Stress Reduction & Healthy Living

Session 5: Existential Aspects
(10) The Existential Triangle: From Meaningless to Meaningful Existence
(11) Tragic Optimism of Logotherapy: Optimism in the Face of Tragedy

Session 6: Suffering and Meaning
(12) "Homo Patiens": Extracting Meaning from Suffering
(13) Noögenic (Spiritual) Neuroses: Logotherapy as a Specific Therapy

Session 7: Personal Growth and Transformation
(14) Post-Traumatic Growth and Possibilities Activated in Logotherapy
(15) The Meaning-Action Triangle: Becoming Existentially Aware
(16) 7-Step Noögenic Activation Method

Session 8: Living Meaningfully
(17) REACH Beyond the Limitations: Sources of Meaning in Life
(18) Connect—Create—Convey: Living Life with Meaning and Purpose
Closing Discussion

- SESSION 1 -

Introduction: Concepts of Logotherapy & Existential Analysis (LTEA)

The primary goal of Session 1 is to summarize the general concepts of Logotherapy & Existential Analysis (LTEA), and to develop familiarity with the topics. In a group setting, both the therapist and members introduce themselves, and if they are comfortable doing so, briefly add additional information; for example, why they enrolled in the program. During this first session, it is important to go over any standard group rules, in particular the expectations and limitations of confidentiality outside of the sessions. Be sure to distribute folders to group participants or clients to be used as a **"Logo-Journey Journal"**—the portfolio that will hold their *"Conceptual Pictographs" — Client Handouts,* as well as session notes, and any other work accumulated during their Logotherapy journey.

It is helpful for the therapist/facilitator of the protocol to become familiar with Section I of this manual, which will provide a detailed overview of Meaning-Centered Logotherapy & Existential Analysis, as well as to have read Viktor Frankl's ***Man's Search for Meaning,*** and any other of his books relating to Logotherapy & Existential Analysis. Additionally, having a copy of Ann Graber's *Viktor Frankl's Logotherapy: Meaning-Centered Counseling*, and Marie Dezelic's *Meaning-Centered Therapy Workbook: Based on Viktor Frankl's Logotherapy & Existential Analysis,* are helpful resource tools for questions that may arise from the therapist/facilitator or from clients throughout the sessions.

- PICTOGRAPH 1 -

What is Viktor Frankl's Logotherapy?

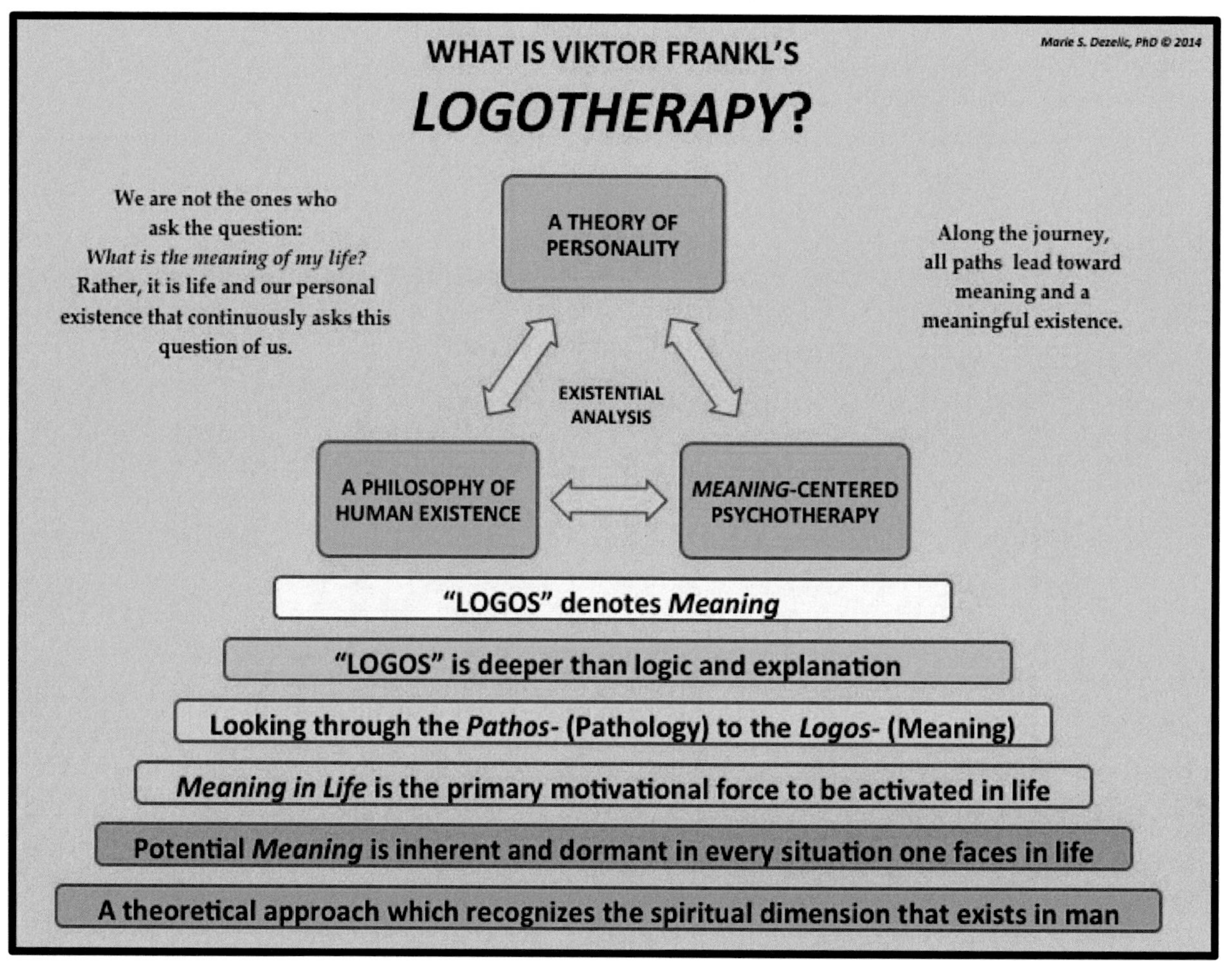

Black-and-White version available in the Appendix p.114

THERAPIST/ FACILITATOR CAN:

- Ask clients or the group to read Frankl's ***Man Search for Meaning*** prior to entering therapy or as part of this first session:
    - Read excerpts from the book for clarification of important concepts.
    - Ask clients to share their reaction to the book, focusing on any parallels to their own lives.
- Use this *Conceptual Pictograph* to elaborate on the general concepts and themes of **Meaning-Centered Logotherapy & Existential Analysis** (LTEA), explaining the general concepts and themes, which will be further developed throughout the 8-session protocol.
- Ask clients/group members to discuss their understanding of the following statements in Pictograph 1:
    - "Logos" denotes *Meaning*
    - "Logos" is deeper than logic and explanation
    - Looking through the *Pathos*—(Pathology) to the *Logos*—(Meaning)
    - *Meaning in Life* is the primary motivational force to be activated in life
    - Potential *Meaning* is inherent and dormant in every situation one faces in life
    - A theoretical approach which recognizes the spiritual that exists in man (all of us)
    - **"We are not the ones who ask the question: *What is the meaning of my life?* Rather, it is life and our existence which continuously asks this question of us."**
- Initiate a discussion based on the readings included in Section 1 of this manual and provide further explanation about Meaning-Centered Logotherapy & Existential Analysis as a theory of personality, a philosophical approach, and a ***Meaning-Centered*** psychotherapy.

- PICTOGRAPH 2 -

Philosophy of Logotherapy:
The Basic Assumptions

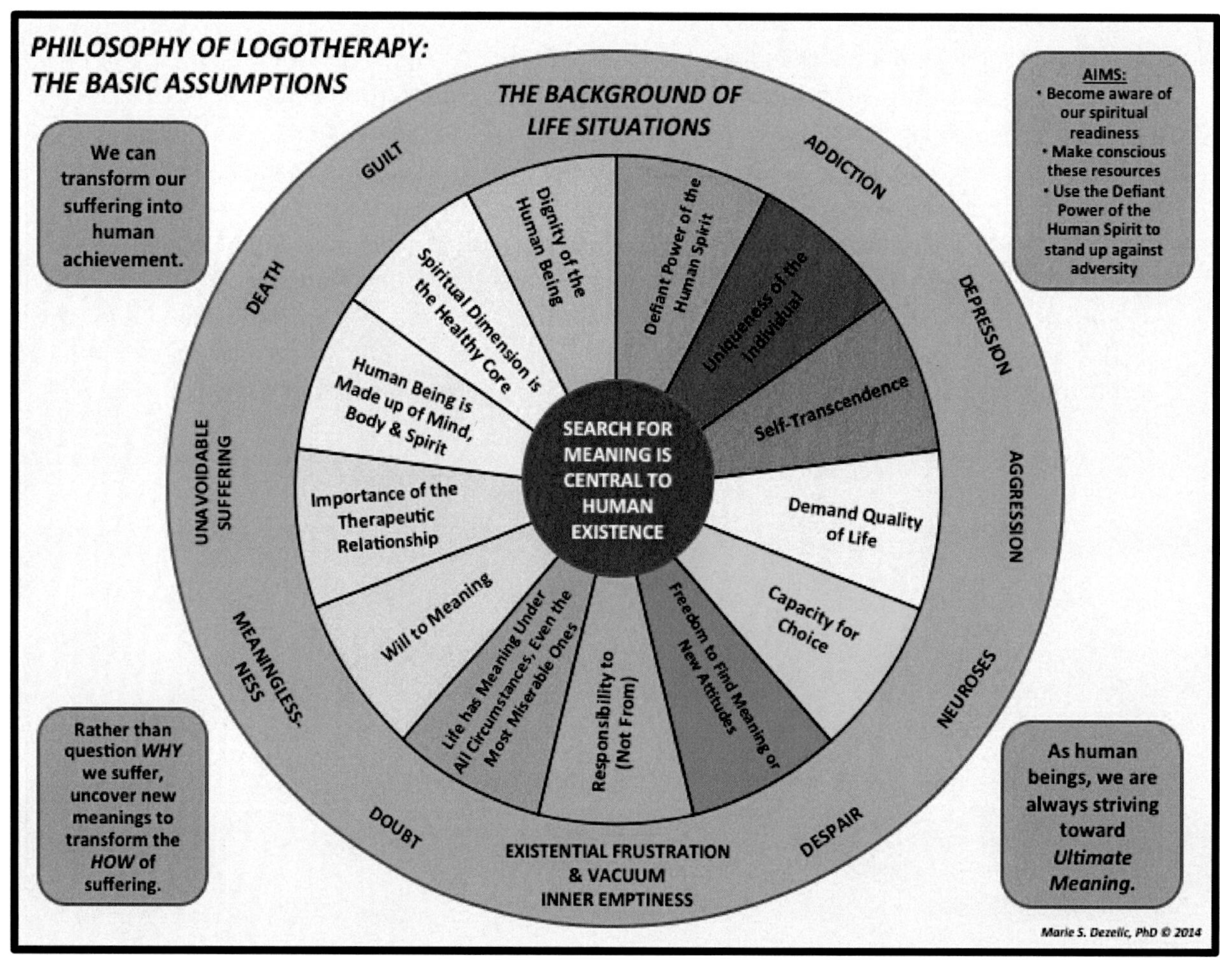

Black-and-White version available in the Appendix p.115

THERAPIST/ FACILITATOR CAN:

- Ask clients to discuss 3 of the following **Basic Assumptions.** Suggest they choose the ones which "speak" to them, and that they intuitively or easily understand:
    - *Defiant Power of the Human Spirit*
    - *Uniqueness of the Individual*
    - *Demand Quality of Life*
    - *Capacity for Choice*
    - *Freedom to Find Meaning or New Attitudes*
    - *Responsibility to (Not from)*
    - *Life has Meaning Under All Circumstances, Even the Most Miserable Ones*
    - *Will to Meaning*
    - *Importance of the Therapeutic Relationship*
    - *Human Being is Comprised of Mind, Body and Spirit*
    - *Spiritual Dimension is the Healthy Core*
    - *Dignity of the Human Being*
- Have clients write about how these **3 Basic Assumptions** could have helped or actually did help them deal with either one or more of the **Background of Life** situations (i.e. addiction, doubt, despair).
- Ask clients to journal about the meaning of this *Conceptual Pictograph* in either an in-session or homework assignment.
- Use the *Conceptual Pictograph* as a psycho-educational piece.
- In the group setting, ask clients to share their thoughts and writings about the messages found in this *Conceptual Pictograph* with other members of the group.
- In a group setting, ask each member to read one of the **Basic Assumptions** out loud; after all have been read, ask other members to offer explanations and personal examples.
- In a group setting, ask members to share when they believe that others in the group have utilized or are now utilizing the **Basic Assumptions.**
- To foster deeper understanding in an individual session, point out when the client is utilizing one or more of the **Basic Assumptions.**
- In group or individual therapy, give a basic overview of the **Background of Life** situations and ask clients or group members to share their own personal examples.
- In group or individual therapy, suggest that clients choose one item from the **Basic Assumptions** that they think addresses one item from the **Background of Life;** discuss how the **Basic Assumption** can help deal with, and even alter their understanding of the **Background of Life** item.
- Facilitate a discussion that furthers our understanding of why we would want to: ***"Transform our human suffering into achievement."***
- Facilitate a discussion about the statement: ***"Rather than question WHY we suffer, uncover new meanings to transform the HOW of suffering."***
    - ***WHY:*** addresses reason; however, since reasoning is part of our intellectual processes, it can sometimes keep us overly focused or even stuck on the "facts" of a situation or event. Having intellectual answers does not always alleviate the pain/suffering.

- ***HOW:*** addresses a search for meaning and is based on the assumption that we can always experience a change in attitude. For example:
    - How do we transform the pain/suffering and move beyond?
    - How do we assimilate the experience and transcend the life-limiting situation or thoughts?
    - How can we experience self-transcendence and discover new meanings?

- PICTOGRAPH 3 -

The Basic Concepts of Logotherapy: The 3 Primary Tenets

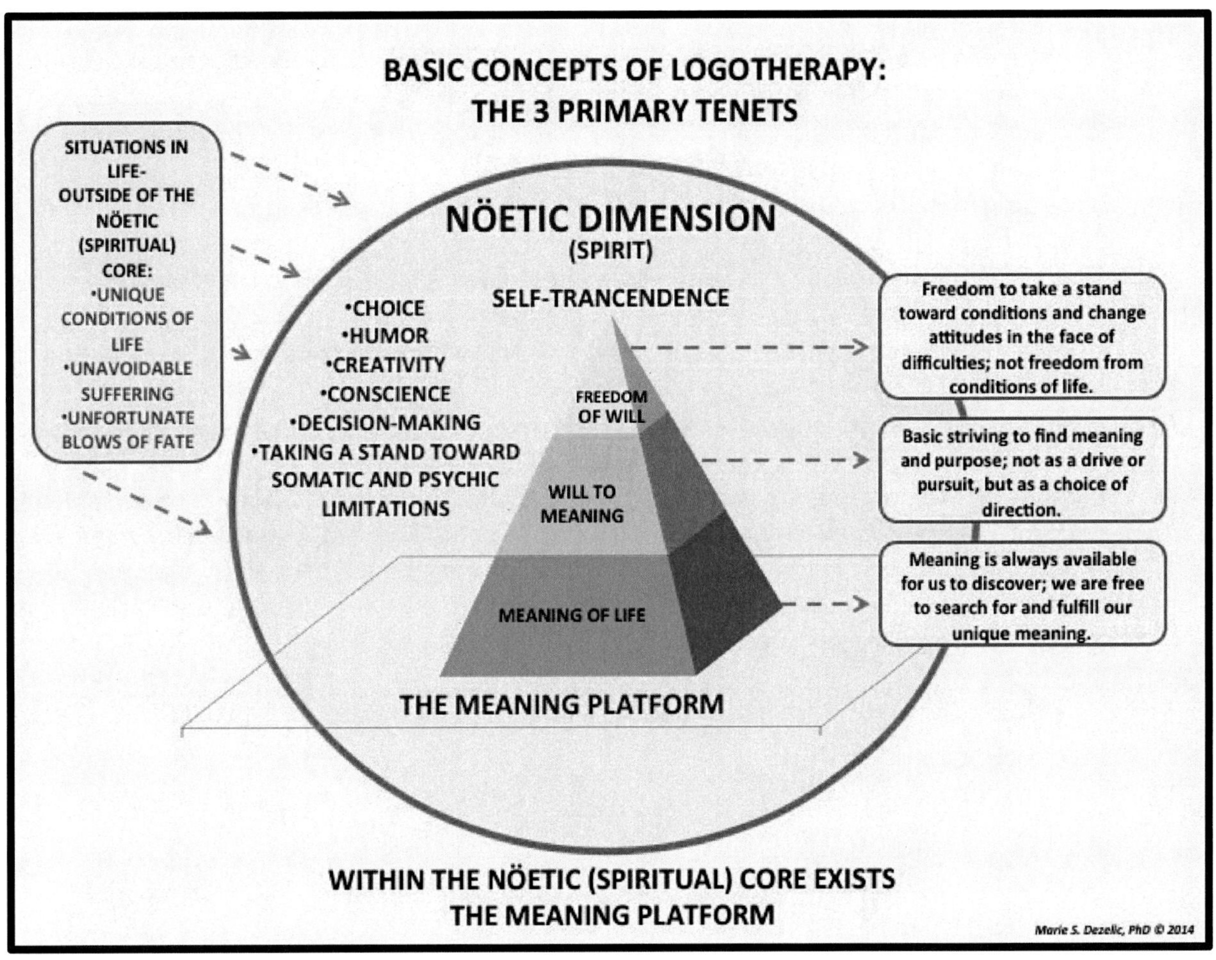

Black-and-White version available in the Appendix p.116

THERAPIST/ FACILITATOR CAN:

- Ask clients to write about **Situations in Life** that have happened to them, been created by them, or have affected them.
- Ask clients to write about how they used some of the **Nöetic Dimension** attributes to deal with these **Situations in Life.**
- Ask clients to write about their understanding of the three areas of the **Meaning Pyramid**, and give examples of each in their lives:
    - ***Meaning of Life:*** Meaning is always available for us to discover; we are free to search for and fulfill our unique meaning.
    - ***Will to Meaning:*** Basic striving to find meaning and purpose; not as a drive or pursuit, but as a choice of direction.
    - ***Freedom of Will:*** Freedom to take a stand toward conditions and change attitudes in the face of difficulties; not freedom from conditions of life.
- Facilitate a discussion focusing on the notion that, regardless of how the **Situations in Life** affect us, we can still access our **Meaning Pyramid.**
- Continue with a discussion of how the **Meaning Pyramid** has changed over the course of the client's life.
- Facilitate a discussion on what **NEW Meanings** have been discovered and how they might fulfilled.
- Facilitate a discussion on how the elements of the **Nöetic Dimension** assist in igniting the different elements of the **Meaning Platform.**
- In individual or group therapy, ask clients or members to discuss how they could begin activating and fulfilling potential **NEW Meanings**.
- In group therapy, ask members to select a partner and have each discuss their own **Meaning Platform,** and how they can work on activating it; then ask group members to share their partner's meanings with the rest of the group. **Note:** If members state that they do not remember any personal meaning or cannot come up with anything, the therapist/ facilitator may assist them in recalling past meanings that do exist in their life.

- SESSION 2 -

Exploring Meaning and Purpose

How do we stay alive in a meaning-centered world? Everything we do, touch, conceptualize, wish for, want, and have a will for is contained within our personal sense of Meaning. To understand human beings is to be able to sit inside our unique Meanings (seeing things from each of our perspectives). The suffering that we experience is beyond only a physical pain, because suffering is an existential angst, and surfaces when Meaning has been lost or our understanding of the world has been ruptured. We help each other by fostering or illuminating each other's unique Meaning of the Moment. By engaging our spirits, we experience a meaningful life in which our unique essence and presence can thrive once more. What a gift it is to be a part of someone's journey toward Meaning Discovery and meaningful existence, and ultimately, self-transcendence.

-M. Dezelic

Session 2 explores concepts related to meaning and purpose in life. An in-depth exploration of Logotherapy's concepts of Meaning, the Meaning Triangle (Creativity, Experiences, Attitude), and opportunities to discover Meaning in Life, provides a framework for being able to find meaning in life at any given moment, regardless of the difficult situations or events we may be experiencing. Logotherapy's main premise is that Meaning is always available to be discovered, even amidst life's tragic elements and events. Session 2 examines our personal identity, and how we can move from merely addressing the "doing" components of our identity toward including the "being" components of living (Breitbart & Poppito, 2014a; Breitbart & Poppito, 2014b; May, 1994). This shift in perspective will allow us to begin living more mindfully and experiencing connection and self-transcendence through meaningful engagement. When we discover our unique meanings of the moment, we often find that life retains a significance and purpose, regardless of the many limitations, difficulties and tragedies we have faced and dealt with in the past or will encounter in the present and future.

- PICTOGRAPH 4 -

Discovering Meaning in Life

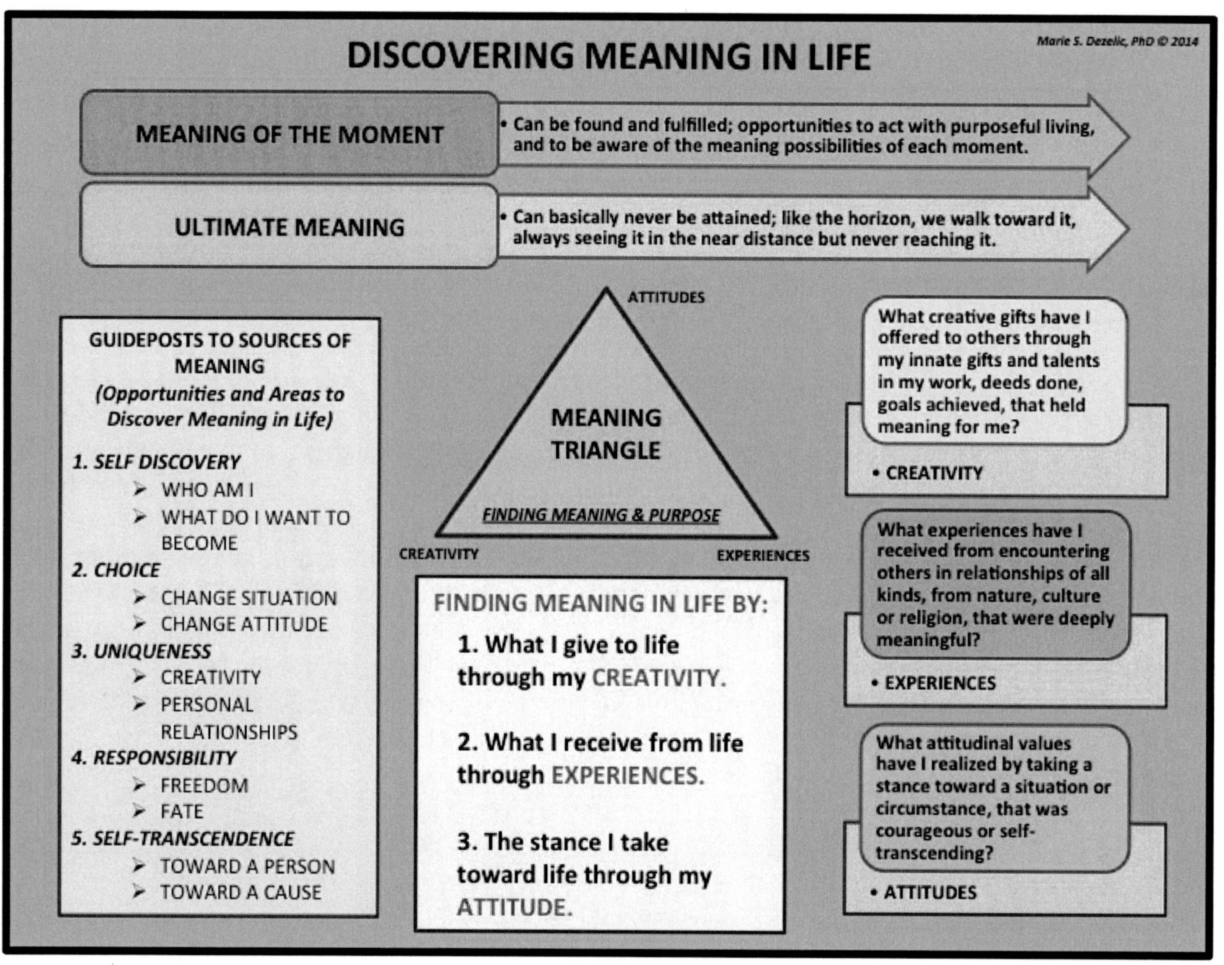

Black-and-White version available in the Appendix p.117

THERAPIST/ FACILITATOR CAN:

- Break this *Conceptual Pictograph* into 3 sections:
  1. **Meaning of the Moment** and **Ultimate Meaning**:
     - ***Meaning of the Moment:*** Can be found and fulfilled; opportunities to act with purposeful living, and to be aware of the meaning possibilities of each moment.
       - Give examples; have clients give examples.
     - ***Ultimate Meaning:*** Can basically never be attained; like the horizon, we walk toward it, always seeing it in the near distance but never reaching it, until facing our last moments of life. In fact, Viktor Frankl stated that we may not even experience Ultimate Meaning until after death; however, we make decisions in the moment based on our personal conscience that hopefully are consistent with the transcendent values found in Ultimate Meaning.
       - Give examples; have clients give examples.
  2. **The Meaning Triangle** and **Finding Meaning in Life through Creativity, Experiences, and Attitudes**, with **Questions on what one experiences through Creativity, Experiences,** and **Attitudes** (Graber, Reflections on the Meaning Triangle: A Strengths Awareness Instrument, 2004):
     - ***Creativity:*** What I give to life through my creativity.
       - What creative gifts have I offered to others through my innate gifts and talents in my work, deeds done, or goals achieved that held meaning for me?
     - ***Experiences:*** What I receive from life through experiences.
       - What experiences have I received from encountering others in relationships of all kinds, from nature, culture or religion that were deeply meaningful?
     - ***Attitudes:*** The stance I take toward life through my attitude in the face of unavoidable suffering, guilt or death.
       - What attitudinal values have I realized by taking a stance that was courageous or self-transcending in response to a situation or circumstance beyond my control?
  3. **Guideposts to Sources of Meaning**- Opportunities and areas to discover meaning in life (Barnes, 2005; Fabry, 1988; Rice et al., 2004; as described in the Logotherapy course manuals of the Viktor Frankl Institute of Logotherapy, USA):
     - ***SELF DISCOVERY-*** Discovering the "Authentic Self" behind any masks or behaviors.
       - Who Am I: Examining myself today, accepting myself along with my past.
       - What Do I Want To Become: Exploring possibilities for the future.
     - ***CHOICE-*** Becoming aware of possibilities for change, even in limiting situations and conditions.
       - Change Situation: Seeing opportunities to choose different options in this situation.
       - Change Attitude: Exploring new attitudes that are possible in this situation.
     - ***UNIQUENESS-*** Recognizing our personal uniqueness in what we offer to the world through our creativity and in our relationships.
       - Creativity: Adding my personal creativity to experiences.
       - Personal Relationships: Experiencing and sharing my uniqueness with others.
     - ***RESPONSIBILITY-*** By responding to situations with the choices we make.
       - Freedom: The ability to make choices or change our attitude.
       - Fate: The choice to change our attitude in the face of unalterable or unavoidable situations or events.

  - ***SELF-TRANSCENDENCE-*** Going beyond ourselves in service and commitments toward people we love and causes we believe in.
    - Toward a Person: Giving of ourselves in relationships with others.
    - Toward a Cause: Giving of ourselves in the causes that are greater than us (e.g., feeding the homeless, non-profit organizations, volunteer work).
- Use each section as a psycho-educational piece or in homework assignments to facilitate orientation toward **Meaning.**
- Ask clients to identify areas in each of the three sections where they have been able to find meaning, as well as where they have struggled; journaling and/or discussing these areas in therapy can be very therapeutic.
- In the areas where the clients have struggled, assist them to review the meaning discovered in the struggle, as well as work on finding additional meaning to derive growth and understanding in the present.
- Specifically in **Guideposts to Sources of Meaning**, ask clients to identify where they have found meaning in the past, where they find meaning today, and where they can find or would hope to find meaning and growth in the future; (extensive work can be done in each of the 5 areas).
- Have clients draw their own **Meaning Triangle**, and make a list under each angle—**Attitudes, Creativity,** and **Experiences.** Facilitate a discussion about those areas that have been meaningful in the past, and assist in identifying new ways meaning can be discovered in each of these areas.
- Ask clients to draw an interactive **Meaning Triangle;** clients can do this project on any size poster-board, construction paper, or regular size paper, draw a visible Triangle in the center with the labels of **Attitudes, Creativity,** and **Experiences** on each angle. Ask clients to insert pictures, cutouts from magazines or books, greeting cards, small mementos or treasures (or pictures of them), sayings, quotes or stories, drawings, and any other meaningful representation of each angle—**Attitudes, Creativity,** and **Experiences**, around the triangle; or create a collage in which the meaningful representations overlap and together create a visible Triangle.
  - Search for meaningful threads to interweave into discussions and therapy.
  - Ask clients to discuss each meaningful representation.
  - Ask clients to discuss the meaning of the entire project; what they were able to derive from it; and how they can use this information to go forward in life.
- In group or individual therapy, facilitate a discussion on each of the angles—**Attitudes, Creativity,** and **Experiences**; in group therapy, based on their new found knowledge of each other, ask members to help each other identify possible examples of meaning; and also highlight new areas of meaning.

- PICTOGRAPH 5 -

Identity: Doing vs. Being

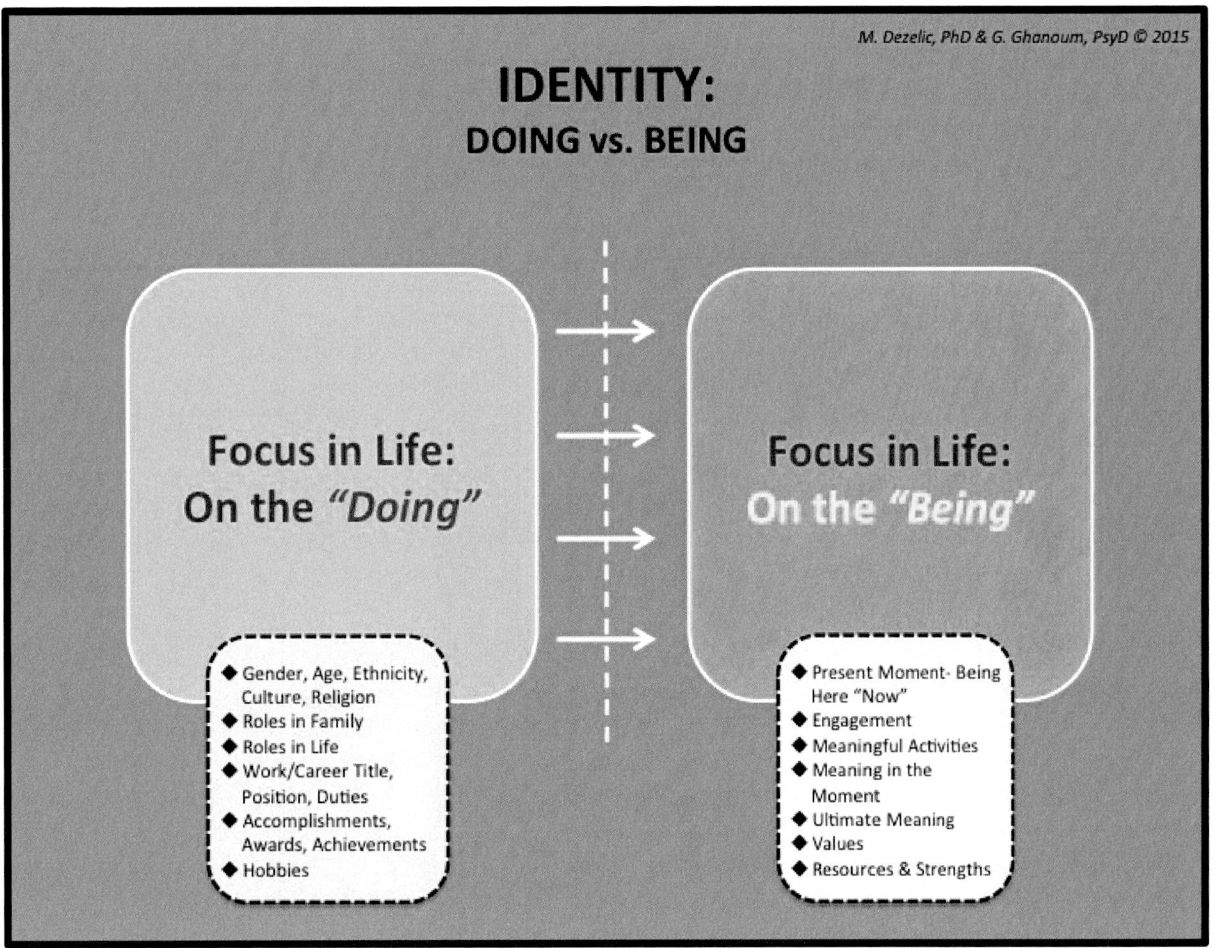

Black-and-White version available in the Appendix p.118

THERAPIST/ FACILITATOR CAN:

- Break this *Conceptual Pictograph* into 2 sections:
    - Focus in Life on the "Doing."
        - Ask clients to describe what "Doing" in relation to life means to them.
        - Ask clients to describe themselves from the "Doing" aspects, journal a list of descriptors.
        - For a group session, ask clients to share their lists with the other members, and continue to add to their list as others share new ideas; if this is an individual session, ask the client to share this list with the therapist, and explore items possibly left out.
    - Focus in Life on the "Being."
        - Ask clients to describe what "Being" in relation to life means to them.
        - Ask clients to describe themselves from the "Being" aspects, journal a list of descriptors.
        - For a group session, ask clients to share their lists with the other members, and continue to add to their list as others share new ideas; if this is an individual session, ask client to share and explore the list with the therapist.
- Ask clients to think of one way each day that they could focus on the "Being" aspects of their list.
- Ask clients to journal, and/or discuss what this exercise of examining "Doing" vs. "Being" aspects of life has made them realize, taught them, and/or inspired them to do differently.

- SESSION 3 -

Ontology of Body, Mind, Spirit (Essence)

Session 3 is intended to increase awareness of and explore Logotherapy's ontological concepts of the human being: the Mind, Body, and Spirit (Unique Essence). Frankl described the unique aspect of being human as having an in-extractable spiritual dimension. This particularly human dimension—the ***Nöetic Dimension***—our spiritual essence, is where we have access to the resources of our own healing and health. Logotherapy maintains that the search for meaning, and the ability to activate our personal ***Meaning Triangle,*** exists within the *Nöetic Dimension*, aiding in the always-possible ***Self-Transcendence*** (reaching beyond ourselves to those we love or causes we serve) and a meaningful existence.

Additionally, Logotherapy aims to bring clients to the awareness of this unique spiritual dimension and the capacities held within it. There is a central point where all three dimensions connect, yet we can separate physical illnesses—*(somatogenic)* and pathological functioning—*(psychogenic)* disorders within each realm. We can have a limitation, or bodily illness originating in the *Soma*, (i.e. cancer, diabetes, heart conditions, pulmonary problems), or a psychological disorder originating in the *Psyche*, (i.e. major depressive disorder, obsessive-compulsive disorder, eating disorders, trauma disorders, personality disorders, ...), or we can experience intense grief or sadness over unavoidable suffering, guilt or death which can limit our normal and adaptive functioning capacity, or a combination thereof *(psychosomatic)*. However, Logotherapy emphasizes that, regardless of these limitations, we can access our *Nöetic Dimension*, where we still have *Freedom*, the possibility of *Meaning-Orientation* through the *Meaning Triangle*, and ultimately *Self-Transcendence*. The areas of the *Nöetic Dimension* are used to activate *Meaning* when one experiences symptoms and effects in any of the five categories of neuroses, which have been described by Frankl in his book: *On The Theory and Therapy of Mental Disorders* (2004) and Lukas in her book: *Logotherapy Textbook* (2000, p.84).

Frankl's Classifications of Neuroses:

- ***Somatogenic Neuroses:*** Originating in the ***Soma***
  - Pathological effects exhibited in the Psyche, usually a 'functional illness'
- ***Psychogenic Neuroses:*** Originating in the ***Psyche***
  - Pathological effects exhibited in the Soma and/or Psyche
- ***Psychosomatic Illness:*** Originating in the ***Soma* AND *Psyche***
  - Pathological symptoms exhibited in the Soma, originally triggered by the Psyche
- ***Reactive Neuroses:*** A reaction to effects of symptoms originating in the ***Soma* OR *Psyche***
  - Pathological reactions in the Psyche, originally triggered by the Soma or Psyche
- ***Noögenic Neuroses:*** Originating in the *Noös*—Spirit, when existential frustration is handled with maladaptive coping mechanisms and access to the Nöetic Dimension is blocked
  - Pathological effects exhibited in the Psyche, originally triggered by the Noös

Frankl frequently used the term "neurosis" to describe anxious, fixated, irrational, or disturbed symptoms that manifested from bodily, spiritual, or sociological-relational causes (Frankl, 2004). Finally, Frankl taught that the *Nöetic Dimension* capacities can assist in bringing the client back to overall health, or if this is not possible, in a modification of attitudes toward his limitations, as noted in his second (psychotherapeutic) credo stated:

> *The belief that not only the nöetic part of the person remains well even if the surrounding psychophysical area has become sick but also that the nöetic self has the power to rise above the affliction of the psychophysical self* (Graber, 2004, p.77).

- PICTOGRAPH 6 -

The Human Being's Multidimensional Aspects: Body (Soma), Mind (Psyche), & Spirit (Noös)

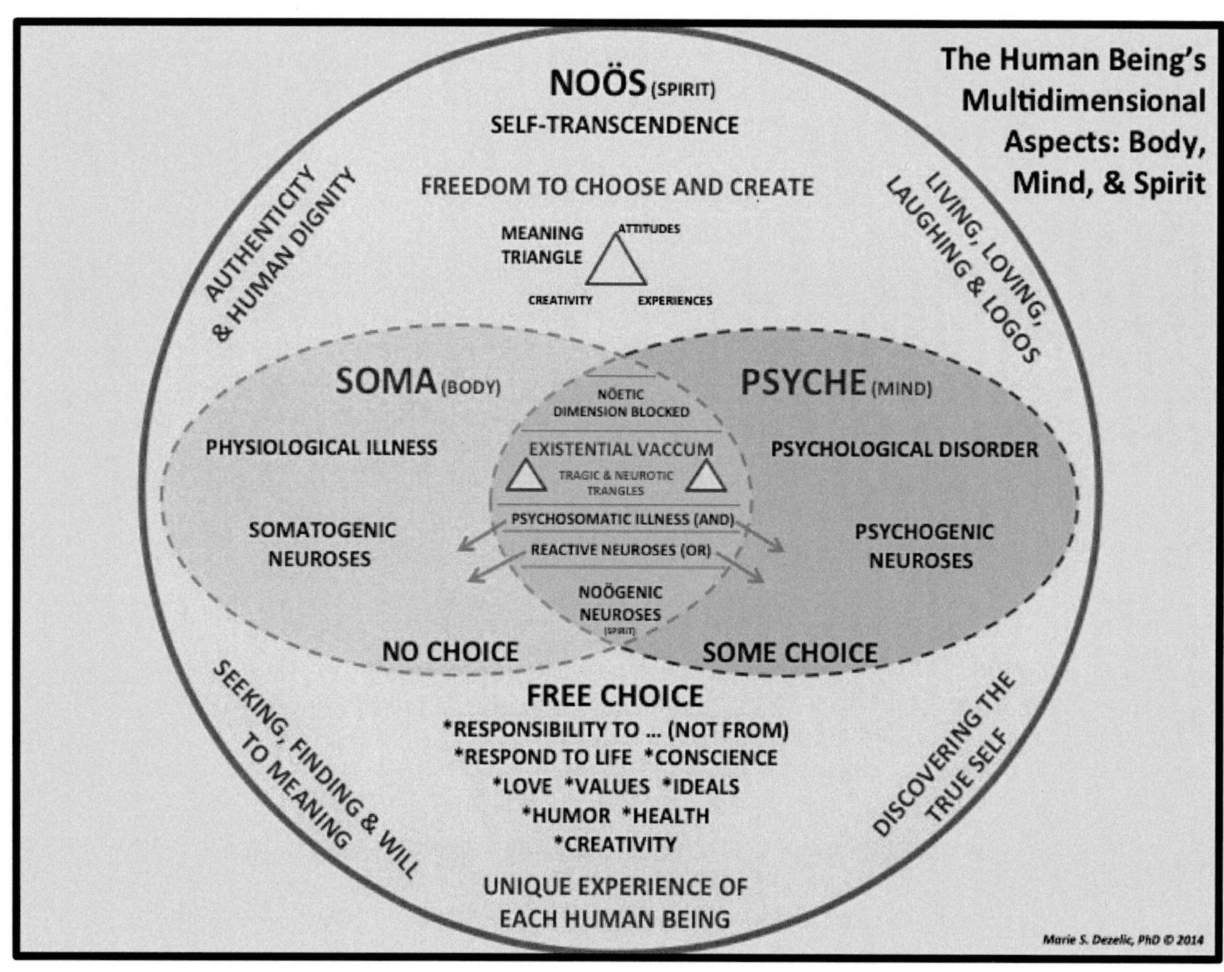

Black-and-White version available in the Appendix p.119

THERAPIST/ FACILITATOR CAN:

- Discuss the multidimensional aspects of the human being—the **Body, Mind,** and **Spiritual Dimensions,** and all of the characteristics that are particular to each (Lukas, 2000):
    - ***Somatogenic Neuroses:*** Originating in the ***Soma (body)***
        - Pathological effects exhibited in the Psyche, usually a 'functional illness'
    - ***Psychogenic Neuroses:*** Originating in the ***Psyche (mind)***
        - Pathological effects exhibited in the Soma and/or Psyche
    - ***Psychosomatic Illness:*** Originating in the ***Soma* AND *Psyche (body and mind)***
        - Pathological symptoms exhibited in the Soma, originally triggered by the Psyche
    - ***Reactive Neuroses:*** A reaction to effects of symptoms originating in the ***Soma* OR *Psyche***
        - Pathological reactions in the Psyche, originally triggered by the Soma or Psyche
    - ***Noögenic Neuroses:*** Originating in the *Noös*—Spirit, when existential frustration is handled with maladaptive coping mechanisms and access to the Nöetic Dimension is blocked
        - Pathological effects exhibited in the Psyche, originally triggered by the Noös
- Break down this *Conceptual Pictograph*, discussing specific issues associated with each area of the human being in detail, giving some examples and asking clients to come up with their own as well; finally, bring the three areas together and show their interaction.
- Draw the **three dimensions—Body, Mind,** and **Spirit** on a board; and ask clients in a group setting to give examples, listing them in each of the appropriate dimensions.
- Ask clients to draw the three overlapping circles of **Body, Mind,** and **Spirit,** and identify their own personal struggles in each area.
- Facilitate a discussion on: **No Choice, Some Choice,** and **Free Choice,** allowing clients to identify areas in their lives where they can relate to each type of choice.
- In group therapy, once clients have identified situations, limitations, and possibilities in **No Choice, Some Choice,** and **Free Choice** areas, or the **Body, Mind,** and **Spiritual Dimensions,** ask members to share these with each other; assist group members in placing situations correctly, and in finding more possibilities. Finally, discuss the various viewpoints.
- In group therapy, pair members and ask them to draw/write out their own individual situations, and then share with the group for a discussion, if they are comfortable. This can also be done in a one-on-one therapy session.
- Discuss the attributes of the **Nöetic Dimension** and ask clients how they might view these attributes differently given their new understanding of the three dimensions.
- Ask clients to journal about new thoughts and/or memories that have surfaced for them when examining this *Conceptual Pictograph*. Ask how they understand or interpret these thoughts and memories.

- PICTOGRAPH 7 -

The Human Being's Unique Aspect: Spiritual (Nöetic) Dimension

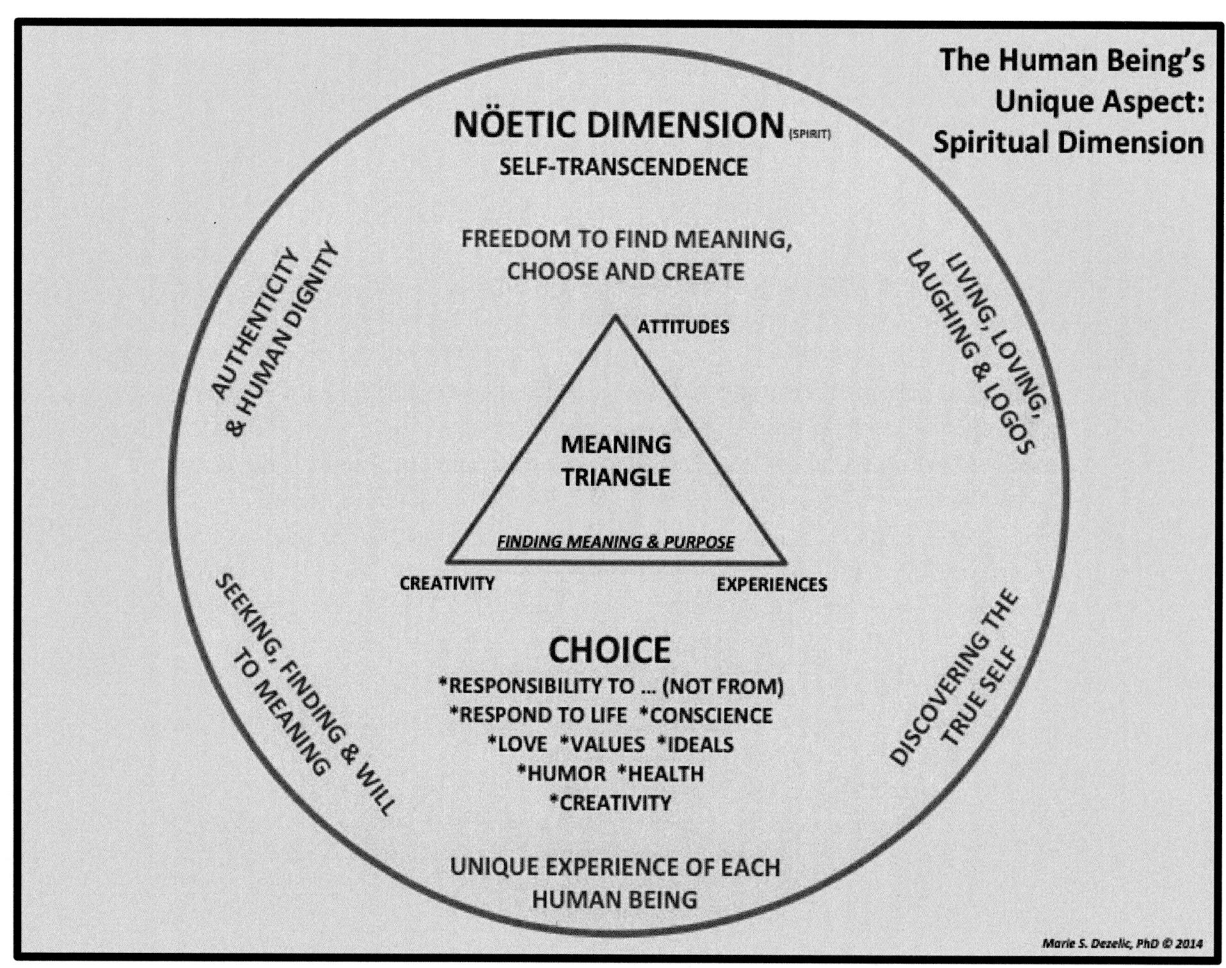

Black-and-White version available in the Appendix p.120

THERAPIST/ FACILITATOR CAN:

- Discuss the unique aspect of the human being—the **Spiritual Dimension** that comes from our unique essence, including all of the characteristics that are particular to this Dimension; this *Conceptual Pictograph* can be used as a **psycho-educational** piece; ask clients to write a personal definition for **Nöetic Dimension Capacities:**
    - ***Meaning Triangle***: Finding meaning and purpose through *Creativity, Experiences*, and *Attitudes*
    - ***Choice***:
      ~ Responsibility to... (not from): Responsibility to ourselves and our actions (as a choice); Not from the responsibility or obligations placed on us by others or by life itself.
      ~ Respond to life
      ~ Conscience
      ~ Love
      ~ Values
      ~ Ideals
      ~ Humor
      ~ Health
      ~ Creativity
      ~ Forgiveness
    - ***Qualities:***
      ~ Freedom to find meaning
      ~ Freedom to choose and be creative
      ~ Unique experiences of each human being
      ~ Authenticity and human dignity
      ~ Seeking, finding, and will to meaning
      ~ Living, loving, laughing, and logos (meaning)
      ~ Discovering the true self
- Ask clients to identify times when having limitations in their lives led them to believe that they did not have access to these particular attributes.
- Ask clients to identify specifics situations that pertain to **each attribute of the Spirit.**
- Ask clients to verbalize or write out how they can now utilize the aspects of the **Nöetic Dimension—**the **Spiritual Dimension**, to overcome obstacles and difficulties in their lives.
- In group therapy, pair members and ask them to share examples of times when they each utilized the various attributes. Come back together in group, and, if no one objects, ask each of them to share what their partner discussed. The group can then make observations about what was shared.
- Offer the **Appealing Technique,** through a guided meditation, which gently draws attention to and accesses the **Defiant Power of the Human Spirit:** (example found following these exercises).
    - The Appealing Technique can be used with any population.
      Important Note: ***Special consideration should be taken with suicidal clients; this technique is not recommended for actively psychotic clients; clients should be under supervised medical and/or psychiatric care.***
    - The Appealing Technique can be used once a week or at every group therapy session, strengthening the clients' access to their **Defiant Power of the Human Spirit** and the **Nöetic Dimension;** likewise it can be added to individual therapy as often as needed (i.e., once a week, every other week, once a month).

- Make a recording of your voice offering the **Appealing Technique** for when clients are outside of therapy and in need of reinforcement.
- Any revised version of the **Appealing Technique** can be designed based on the specific population and the specific areas clients are addressing.
    - For **"Your Spirit States..."** have the group members or individual clients substitute additional phrases that they would like to strengthen for themselves.

Appealing Technique:
"Accessing the Defiant Power of the Spirit"
(Marie S. Dezelic © 2014)

The use of the Appealing Technique, an "appeal" to the client's spiritual dimension, is a guided meditation and autogenic training approach which encourages clients to connect with their inner resources, as well as to develop and strengthen a sense of inner calmness.

Preparation:
Ask client(s) to lie down or sit back in a comfortable position, with their back supported, placing their hands gently in their lap or on their abdomen, and to close their eyes when they feel comfortable.

You may have soft music (meditation music) or the sound of gentle running water playing in the background.

Proceed in a slow, softly spoken, gentle voice; taking slow pauses between sentences. *Any words in bold and italic should be emphasized.*

Therapist to client(s):
As you place your body in a comfortable position, begin to gently close your eyes, allowing your body to relax and quiet down. Begin to take deep, full breaths, allowing your breath as you exhale through your mouth or nose, to wash over your body in warm soothing waves. Notice any noises happening around you, and let them fade gently into the distance. Feel any tension throughout your body begin to slowly soften and dissipate as your warm breaths wash over your body. I will begin to slowly count backward from 10 to 1, and as I get closer to 1, your body will be feeling more and more relaxed, and all tension will be released from your body.

10 – 9 – 8 – 7 – 6 – 5 – 4 – 3 – 2 – 1... (tone of voice in a decrescendo). You are now in a state of deep and gentle relaxation. Your body is resting quietly while your spirit, the essence of you, is ever present.

As you take notice of the different parts of your body, you notice them getting more and more relaxed. Your head and neck have become completely relaxed; all tension has left this area... Your shoulders and both of your arms have become completely relaxed; all tension has left this area... Your chest and stomach area have become completely relaxed; all tension has left this area... Your hips and pelvis area have become completely relaxed; all tension has left this area... Your legs have become completely relaxed; all tension has left this area... Your entire body feels relaxed and calm. Nothing disturbs you now, you are completely relaxed. If any tension, thoughts, images or feelings arise, whatever they may be, simply notice them as if they are engulfed in a soft, puffy cloud, and let them gently pass by, paying no attention to them and offering no judgment as they pass and dissipate in the distance. You are completely relaxed.

As your body is resting gently and quietly, and feeling complete calmness and safety, your spirit is ever present. Your spirit states: ***I have willpower, I am strong, I am able, I am well.*** Again, as your body is resting quietly and feeling complete calmness and safety, your spirit is ever present. Your spirit states: ***I have willpower, I am strong, I am able, I am well.***

A color of your choice comes to mind, for which when you see this particular color of yours, you become ***empowered, resilient, full of strength, wellbeing and joy.*** Picture this color all around you like flowing scarves in the wind of your soft and soothing breath. See this color vividly, which awakens your spirit, and your spirit states: ***I have willpower, I am strong, I am able, I am well.***

Now allow your attention to drift back to your resting and calm body. Your color has gradually permeated the air around you and you are now able to breathe this color in and out, which washes over your body in gentle waves as you exhale. As you breathe your color in and out, you are feeling ***empowered, resilient, full of strength, wellbeing and joy.*** See and feel that your resilient spirit allows your body to feel calm, at peace, and full of joy. Your body and your spirit alike state: ***I have willpower, I am strong, I am able, I am well.***

Now as I count forward from 1 to 10, climbing from the deeply relaxed state of wellbeing to the awake consciousness of 10, notice that your body and spirit bring with it the thoughts and feelings of: ***I have willpower, I am strong, I am able, I am well.*** As we climb toward 10, notice your body beginning to wake up slowing, so that when we arrive to 10, you open your eyes, feeling fully awake and alive, and are filled with the thoughts and feelings of: ***I have willpower, I am strong, I am able, I am well.***

Let us begin our soft and gentle climb to becoming fully awake and conscious in this room...
1 – 2 – 3 – 4 – 5 – 6 – 7 – 8 – 9 – 10! (tone of voice in a crescendo). Gently open your eyes, move your arms and fingers, your legs and toes, head and neck around. Recall your thoughts and feelings from the combined sense of your body and spirit of: ***I have willpower, I am strong, I am able, I am well.*** Carry with you for the rest of the day: ***I have willpower, I am strong, I am able, I am well.***

This concludes the Appealing Technique session. Ask client(s) to describe how they are feeling and what they will take away with them from this exercise for the day. Ask client(s) to recall their color, and to begin to notice it throughout the day.

An additional ***Appealing Technique,*** **"7-Step Noögenic Activation Method,"** is found in Session Seven on p.89.

- SESSION 4 -

Inner Resources and Strengths

Session 4 is intended to increase awareness of and to explore internal resources and strengths that enable us to better handle everyday life situations, hardships, medical illnesses, psychological effects, traumas, tragedies and difficulties. We often overlook our inner resources, which makes us vulnerable to focusing on the capabilities we think we lack, as well as on the things we cannot do because we believe that we are missing the inner resources that would help us to accomplish them. When we are able to access interior strengths, we begin to feel differently about our lives and ourselves in general. We all want to live healthier, stress free lives, but what does that actually mean and how do we go about achieving it? We sometimes take it for granted that we possess all of the resources (to varying degrees) necessary to accomplish these tasks. We do not have to go out and acquire something specific, or spend a lot of wasted money on unnecessary items. In an age where scientists and researchers are finally recognizing what religious and spiritual leaders have known for centuries: that we are more than just body and mind; we see a greater movement toward wholeness and unity. Currently, advocates of holistic-integrative medicine, and energy psychology are bringing forth invaluable information documenting the powerful effects that our spirits have on the healing of our other dimensions, namely, our bodies and minds.

A simple way to understand the ***Mind-Body-Spirit Harmony*** is to view ourselves as a WHOLE of three inseparable and integrated parts. As Viktor Frankl (Dezelic, 2014; Frankl, 2006; Frankl, 2004; Frankl, 2000; Frankl, 1988; Frankl, 1986; Frankl, 1978; Graber, 2004) described through his dimensional ontology of the mind, body, and spirit: We are beings comprised of **Mind**—the conceptual thinking part of ourselves, otherwise known as our psyche, which governs our physiology, cognitions and behaviors; **Body**—the physical and physiological part of ourselves, which in biological terms is the living and breathing organism; and **Spirit**—the essence of ourselves, which is comprised of our particular uniqueness in this world and lifetime, our exclusive existence (in a non-religious context yet well-known to religious and faith beliefs).

Creating a healthier lifestyle will automatically lead to less stress in our daily lives; less stress will lead to less psychological and physiological issues, and spiritual/existential distress, thus allowing us to be more energized and free to follow creative and meaningful pursuits. By balancing these three dimensions of ourselves—the Mind-Body-Spirit, we create a triangular effect of energy movement, what we have coined as the ***"Mind-Body-Spirit Rejuvenation Method."*** When we feel more rejuvenated in and connected to all of our dimensions, we can ultimately discover, develop and embrace a healthier lifestyle. With a few simple exercises, we can start to develop a new shift in our lives; create a healthier lifestyle and begin to feel re-energized and recharged, rather than energetically depleted, fatigued, irritable, depressed, or anxious. Chronic pain will be less intense or may even disappear, and our overall stress level will begin to diminish. We can begin to discover and become more engaged in the specific areas of Meaning as a result of our more balanced Mind, Body and Spirit.

Discovering a method for achieving a healthier way to take care of ourselves, and facilitating a balance in Mind, Body, and Spirit, allows us to experience and appreciate life more fully, take better care of ourselves and our loved ones, find new purposes and goals, discover new meanings, and feel rejuvenated. The resources to improved health and healthy, stress-free living exist within ourselves; and we have the ability and freedom to access these inner resources and capitalize on the assets we have available at our fingertips—our Mind, Body, and Spirit.

- PICTOGRAPH 8 -

Nöetic Dimension: The Medicine Chest of Logotherapy

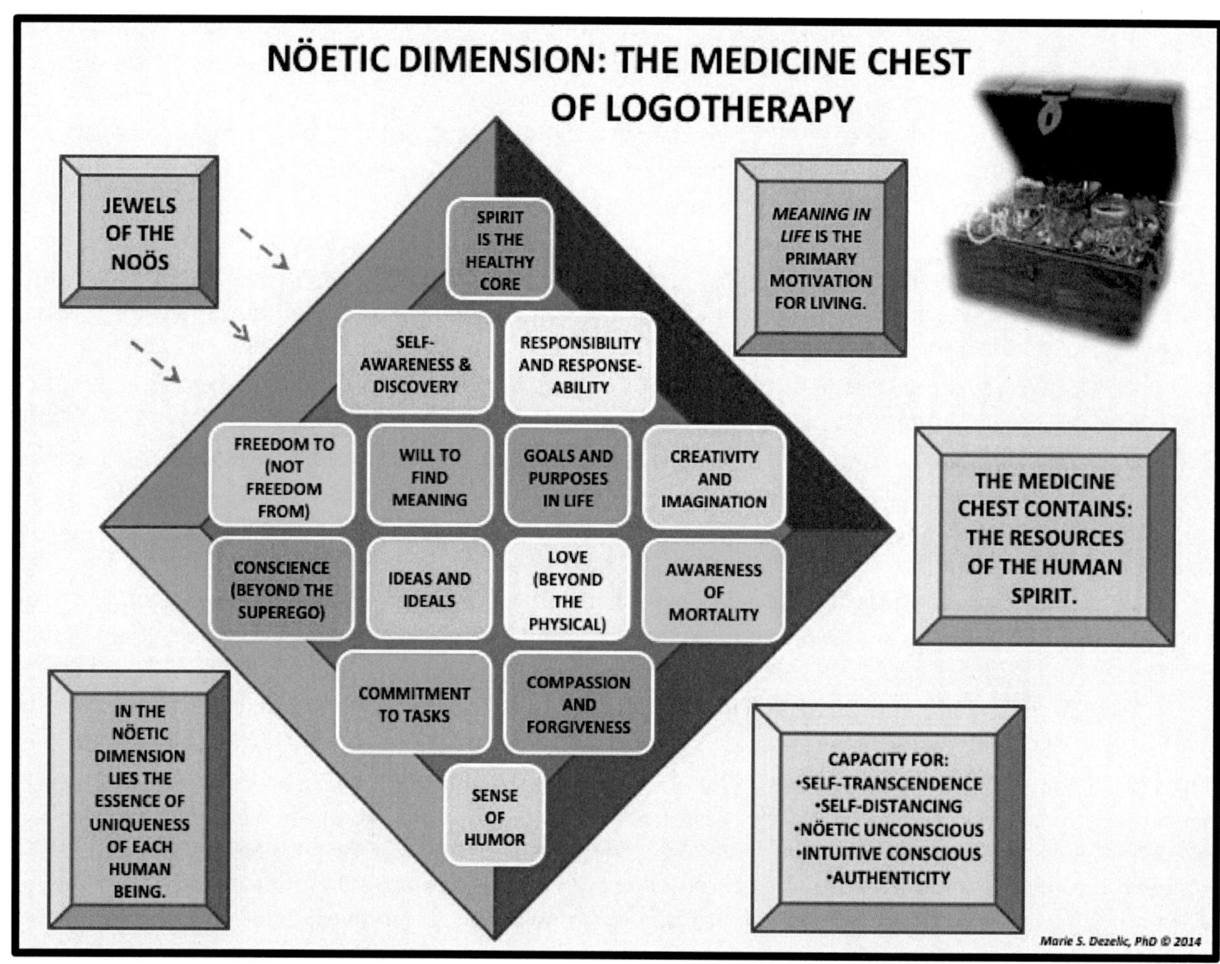

Black-and-White version available in the Appendix p.121

THERAPIST/ FACILITATOR CAN:

- Discuss the contents or "jewels" contained in the **Medicine Chest**, found in the **Nöetic—Spiritual Dimension** (Barnes, 2005; Graber, 2004; Dezelic, 2014):
    - *Spirit is the Healthy Core*
    - *Self-Awareness and Discovery*
    - *Responsibility and Response-ability*
    - *Freedom to (Not freedom from)*
    - *Will to Find Meaning*
    - *Goals and Purposes in Life*
    - *Creativity and Imagination*
    - *Conscience (Beyond the Superego)*
    - *Ideas and Ideals*
    - *Love (Beyond the Physical)*
    - *Awareness of Mortality*
    - *Commitment to Tasks*
    - *Compassion and Forgiveness*
    - *Sense of Humor*
- Ask clients to write about each aspect—or **Jewel,** giving examples from their lives.
- At the beginning or end of each session, ask clients to pick one aspect of the **Medicine Chest** and describe how they see it in themselves, or how they will foster this aspect in the coming days or week.
- In group therapy, cut out all of the jewels, place them in a hat or bowl. Ask clients to pick one and write or think about what comes to mind. Follow this with a group discussion. Group members can share their own experiences with each other's topic, or assist other members in furthering their understanding of the jewel.
- Ask clients to draw their own **Large Jewel;** fill the jewel with descriptions of its many facets, using examples from their own lives. Clients can color or decorate the different facets as shown in the *Conceptual Pictograph.*
- Instruct clients to cut out the **Large Jewel,** and keep it in their wallet or place it in a location where they can see it every day; suggest that they read it every day to remind themselves of their own facets and strengths.
- Ask clients to write a short story about a **fictional character** who used some of the aspects of the **Medicine Chest** to overcome a difficulty in their life; (i.e., short story, poem, musical lyrics, drawings, cartoons, etc.).
    - Look for projections—the clients' internal feelings and behaviors expressed/projected onto the character.
    - Facilitate a discussion about how the clients are similar or different from their fictional character, and what this may teach them about their own personality.
    - Ask clients how they can utilize some of the same strengths in their own life.
- Ask clients to identify additional strengths—**Jewels** held within the **Medicine Chest**—that they or others they view as role models have used within their lives to overcome difficulties, tragedies and adversities.

- PICTOGRAPH 9 -

Mind-Body-Spirit Rejuvenation Method: Simple Techniques for Stress Reduction and Healthy Living

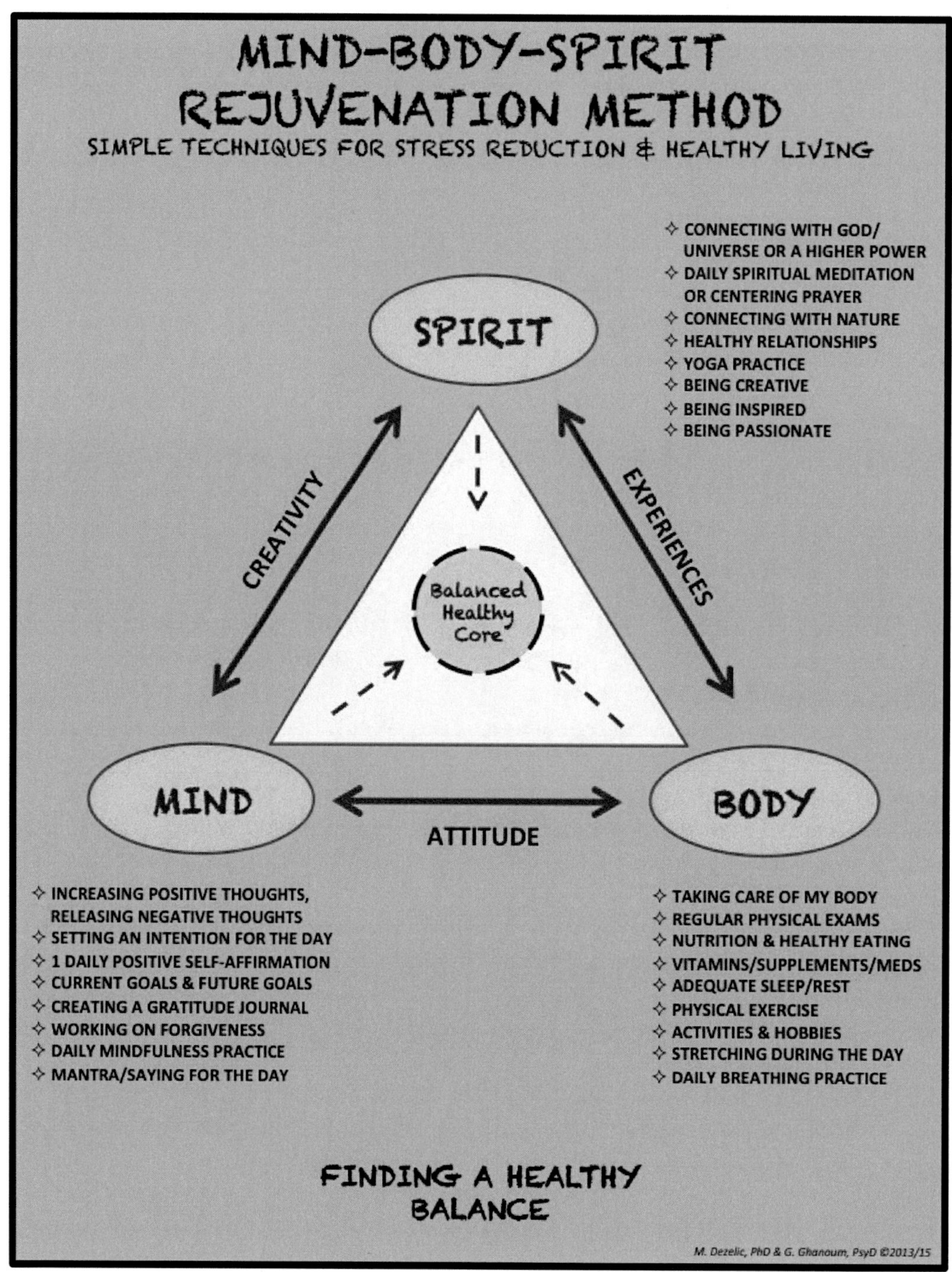

Black-and-White version available in the Appendix p.122

THERAPIST/ FACILITATOR CAN:

- Facilitate a discussion on the possible circular flow and effects of a healthier lifestyle:
  Healthier Lifestyle → Less Stress
  Less Stress → Less Psychological and Physiological Issues, and Spiritual/Existential Distress; More Energy to Follow Creative and Meaningful Pursuits
  Balance the Triangle of Mind-Body-Spirit → Rejuvenation Method
  Rejuvenation Method → Healthier Lifestyle → ... (repeat) →
- Facilitate a discussion on what behaviors and actions would interrupt this flow, or take away from healthy living.
- Facilitate a discussion on how, with a few simple exercises, we can start to develop a new shift in our lives; create a healthier lifestyle and begin to feel rejuvenated, rather than energetically depleted, fatigued, irritable, depressed, or anxious. Chronic pain will be less intense or may even disappear, and our overall stress level will begin to diminish.
- Ask clients to describe how, as a result [byproduct] of a balanced and healthy system, they might start becoming more engaged in the specific areas of Meaning: Creativity, Experiences, and Attitude.
- Suggest using of the ***"Mind-Body-Spirit Rejuvenation Method"*** Conceptual Pictograph as a daily check-in. For example, clients can keep the *Conceptual Pictograph* handout handy for at least 30-90 days, looking at it at a designated time every day. This action promotes brain-memory integration, as well as creates new neural pathways and habitual patterns. Have a discussion of ways and times clients can begin this process.

Daily **"Check-In with Yourself"** method:

- We can pick one (or several) item(s) in each dimension, (mind, body, spirit), and work on it (or them) throughout the day. It is usually easier to begin with one task in each area, so that it does not feel overwhelming or appear as an impossible task to accomplish.
- In the evening, we can review our day to see how well we did with following through on our chosen tasks.
  - Congratulate ourselves for the efforts that we have made.
  - We can be gentle with ourselves by not feeling badly about tasks that we did not complete; we can simply try to take note of them and possibly attempt them the next day, or move on to a different, more favorable task.
- Try new tasks once we have mastered or have a continued practice with other tasks.
- If there are any tasks that make us feel uncomfortable, we can disregard them.
- If we choose to use the *Check-In with Yourself* method a few times throughout the day, it would be good to pick the most opportune times to have a few moments to ourselves, (i.e. after waking up, lunch break, coffee break, prior to or after work/school/social hobbies, before going to bed).
- Remember to have fun! This is about feeling good, being energized, building our self-esteem, recognizing our choices, being creative, and creating new, healthy patterns.
- Have clients write out examples for each area in the Overview, or directly on the *Conceptual Pictograph.*

Overview of the ***Mind-Body-Spirit Rejuvenation Method*** Conceptual Pictograph:

MIND:

- INCREASING POSITIVE THOUGHTS, RELEASING NEGATIVE THOUGHTS
- SETTING AN INTENTION FOR THE DAY
- ONE DAILY POSITIVE SELF-AFFIRMATION
- CURRENT GOALS & FUTURE GOALS
- GRATITUDE JOURNAL
- FORGIVENESS
- MINDFULNESS PRACTICE
- MANTRA/SAYING FOR THE DAY

BODY:

- TAKING CARE OF MY BODY
- REGULAR PHYSICAL EXAMS
- NUTRITION
- VITAMINS/SUPPLEMENTS/MEDICATIONS
- ADEQUATE SLEEP/REST
- PHYSICAL EXERCISE
- ACTIVITIES & HOBBIES
- STRETCHING DURING THE DAY
- DAILY BREATHING PRACTICE

SPIRIT:

- CONNECTING WITH GOD/UNIVERSE OR A HIGHER POWER
- DAILY SPIRITUAL MEDITATION OR CENTERING PRAYER
- CONNECTING WITH NATURE
- HEALTHY RELATIONSHIPS
- YOGA PRACTICE
- BEING CREATIVE
- BEING INSPIRED
- BEING PASSIONATE

MEANING TRIANGLE:

- CREATIVITY—utilizing our creativity, having creative pursuits
- EXPERIENCES—with others, nature, animals, the arts
- ATTITUDE—that we can choose to have in difficult or unalterable situations

- Discuss the statement: ***Finding a Healthy Balance in life begins with you!***

- SESSION 5 -

Existential Aspects

Session 5 explores the existential experiences of *Unavoidable Suffering—Pain, Guilt,* and *Death,* and the existential aspects of various levels of *Depression, Aggression,* and *Addiction.* These experiences that are all aspects of ***The Tragic Triad*** and ***The Neurotic Triad,*** can often lead to ***Existential Frustration*** followed by the ***Existential Vacuum.*** When we are in the throes of the emotional and behavioral turmoil of these two Triads, we may experience ***Existential Frustration***—the disturbance that results when our *Will to Meaning* has become frustrated. This can lead to an ***Existential Vacuum***—the internal pulling effect of despair and hopelessness, which is experientially sensed as a bottomless pit and dark hole. Using Logotherapeutic techniques, therapists can address this existential suffering by assisting clients to activate and enter into their own ***Meaning Triangle—Creativity, Experiences,*** and ***Attitudes.*** This can ultimately lead toward discovering meaning and purpose in life, and ***Self-Transcendence,*** *connecting to a greater whole and purpose.*

The "Existential Triangle," a concept coined by Dr. Marie Dezelic, co-author of this manual, is comprised of Frankl's three triangles. This encompassing triangle is depicted in Pictograph 10. The lower half of the Existential Triangle contains the difficult aspects, which can produce suffering and despair; movement to the upper part of the Existential Triangle can activate the meaning of the moment regardless of life's conditions, happenings or events. The theory behind the Existential Triangle is that there is a constant movement between the two halves of the triangle throughout life. How can we keep Meaning as our focus? How do we alleviate or relieve suffering? The answers lie in moving from a position of "meaninglessness" to an overall feeling of "meaningfulness." Likewise, Logotherapy calls for *Tragic Optimism,* a positive outlook or optimism in the face of tragedy and setbacks. How can we feel motivated to change direction or have new beliefs and awareness when faced with life's limiting and difficult experiences?

- PICTOGRAPH 10 -

The Existential Triangle:
From Meaningless to Meaningful Existence

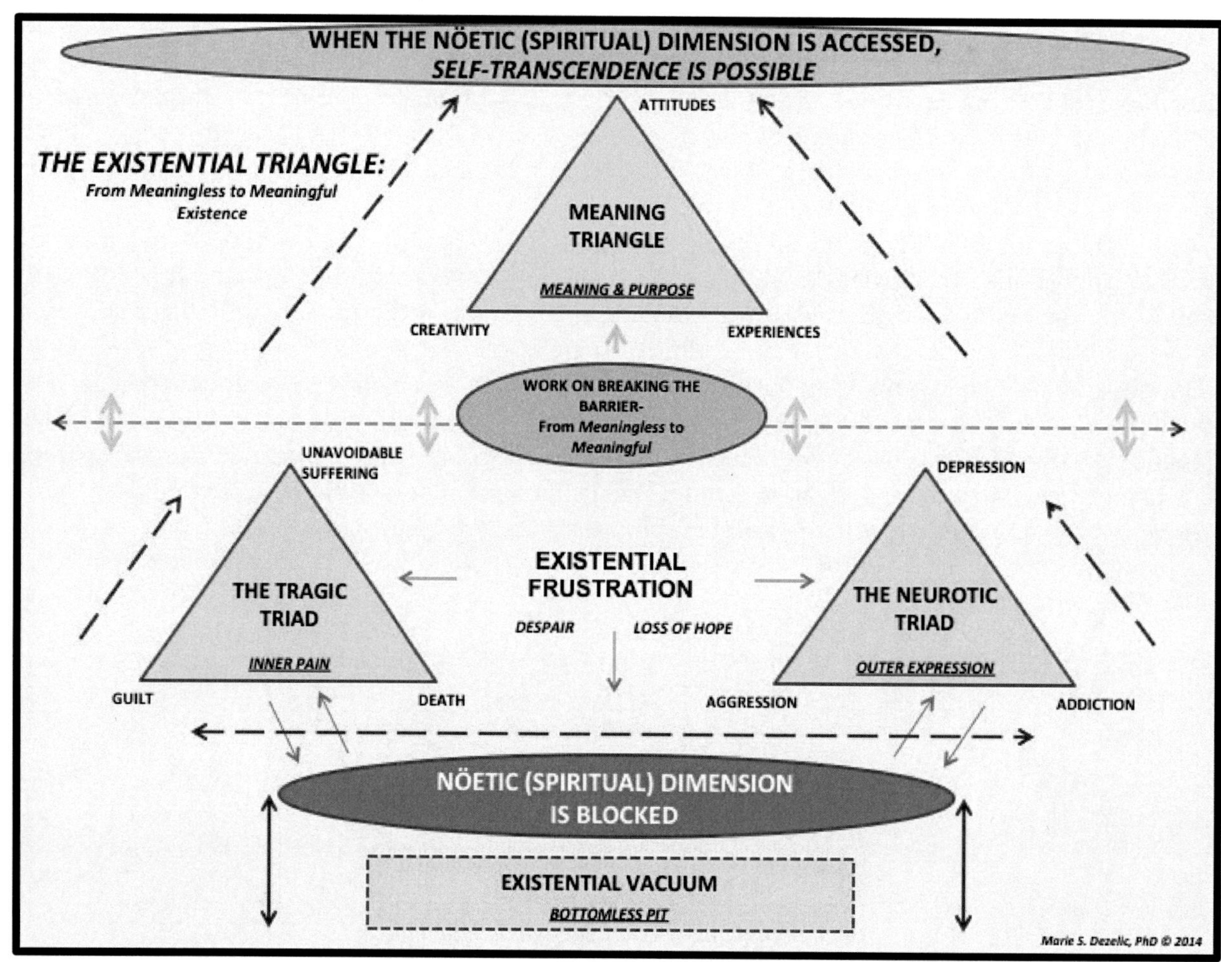

Black-and-White version available in the Appendix p.123

THERAPIST/ FACILITATOR CAN:

- Utilize this *Conceptual Pictograph* as a psycho-educational piece describing **The Existential Triangle**, and the 3 sub-triangles, which comprise it.
- As **The Meaning Triangle** has already been introduced to clients, work extensively on the lower half of **The Existential Triangle—The Tragic Triad** and **The Neurotic Triad**.

The Tragic Triad—people in ***despondency*** experience:

- ***Unavoidable Suffering***: Emotional Pain experienced from events that could not be prevented, such as if we have been violated by physical, emotional, psychological, and/or sexual abuse or aggression; when we are caught in a natural or technological disaster, act of terror or war time trauma; or when we experience a personally tragic situation, such as a major illness, loss, or a death or prolonged illness of a loved one.
- ***Guilt***: Responsibility, fault, or self-blame that we experience which is caused by decisions we have been a part of, caused, or that have affected us or others in some way. In the cases of death of or abuse to a loved one, we often experience guilt, feeling that we "should have" or "could have" done something more to prevent the tragedy. When our loved ones are dying or we are experiencing grief after their death, we may feel guilty that we are also feeling happiness and joy in life. This is especially true if we believe that it is unfair or uncaring to experience such positive emotions when our loved ones are no longer alive and therefore unable to have these same opportunities.
- ***Death***: The deep sadness or questioning experienced when we are faced with the transitoriness of life because of the reality of our own mortality, the death of someone, or the ending of a relationship, a job, a lifestyle, or a dream. The death itself can foster feelings of *Unavoidable Suffering* and *Guilt,* as well as aspects of the *Neurotic Triad.*

The Neurotic Triad—people in ***despair*** experience:

- ***Depression***: Depression is often experienced as a sense of hopelessness or helplessness; inner symptoms are expressed in visible behaviors and symptoms such as a decreased/increased appetite and sleep, and/or a decrease in libido, personal hygiene, motivation, interest in activities and relationships. These behaviors can sometimes lead to feelings of hopelessness and despair that can manifest itself as a loss of the will to live.
- ***Aggression***: An outward expression of violence/rage/anger/hostility, possibly as a way to control others (to be able to) and/or to feel a sense of personal control over internal powerlessness, uncertainty or discomfort. Aggression can be triggered by such things as abuse, natural disasters, death of a loved one, or feelings of frustration due to a major loss or even mental illness. This aggression is usually the result of internal anger and rage originating from fear, frustration and/ or hurt; in the case of mental illness, some forms of aggression may be triggered by delusions or paranoia. Aggression can also be turned inward—the attempt to harm ourselves through self-mutilation or, at the extreme end, by a suicide attempt or completion—to extinguish one's existence from this world completely.
- ***Addiction***: The use of maladaptive, extreme, or repetitious acts manifested by a loss of personal control over the behaviors that negatively affect our lives. Examples include excessive alcohol use, drug abuse, over-eating/food restriction/purging, gambling, sexual behaviors, and self-harming behaviors in an attempt to avoid, numb or dull our inner pain and despair. In addition, thrill-seeking behavior, outside of normal limits, and without safety precautions, is often used in order to experience invincibility and appear larger-

than-life. These thrill-seeking acts are done without regard to the negative consequences; such as our possible death or the death of someone else, (i.e. racing cars/motorcycles on a busy highway).

- Explain the aspects of **The Tragic Triad**, facilitating discussions or journaling on the **3 components—Unavoidable Suffering, Guilt,** and **Death**; explain the aspects of **The Neurotic Triad**, facilitating discussions or journaling on the **3 components—Depression, Aggression,** and **Addiction**.
    - Ask clients to describe a past or current time where they have experienced a sense of **Inner Pain** or **Outer Expression** with any/all of the 3 components of either Triad.
    - Describe how this has affected their past or present levels of functioning, maladaptive or adaptive behaviors.
- Facilitate a discussion on **Existential Frustration, Despair** and **Loss of Hope,** which can lead to blocking the **Nöetic Dimension** and also to experiencing the **Existential Vacuum.**
    - ***Existential Frustration:*** Our *Will to Meaning* is in a state of uncertainty or insecurity triggered by elements of the *Tragic Triad (Unavoidable suffering, Guilt, Death);* frustration in one's *Search for Meaning,* can also be caused by affluence, homeostasis, elimination of stress, or release from commitments and responsibility. Symptoms include boredom, discontent, feelings of meaninglessness, extreme sadness, lack of interest, and a frantic desire to fill an internal emptiness, which can lead to an overemphasis on pleasure seeking, drug addiction or violence.
    - ***Existential Vacuum***: An internal pulling force triggered by Existential Frustration and characterized by a feeling of inner emptiness, boredom, apathy, struggle, and meaningless existence.
    - Focus on:
        - What it feels like for clients.
        - What behaviors and attitudes they notice about themselves.
        - What signs or symptoms they can recognize as clues that they are possibly experiencing the lower half of **The Existential Triangle.**
        - Ask clients to journal their reflections and thoughts.
- Discuss what **"Work on Breaking the Barrier—From Meaningless to Meaningful"** means to clients.
    - Ask clients to identify ways/tools they have learned so far which will facilitate "breaking the barrier" and that will allow them to access their **Meaning Triangle.**
    - Ask clients to identify signs and indications that they are living/ experiencing the upper half of **The Existential Triangle.**
    - Ask clients to identify differences between the lower half of **The Existential Triangle** and the upper half.
- Facilitate a discussion on **Self-Transcendence:**
    - What this means to them.
    - How they can go about accessing it.
    - How they will know if they have accessed it.
    - Identify goals that will be accomplished when they access it.
    - In what ways have they seen others experiencing Self-Transcendence.

- After time has been spent in each area of **The Existential Triangle,** facilitate a discussion on the overview and meaning of the entire Existential Triangle and its 3 inner Triangles.
    - Explore how situations, events, patterns, and behaviors in our life's experience/ journey can cause us to move back and forth between the lower and upper half of **The Existential Triangle.**
    - Ask clients to write clues or notes along the sides of each Triangle as reminders of what they have noticed in their lives.
    - Ask clients to journal about the entire experience of **The Existential Triangle,** and what choices/possibilities they have gained from this exercise.

- PICTOGRAPH 11 -

Tragic Optimism of Logotherapy: Optimism in the Face of Tragedy

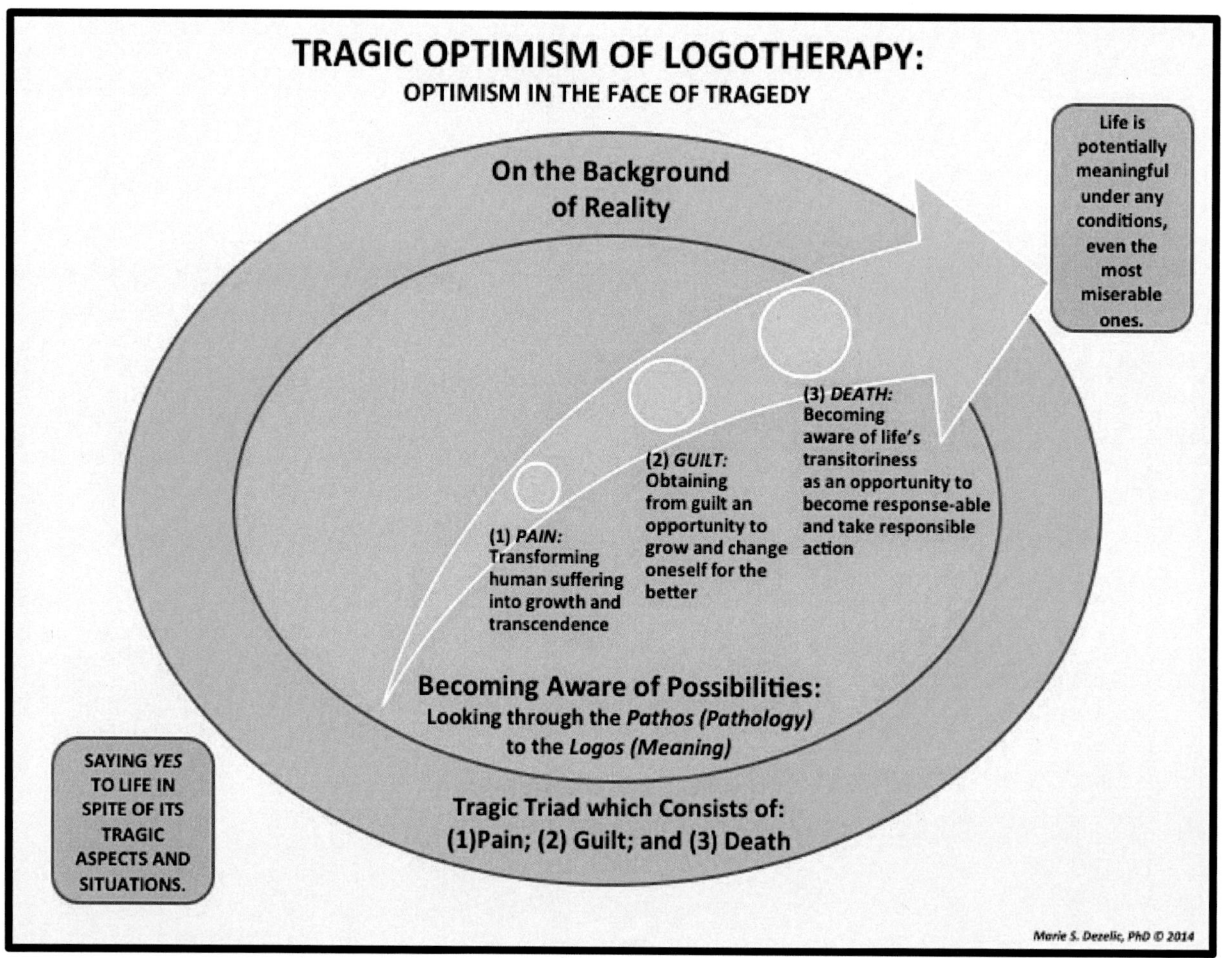

Black-and-White version available in the Appendix p.124

THERAPIST/ FACILITATOR CAN:

- Utilize this *Conceptual Pictograph* as a **psycho-educational** piece describing **The Tragic Triad** and the results of **Pain, Guilt,** and **Death**, followed by ways to transcend the suffering inherent in each area:
    - **(1) Pain:** Transforming human suffering into growth and transcendence
    - **(2) Guilt:** Obtaining from guilt an opportunity to grow and change ourselves for the better
    - **(3) Death:** Becoming aware of life's transitoriness as an opportunity to become response-able and take responsible action
- Ask clients to describe times in their life where they used the three areas of **Becoming Aware of Possibilities** found in the *Conceptual Pictograph* to transcend difficult moments.
- Ask clients to journal or verbalize what **"Saying *yes* to life in spite of its tragic aspects and situations"** means to them.
- Ask clients to journal or verbalize how they have experienced **"Life is potentially meaningful under any conditions, even the most miserable ones."**
    - In group therapy: Ask other group members to identify additional areas of meaning, which the person sharing may have overlooked.
    - In individual therapy: Explore additional areas of meaning, which may have been overlooked by the client.
- On the actual *Conceptual Pictograph* handout (next to **points (1) Pain, (2) Guilt,** and **(3) Death**), ask clients to fill in a life situation on **The Background of Reality,** as well as a brief description of how they did/could turn the **Pain, Guilt,** and/or **Death** experienced from the life situation into meaningful actions.
    - Ask clients to look at the arrow and come up with a **new statement** about themselves and/or their life based on what they have experienced and derived from this exercise.
- Have clients discuss the meaning of: **"Looking through the Pathos (Pathology) to the Logos (Meaning),"** identifying areas in their life where they can use this statement.

- SESSION 6 -

Suffering and Meaning

Session 6 explores suffering in relation to meaning, and how we can discover meaning within suffering. Frankl spoke and wrote often about ***"Homo Patiens"***—persons who ***"can find fulfillment even in the most extreme failure, in defeat"*** (Frankl, 2004). He contrasted these individuals with "*Homo Faber*," those successful people who think only in terms of success and failure. This perspective results in a continual movement between success and failure. "*Homo Patiens*," on the other hand, are individuals who have moved beyond this success and failure polarity to another level or dimension, namely the level that contains fulfillment and despair. As these two levels exist on different planes, it is easier to visualize them as perpendicular lines, making a cross, one on top of the other in a three-dimensional view.

According to Viktor Frankl, "suffering ceases to be suffering at the moment it finds a meaning." Logotherapy offers the hope that suffering persons, ***"Homo Patiens,"*** can discover the highest meaning even in the most extreme failure or defeat. In this sense, Logotherapy assists clients in activating ***Modification of Attitudes,*** in order to discover meaning in and through suffering. When we view these two categories as perpendicular lines, making a cross, we see four quadrants, and can examine the quadrants as four areas where possible meaning can be found.

Additionally, when we feel that we are going against our internal value system and moral code (essentially, going against our own grain), in order to please another person or a group, to be accepted by others, to follow others' rules and views, or to stand against the culture of an organization, we may experience an existential crisis and frustration, a spiritual crisis—symptoms of suffering resulting from going against our essence. Examining these aspects of who we are, what we stand for, how we want to live our lives, allows us to become responsible to and for our own existence, and find ways of extracting meaningful opportunities of authenticity.

- PICTOGRAPH 12 -

"Homo Patiens": Extracting Meaning from Suffering

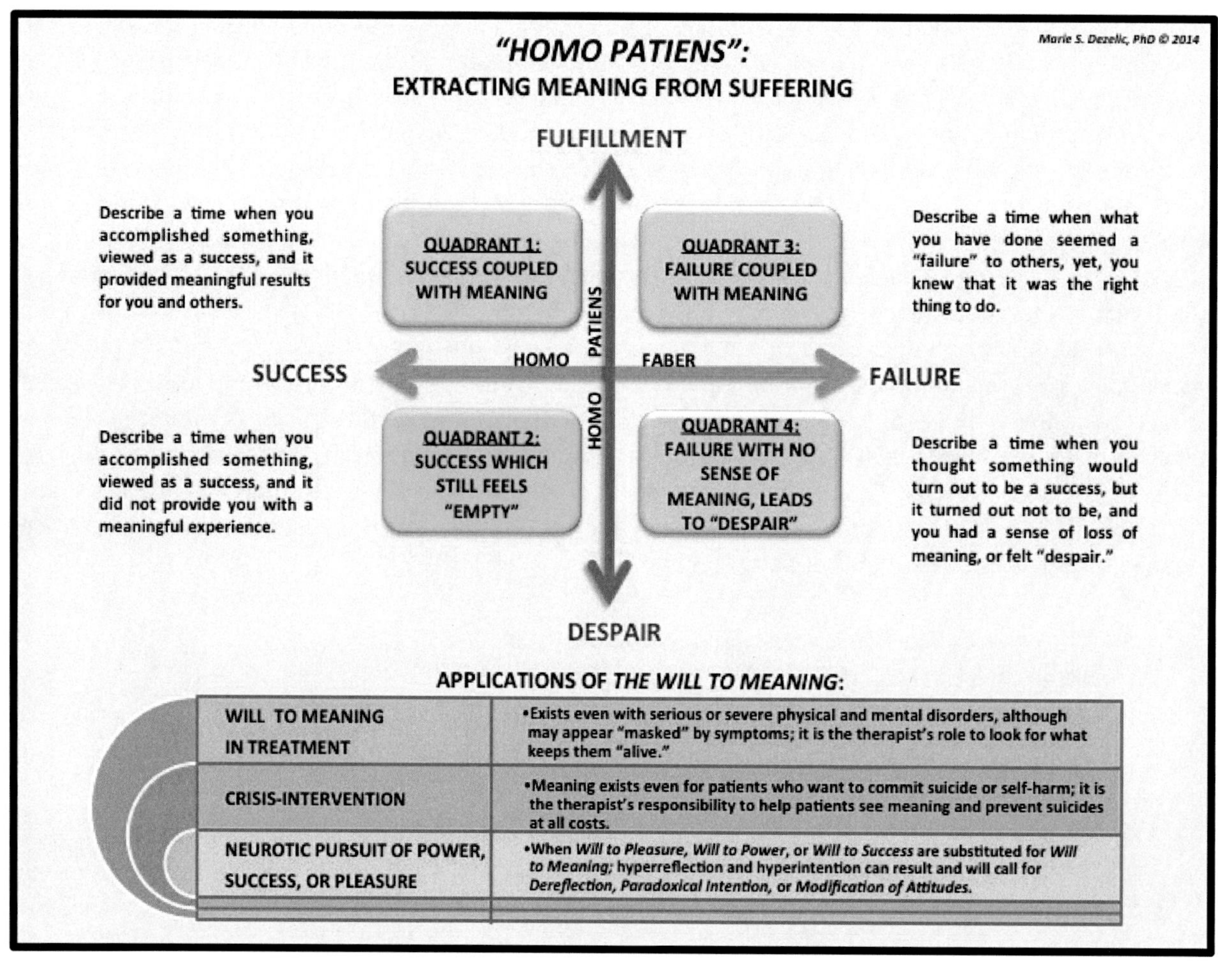

Black-and-White version available in the Appendix p.125

THERAPIST/ FACILITATOR CAN:

- Describe the **4 Quadrants: Success-Failure** and **Fulfillment-Despair**.
- Explain Frankl's description of the person who discovers or extracts meaning in suffering—**"Homo Patiens."** Frankl stated that suffering ceases to be suffering at the moment it finds a meaning.
- Address the questions and create a discussion on the **Quadrants of the Fulfillment-Despair/ Success-Failure Indices** (Dezelic, 2014b; Frankl, 2004; Lukas, 2014):
    - ***Quadrant 1: Success and Meaning*:** (Success and Fulfillment)
        - Describe a time when you accomplished something, viewed it as a success, and it provided meaningful results for yourself and others.
        - Discuss the aspects that made this event/time successful; discuss the aspects that made this event/time meaningful.
    - ***Quadrant 2: Success without Meaning*:** (Success and Despair)
        - Describe a time when you accomplished something, viewed it as a success, and yet it did not provide you with a meaningful experience.
        - Discuss the aspects that made this event/time successful; discuss the aspects that made this event/time not meaningful.
    - ***Quadrant 3: Failure and Meaning*: (**Failure and Fulfillment)
        - Describe a time when what you have done seemed a "failure" to others, yet you knew it was a meaningful action.
        - Discuss the aspects that made this event/time a failure; discuss the aspects that made this event/time meaningful.
    - ***Quadrant 4: Failure without Meaning*:** (Failure and Despair)
        - Describe a time when something turned into a failure, which possibly brought a loss of meaning and/or despair.
        - Discuss the aspects that made this event/time a failure; discuss the aspects that made this event/time lack meaning.
- Ask clients to journal about or verbalize descriptions of each associated question in the four quadrants.
- Suggest that clients assign a personalized **Label** or **Name** to each quadrant.
- Have clients create their own **Quadrants** and **Indices,** which relate to patterns in their own life. Ask them to discuss the meaning and implications of these patterns.
- Ask clients to identify how they can move along the **Indices** using experiences in their daily lives to arrive in the upper **Quadrants**. In group therapy, members can share ideas on ways to achieve this goal.
    - Regarding Quadrant 1, have group members identify ways to experience success coupled with meaning.

Applications of "The Will to Meaning" (Marshall & Marshall, 2012):

- Utilize this portion of the *Conceptual Pictograph* as a psycho-educational piece describing the **Three Applications of The Will to Meaning**. This will enable clients to better understand that they can access their own **Will to Meaning:**
    - ***Will to Meaning in Treatment:*** Exists even with serious or severe physical and mental disorders, although may appear "masked" by symptoms; it is the therapist's role to look for what keeps this Will to Meaning "alive."
    - ***Crisis-Intervention:*** Meaning exists even for clients who want to commit suicide or self-harm; it is the therapist's responsibility to help clients find or uncover Meaning and always endeavor to prevent suicide.
    - ***Neurotic Pursuit of Power, Success, or Pleasure:*** When *Will to Pleasure, Will to Power*, or *Will to Success* are substituted for *Will to Meaning;* hyperreflection and hyperintention can result. Interventions include *Dereflection, Paradoxical Intention,* or *Modification of Attitudes.*
- Ask clients to journal or verbalize how they see **The Will to Meaning** as an ever-present aspect of their Nöetic Dimension that they can access in each of the **three applications.**
- In group therapy, facilitate a discussion of the responses to each of the three applications.
- Facilitate a discussion of how **"Homo Patiens"** can be utilized in the three applications of **The Will to Meaning.**
- Ask clients to identify other areas in life that can be utilized as applications of **The Will to Meaning.**

- PICTOGRAPH 13 -

Noögenic (Spiritual) Neuroses: Logotherapy as a Specific Therapy

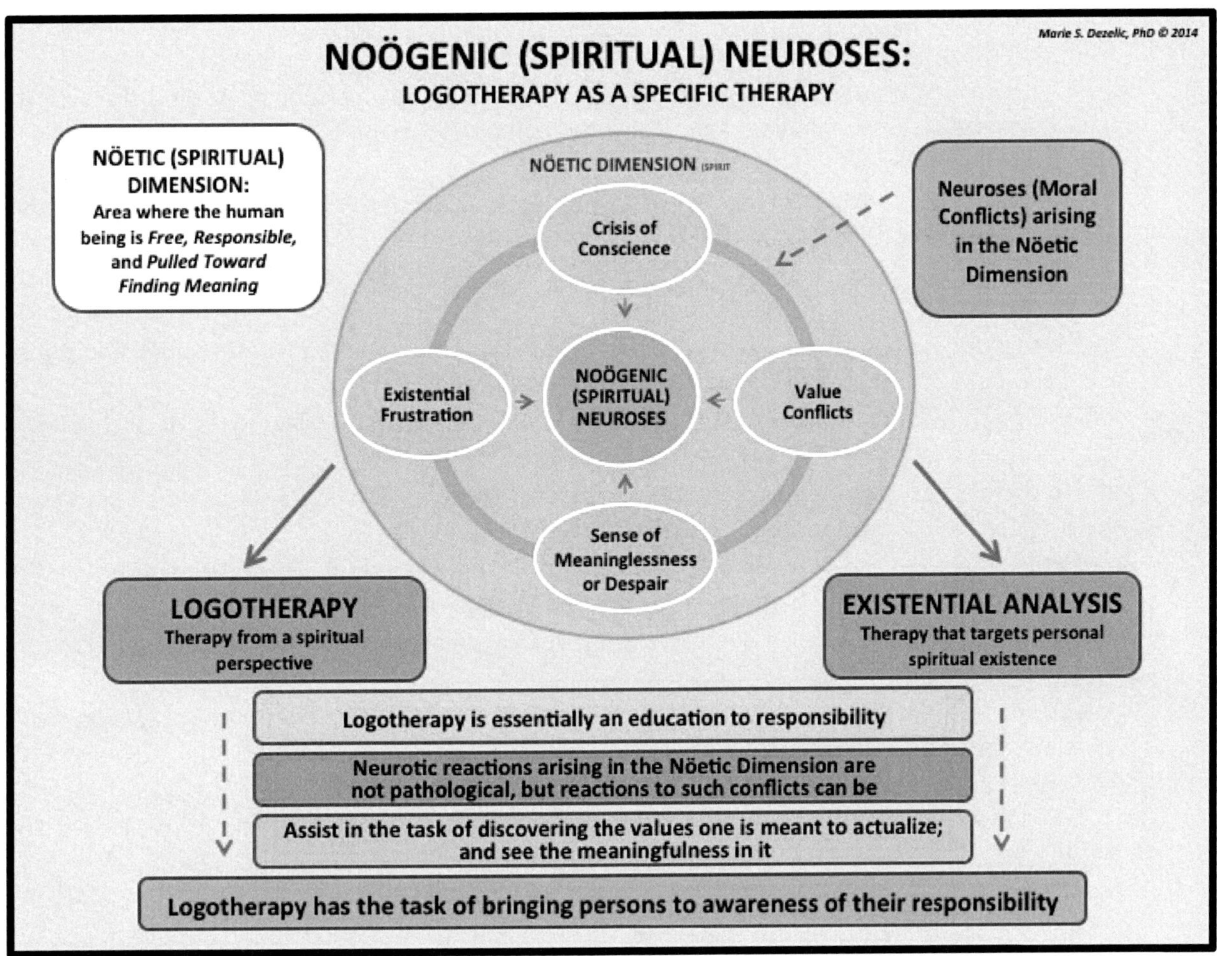

Black-and-White version available in the Appendix p.126

THERAPIST/ FACILITATOR CAN:

- Utilize this *Conceptual Pictograph* as a psycho-educational piece to define **Noögenic (Spiritual) Neurosis:** Neurosis caused by value collisions between our *nöetic* (spiritual, inner) knowing and outer mandates, resulting in conflicts of conscience, existential frustration, or the existential vacuum.
- Discuss the origins of Noögenic Neurosis as well as the therapeutic use of **Logotherapy & Existential Analysis** as a treatment option.
- Ask clients to discuss or journal about their own **Moral Conflicts** (Frankl, 1986):
    - ***Crisis of Conscience:*** A flight from responsibility and a fear of freedom regarding **our** meaning in life; a conflict between a potential action and our own personal moral code.
    - ***Value Conflicts:*** Internal conflicts and struggles arising when we are not acting in line with our own developed value system.
    - ***Sense of Meaninglessness or Despair:*** The overall, overwhelming feeling that life has ceased to have meaning, along with the complete loss of hope that a meaning will ever be discovered.
    - ***Existential Frustration:*** An internal experience in which our *Will to Meaning* has become frustrated or halted due to experiences of or reactions to *The Tragic Triad* (Unavoidable Suffering, Guilt, and Death) and *The Neurotic Triad* (Depression, Aggression, and Addiction).
- Facilitate a discussion on how clients can access resources found in the **Nöetic Dimension** to help them combat or overcome **Noögenic Neuroses.**
- Ask clients to identify a time when they have experienced **Noögenic Neuroses** or an Existential Vacuum.
- In group therapy, ask members to offer possible Meanings that are present in a difficulty experienced, which previously led to **Noögenic Neuroses.**
- In group therapy, ask members to journal or comment about each listed statement of **Logotherapy & Existential Analysis,** including its meaning for them.
- Ask clients to recall how they successfully overcame or alleviated the symptoms of **Noögenic Neuroses.**
- Ask clients to identify their new tools, which can facilitate growth, awareness of responsibility, meaning-discovery, and **Self-Transcendence.**
- **Additional Exploration for relief of Noögenic Neuroses** (Lukas, 2000):
    - The search for role models
    - The search for persons that the client might or does find important
    - Visualization techniques that can awaken the dormant imagination within the client
    - Sensitization training for Meaning:
        - What current problem am I facing?
        - What "scope of free action(s)" do I have at this moment?
        - What options do I have now?
        - What option is the most meaningful to me ***(Creative Values, Experiential Values, and/or Attitudinal Values)?*** This is the option I want to put into action!

- Assist clients to address the following:
    - What areas of freedom still exist within their current circumstances?
    - What goals and possibilities were once mentioned, never completed, and could be reactivated?
    - What new possibilities can be discovered and become meaningful?
    - What meaningful tasks can be accomplished as part of a personal ***Legacy Project*** of one's human existence?
- Ask clients to make a list of 3 columns on a page titled: ***Creativity, Experiences,*** and ***Attitudes.***
    - Identify **"new items"** under each category title that may be possible areas of Meaning in their lives.
    - Identify **"previous items"** which have given them Meaning in the past, which they can reinstate in their lives.
    - Facilitate a discussion of how clients can put these "new" and "previous" items into practice.

- SESSION 7 -

Personal Growth and Transformation

Session 7 explores personal growth and transformation over the lifespan, including how we can work toward taking new actions. Through examining the three phases of life—the ***Past,*** the ***Present,*** and the ***Future,*** therapists can assist clients in discovering meaningful interpretations of past life-altering events; in activating Meaning-possibilities in the present; and in creating goals for the future that have Meaning potential—thereby leading them toward ***Self-Transcendence*** and ***Ultimate Meaning.***

Logotherapy & Existential Analysis (LTEA) emphasizes that we have free will, we are ***Pushed by our Past*** while simultaneously being ***Pulled toward our Future,*** concurrently fully existing and living in the ***Present Moment,*** with inherent ***Choices, Freedom, Meaning*** and ***Responsibility***. We are not pre-determined beings, reduced and fated by intrinsic drives. While it is true that genetics and our past shape many aspects of our personality, interpersonal relationships and behavioral functioning; nevertheless, it does not define our ***Being*** (existence and physical nature) in the world and our ***Well-Being*** in life.

Logotherapy looks to our past, not for a catharsis, but for ***Meaningful Cues*** and areas where ***Freedom*** still exists, for suffering which can be turned into Meaning and healing, and experiences that can be used as meaningful lessons and growth-propelling possibilities. Logotherapy helps therapists and their clients to look at themselves as the **"Me" of the Past**, the **"Me" I am Today**, and the **"Me" I Want to Become**, while recognizing the inherent possibilities of ***Choice, Freedom, Will to Meaning, Meaning in the Moment,*** and ***Responsibility To (Not From).***

Frankl often quoted the aphorism of Goethe: ***"If we take people as they are, we make them worse. If we treat them as if they were what they ought to be, we help them to become what they are capable of becoming."*** We can help people and ourselves in the "becoming" by being **Conscious**—Aware, taking **Responsibility** for our lives, and then taking **New Action.** The concept of "becoming" is a self-discovery process of our inner resources and potentials, and is a forward action that leads to transformation—to becoming the **"Me" I Want to Become.**

- PICTOGRAPH 14 -

Post-Traumatic Growth and Possibilities Activated in Logotherapy

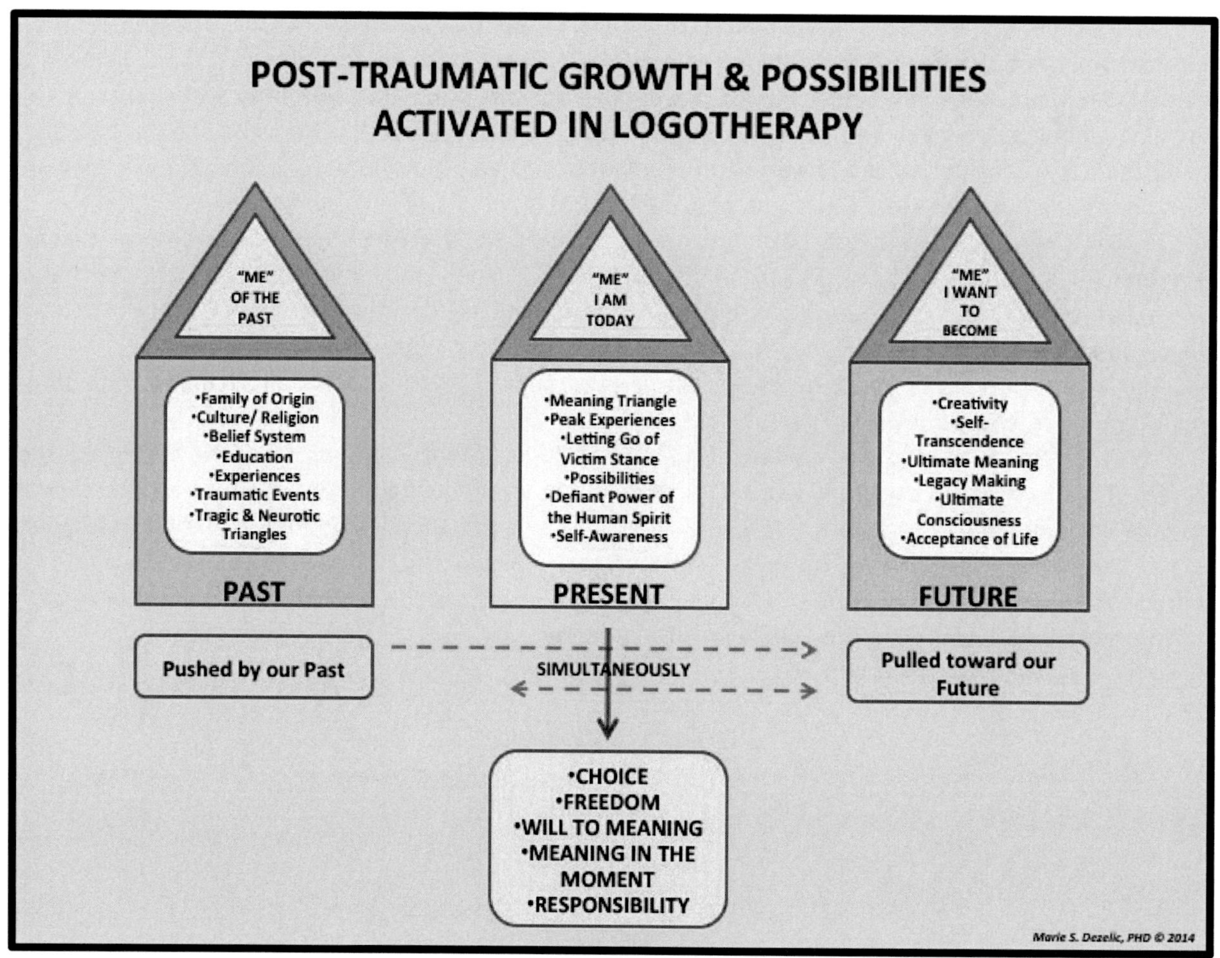

Black-and-White version available in the Appendix p.127

THERAPIST/ FACILITATOR CAN:

- Review each of the houses and their aspects in this *Conceptual Pictograph* with the clients to determine what they have learned about the **Logotherapeutic Encounter.**
- Ask clients to **draw all three houses,** and write about how they see themselves in each of these areas (such as: representations, experiences, people, accomplishments in each house). Afterward, have the clients journal and/or discuss how this exercise has helped them make connections and move forward in life.
- In group therapy, have members comment on each other's descriptions of houses, and how they can extract meaning for their life going forward.
- Have clients **create a collage** of pictures, magazine cutouts, drawings, phrases, mementos, etc., to represent each house. This can be done on a large poster board or on a computer, electronic tablet or iPad using personal photos, sayings, articles, etc.
- Make a small **Pocket Card** copy of this *Conceptual Pictograph* for clients to carry with them as a reminder that they are not stuck in their past, are not victims of their past, nor do they need to keep living in the past; clients can create their own Pocket Card, depicting representations and experiences of each house and the goals they are working toward, or make a list of each house in their smart phone notes.
- Ask clients to use any mode of artistic expression to demonstrate their own meaningful representations of the **"Me of the Past," "Me I Am Today,"** and **"Me I Want to Become."**
- On the copy of this *Conceptual Pictograph,* ask clients to write goals next to the **"Me I Want to Become"** House, and use this as a reminder of what they are working toward in therapy, to ignite possibilities of what they can and hope to achieve.
- Have clients create a **Legacy Project—Logotherapeutic Autobiography**:
    - In Group therapy, this project can be completed in session or assigned as homework; in individual therapy this project can be assigned as homework; clients can share their work in session and process their feelings associated in each Chapter.
    - Clients can write in paragraph format or bullet points as much or as little as they want, depending on the scope of their personal situations.
    - Clients can add pictures or sayings, or decorate each Chapter as they would like.
    - This project can be done on loose-leaf paper, a special journal specifically for this project, or digitally.
    - Clients can incorporate other projects or exercises from this Manual within each chapter.
    - Clients can create their own titles for each Chapter.

- **Suggested Chapter Headings** (adapted from Lukas, 2000):
  - Chapter 1: My Background
    (My Parents, My Extended Family, My Culture, My Religious/ Faith/ Spiritual Background)
  - Chapter 2: My Pre-School Years
  - Chapter 3: My Elementary/Middle School Years
  - Chapter 4: My High School/Teenage Years
  - Chapter 5: My Adult Years (Up to the current point in time)
  - Chapter 6: **MY PRESENT (My Values, Beliefs, Existence)**
  - Chapter 7: My Near Future Years
  - Chapter 8: My Distant/Older Years
  - Chapter 9: My Passing and Transition
  - Chapter 10: My Legacy/Imprint on this World (Where I felt most alive, Where I felt a difference in me, Where I made a difference, Where I acknowledged my unique existence)

- PICTOGRAPH 15 -

The Meaning-Action Triangle: Becoming Existentially Aware

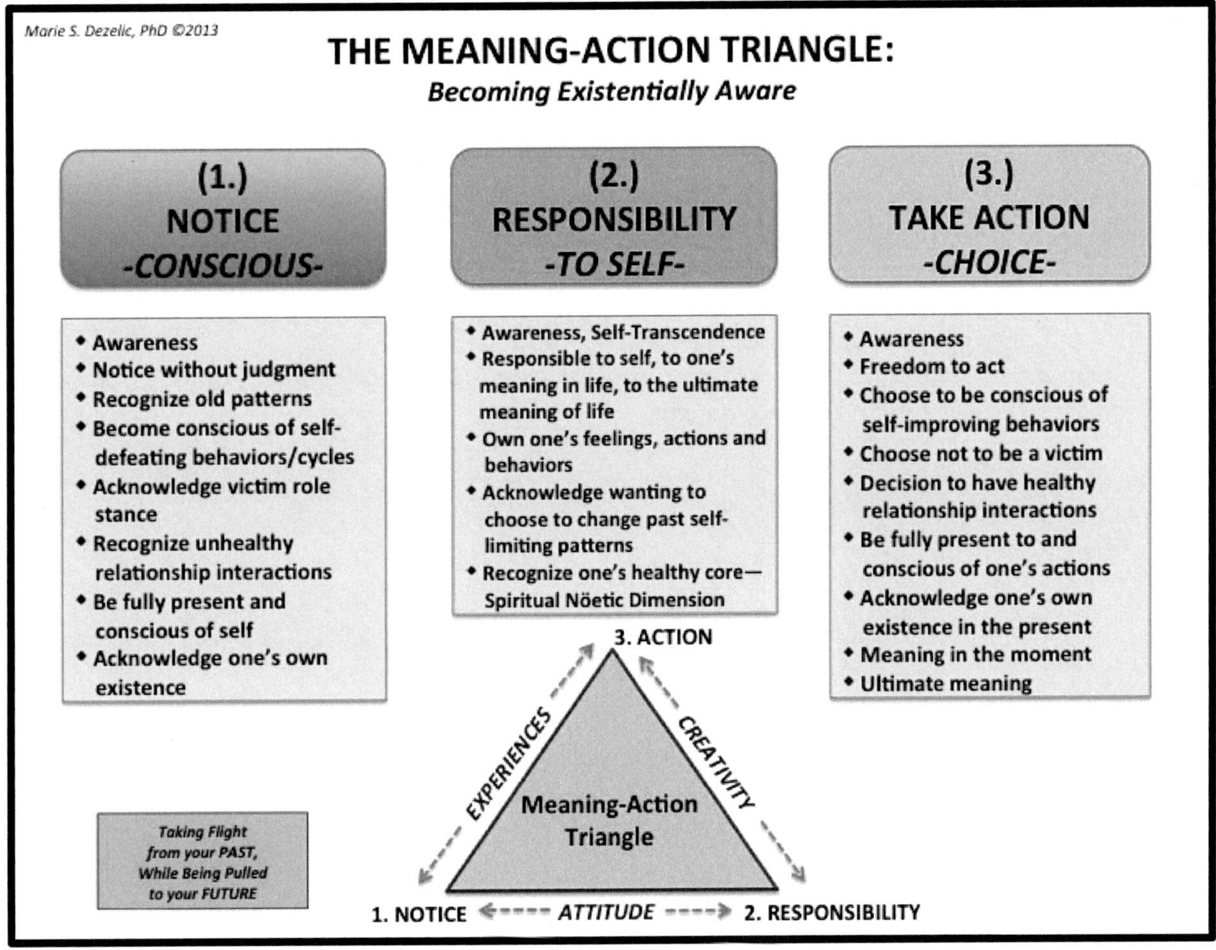

Black-and-White version available in the Appendix p.128

THERAPIST/ FACILITATOR CAN:

- Review each of the three areas and discuss their aspects with the clients to determine what they have learned about each of the existential concepts:
    - **(1) Being Conscious:** Becoming aware and noticing who we are—our beliefs and self concepts, behaviors, and life.
    - **(2) Responsibility:** Taking ownership of actions and attitudes towards our personal life and our relationships with others.
    - **(3) Choice:** Having the freedom to take action or have different attitudes in the face of any situation or life circumstance.
- Ask clients to **draw/write out each of the three areas,** and write about how they see themselves in each of these areas (such as: representations, experiences, people, accomplishments in each area); Afterwards, have the clients journal and/or discuss how this exercise has helped them make connections to move forward in life, and take new action.
- In group therapy, have members comment on each other's descriptions of each area, and how they can extract meaning for their life going forward.
- Ask clients to describe how the Meaning aspects fit in combination with each area and give examples:
    - Notice and Action: *Experiences*
    - Notice and Responsibility: *Attitude*
    - Responsibility and Action: *Creativity*
- Discuss the notion that the three areas **(Notice, Responsibility, Action),** are steps of an ongoing process throughout life and development.

- PICTOGRAPH 16 -

7-Step Noögenic Activation Method: Igniting the Defiant Power of the Spirit

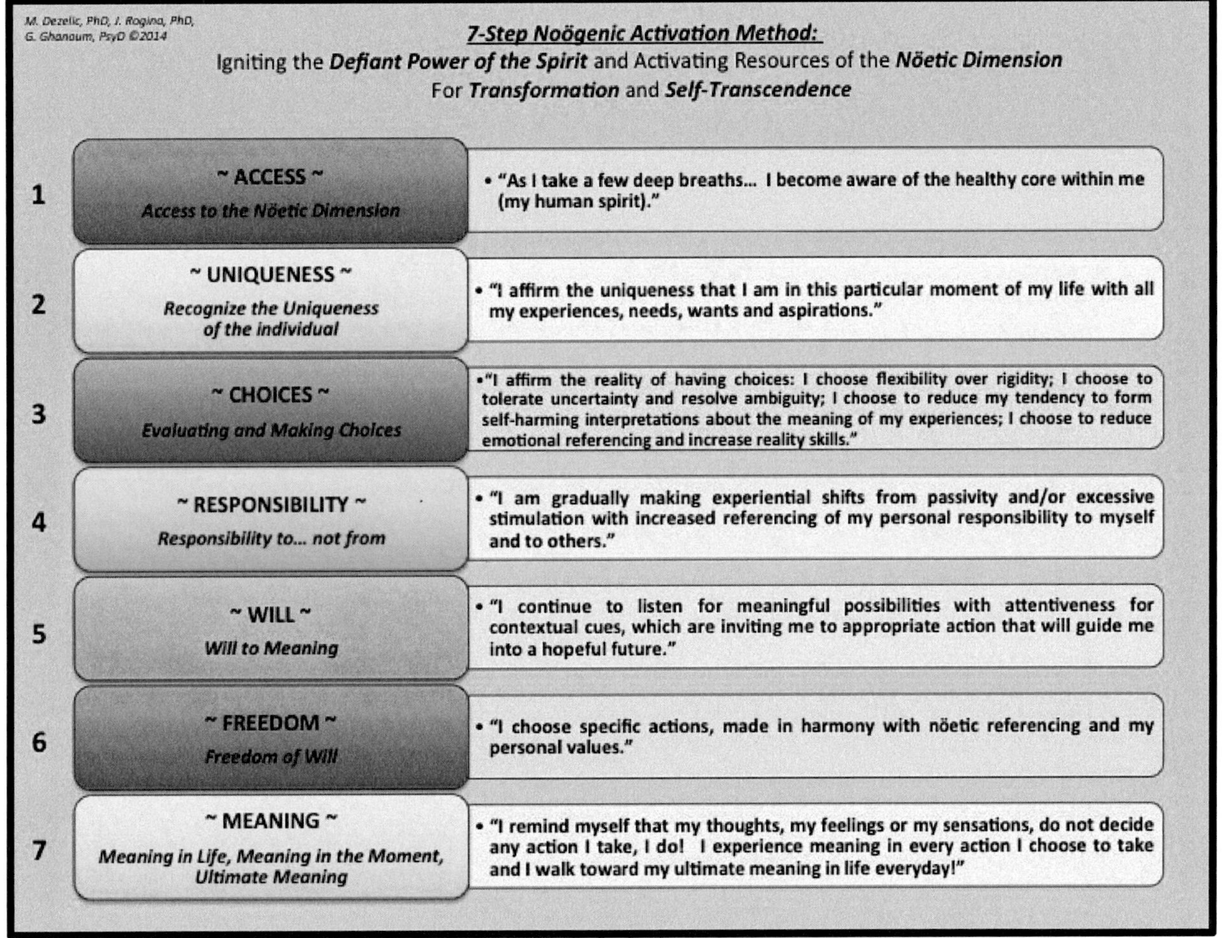

Black-and-White version available in the Appendix p.129

THERAPIST/ FACILITATOR CAN:

- Offer this Appealing Technique, "7-Step Noögenic Activation Method," that was developed by Rogina and expanded by Dezelic and Ghanoum, as a supplemental or closing exercise.
- The Appealing Technique can be used with any population.

  Important Note: ***Special consideration should be taken with suicidal clients; this technique is not recommended for actively psychotic clients; clients should be under supervised medical and/or psychiatric care.***
- The Appealing Technique can be used once a week or at every group therapy session, strengthening the clients' access to their **Defiant Power of the Human Spirit** and the **Nöetic Dimension;** likewise it can be added to individual therapy as often as needed (i.e., once a week, every other week, once a month).
- Make a recording of your voice offering the **Appealing Technique** for when clients are outside of therapy and in need of reinforcement.
- Any revised version of the **Appealing Technique** can be designed based on the specific population and the specific areas clients are addressing.

7-Step Noögenic Activation Method

© Julius Rogina, PhD

Noögenic Activation is divided into two parts:

Part I:

(1) Assess the patient/client for readiness to experience Noögenic Activation. This readiness should include an awareness of the Nöetic (Spiritual) Dimension.
(2) Invite the patient/client to become aware of ways he or she already utilizes Noögenic (Spiritual) resources.
(3) Ask direct permission to engage the application of formal Noögenic Activation.

Part II:

Formal Noögenic Activation: All seven steps are integral to the process; sometimes the focus is "choices." Other times, the focus could be hope, forgiveness, gratefulness, compassion, freedom, meaning, etc.

- The **"7-Step Noögenic Activation Method"** can be combined and used daily as an ***Appealing Technique*** in Noögenic (Spiritual) Training to ignite the ***Defiant Power of the Spirit*** and activate resources of the ***Nöetic (Spiritual) Dimension.***
- And/or each of the 7 Steps can be explored within the context of the LTEA 7 Stages of Change

LTEA Stages of Change

LTEA adaptation and expansion of Prochaska and DiClemente's **"Stages of Change in the Transtheoretical Model (TTM)":**
(Prochaska, J., Norcross, J. & DiClemente, C., 1994)

LTEA aspects and terminology are described in purple

- **Stage One: "Precontemplation"**
  LTEA Stage One: *Possibly experiencing the Tragic and Neurotic Triads- Existential Frustration*
  People are not thinking seriously about changing and are not interested in any kind of help.
  - "I don't want to."
  LTEA Task: Educate on Dimensional Ontology

- **Stage Two: "Contemplation"**
  LTEA Stage Two: *Possibly experiencing the Tragic and Neurotic Triad- Existential Frustration*
  People are more aware of the personal consequences of their bad habit and they spend time thinking about their problem. Although they are able to consider the possibility of changing, they tend to be ambivalent about it.
  - "I may try."
  LTEA Task: Educate on Nöetic Dimension

- **Stage Three: "Preparation/ Determination"**
  LTEA Stage Three: *Freedom of Will*
  People have made a commitment to make a change. Their motivation for change is reflected by statements such as: "I've got to do something about this – this is serious. Something has to change. What can I do? What do I want to do?"
  -"I will try."
  LTEA Task: Explore Meaning in Life, Freedom of Will, Will to Meaning

- **Stage Four: "Action"**
  LTEA Stage Four: *Will to Meaning*
  People believe they have the ability to change their behavior and are actively involved in taking steps to change their undesirable behaviors by using a variety of different skills.
  -"I am making changes."
  LTEA Task: Activate Meaning Triangle, Defiant Power of the Spirit

- **Stage Five: "Maintenance"**
  LTEA Stage Five: *Meaningful Living*
  Maintenance involves being able to successfully avoid or overcome any temptations to return to the undesirable behaviors. The goal of the maintenance stage is to maintain the new status quo. People in this stage tend to remind themselves of how much progress they have made.
  -"I have made a new habit and choices."
  LTEA Task: Explore Meaning, Transformation, Self-Transcendence

- **Stage Six: "Relapse"**
  LTEA Stage Six: *Existential Distress & Frustration*
  Along the way to permanent cessation or stable reduction of undesirable behavior, most people experience relapse. In fact, it is much more common to have at least one relapse than not. Relapse is often accompanied by feelings of discouragement and seeing oneself as a failure.
  -"I went back to my old pattern."
  LTEA Task: Explore Existential Despair & Frustration—Tragic & Neurotic Triads

- **Stage Seven:** (not in original "Stages of Change, TTM")
  LTEA Stage Seven: *Noö-dynamics and Self-Transcendence*
  If maintenance is successful for a long period of time, we reach a point where we are able to work with our emotions and understand our own behaviors and view them in a new light. Self-Transcendence is manifested in the human spirit's ability to reach beyond the present problems and visualize how we want to be in order to actualize meaning possibilities. Noö-dynamics create a tension between who we are and who we could be.
  -"I am responsible to my life, and am consistently making healthy choices."
  LTEA Task: Explore Living Meaningfully, Meaning in Life, Existential Analysis, Self-Transcendence

Formal "7-Step Noögenic Activation Method":
(Therapist/ Facilitator can read the following statements with a slow-paced, relaxed voice and gentle tone.)

1. As I take a few deep breaths... I become aware of the healthy core within me (my human spirit).
   (Access to the Nöetic Dimension)

2. I affirm the uniqueness that I am in this particular moment of my life with all my experiences, needs, wants and aspirations.
   (Recognize the Uniqueness of the individual)

3. I affirm the reality of having choices: I choose flexibility over rigidity; I choose to tolerate uncertainty and resolve ambiguity; I choose to reduce my tendency to form self-harming interpretations about the meaning of my experiences; I choose to reduce emotional referencing and increase reality skills.
   (Choices)

4. I am gradually making experiential shifts from passivity and/or excessive stimulation with increased referencing of my personal responsibility to myself and to others.
   (Responsibility to... not from)

5. I continue to listen for meaningful possibilities with attentiveness for contextual cues, which are inviting me to appropriate action that will guide me into a hopeful future.
   (Will to Meaning)

6. I choose specific actions, made in harmony with nöetic referencing and my personal values.
   (Freedom of Will)

7. I remind myself that my thoughts, my feelings or my sensations, do not decide any action I take, I do! I experience meaning in every action I choose to take and I walk toward my ultimate meaning in life everyday!
   (Meaning in Life, Meaning in the Moment, Ultimate Meaning)

The Key to Meaningful Changes In Logotherapy & Existential Analysis (LTEA) is to:
*Explore with the patient/client the reality of nöetic resources as related to unique human qualities.
*Help the patient/client to become aware of his/her unique nöetic qualities already in place.
*Assist the patient/client to explore his/her values that support and guide towards activation of nöetic (spiritual) resources.
*Encourage the patient/client to choose contextually his/her activities corresponding with resources and abilities.

More Information on the **Noögenic Activation Method** is found in:
Dezelic, 2014. *Meaning-Centered Therapy Workbook: Based on Viktor Frankl's Logotherapy & Existential Analysis.* San Rafael, CA: Palace Printing and Design.

- SESSION 8 -

Living Meaningfully

To summarize, the philosophy and theory Frankl's philosophical, phenomenological and anthropological approach, Logotherapy & Existential Analysis expresses the unique quality of the human being through its dimensional ontology—comprised of *Soma* (Body), *Psyche* (Mind), and *Noös* (Spirit). It teaches that we are motivated and pulled toward our future by our (1) *Freedom of Will*, (2) *Will to Meaning*, and (3) *Meaning of Life,* culminating in *Self-Transcendence*, all of which exist within the *Nöetic—Spiritual Dimension*. Logotherapists can reorient clients who are suffering back toward these *Three Tenets of Logotherapy* through activating and discovering their ***Meaning Triangle*—with *Creativity, Experiences*,** and ***Attitudes*;** and use the unique qualities held within the *Nöetic Dimension—the Medicine Chest,* to address the difficulties in life, as well as the *Somatic*, *Psychic*, or *Noögenic* illnesses/ disorders/ neuroses/ frustrations that are part of human existence.

Session 8 is not only a culmination of the Meaning-Centered Therapy Manual's group or individual therapy process; it also marks a key transitioning point for individuals to begin examining their lives from a new perspective, through new lenses, with a new **self-awareness,** through **self-reflection,** and **self-discovery,** to a place of **self-connection, self-acceptance, self-compassion** and an ability for **self-transcendence.**

All of us experience ***Unavoidable Suffering—Pain, Guilt,*** and ***Death***. We are also likely to feel or experience various levels of ***Depression, Aggression,*** and ***Addiction,*** all of which are symptoms of ***The Tragic Triad*** and ***The Neurotic Triad,*** which can lead to ***Existential Frustration*** followed by the ***Existential Vacuum.*** However, it is not the question of ***"Why"*** *we have* experienced these difficulties that is important; rather; it is the **"How," "What," "Where," "When,"** and **"Who"** ... of the experience that ultimately matters most. This final session explores those questions and provides suggestions and ways for clients to bring together the most salient topics discussed and explored in this Meaning-Centered Therapy Manual.

- PICTOGRAPH 17 -

REACH Beyond the Limitations: Sources of Meaning in Life

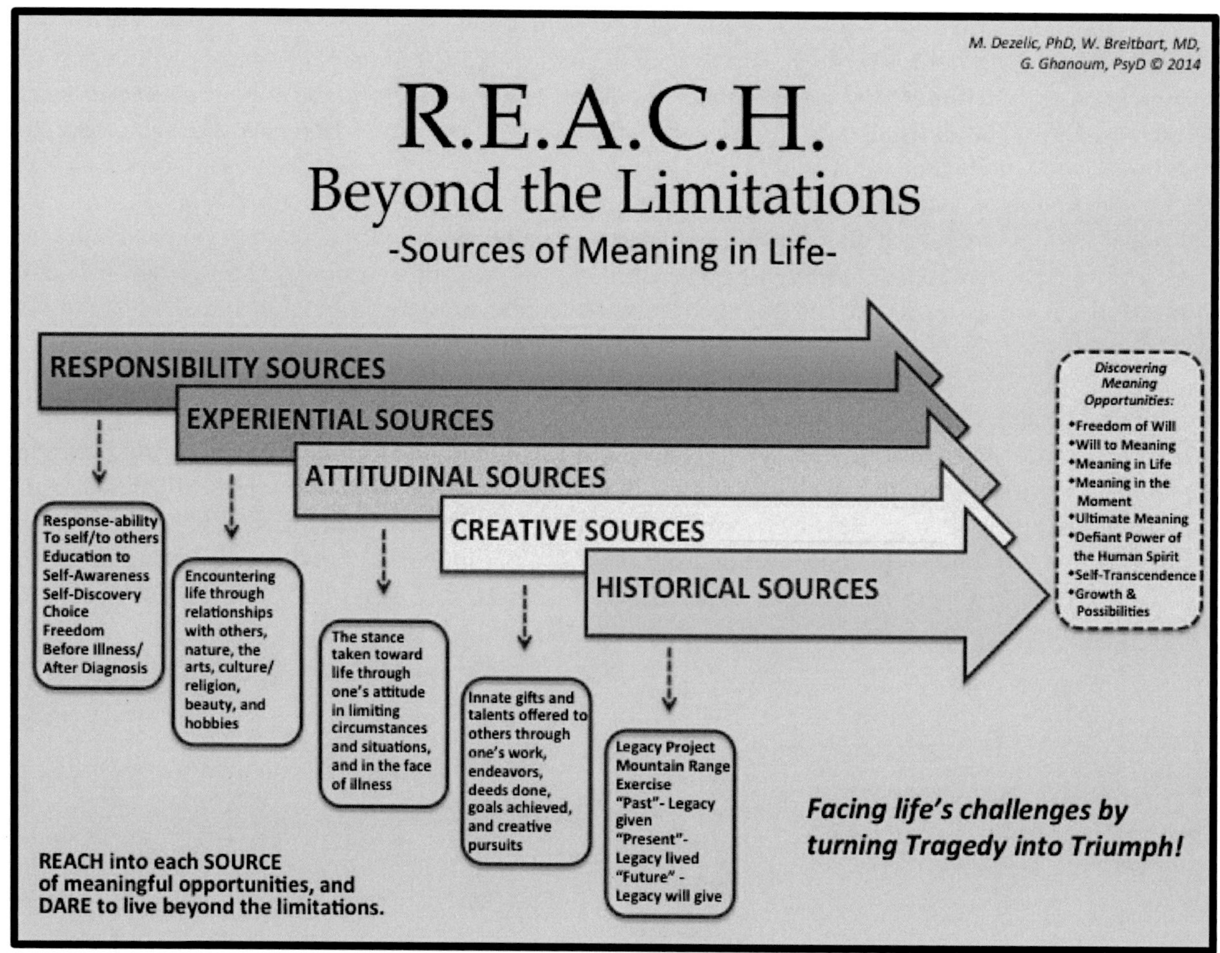

Black-and-White version available in the Appendix p.130

The "REACH Beyond the Limitations: Sources of Meaning in Life" Conceptual Pictograph—Client Handout, was designed by M. Dezelic, PhD, W. Breitbart, MD, and G. Ghanoum, PsyD, based on Dr. William Breitbart's work and clinical research with randomized controlled trials of his Meaning-centered group psychotherapy (MCGP) and Individual meaning-centered psychotherapy (IMCP) (Breitbart et al., 2010; Breitbart et al., 2012; Breitbart et al., 2015). The REACH acronym has the following components: R) Responsibility; E) Experiential sources; A) Attitudinal sources; C) Creative sources; H) Historical sources. Dr. Breitbart's manualized treatment workbooks for MCGP and IMCP, informed by his clinical research are entitled: ***Meaning-Centered Group Psychotherapy for Clients with Advanced Cancer: A Treatment Manual*** (Breitbart & Poppito, 2014a); and ***Individual Meaning-Centered Psychotherapy for Clients with Advanced Cancer: A Treatment Manual*** (Breitbart & Poppito, 2014b).

The key concepts of Viktor Frankl's Logotherapy and Existential Analysis (LTEA): meaning in life, responsibility to life, and the spiritual aspects of the human being, inspired the applications and novel exercises in Bretibart's psychotherapeutic work with people in the advanced stages of cancer. Many who are diagnosed with cancer seek guidance and support in addressing the following issues: Sustaining meaning in life despite their life-limiting diagnosis; finding hope in the face of death; understanding their cancer diagnosis and progression; and facing or coming to terms with their impending death.

The particular interventions, developed and rigorously tested by Breitbart and his colleagues at the Department of Psychiatry & Behavioral Sciences at Memorial Sloan-Kettering Cancer Center in New York City, NY, USA, and found within the eight sessions for group psychotherapy and seven sessions for individual psychotherapy, utilize a mixture of didactics, discussion and experiential exercises that focus on particular themes related to meaning in life and advanced cancer. The themes of the REACH components: Responsibility, Experiential values, Attitudinal values, Creative values, and Historical values, are found within each session. Clients are assigned readings and homework that are specific to each session's theme. These assignments are then utilized in the sessions, with the goal of motivating clients to discover meaning and purpose in life in the face of terminal illness and impending death.

THERAPIST/ FACILITATOR CAN:

- Explore the questions in regards to the entire 8-session therapy process of this Manual:
    - ***"How"*** have I grown from the experience?
    - ***"What"*** have I taken away and learned from the difficulties in life?
    - ***"Where"*** do I see new possibilities in the face of setbacks?
    - **"When"** will I actualize the new possibilities?
    - ***"Who"*** is making a difference in my life and am I making a difference in someone's life?
- Explore the Sources of Meaning in Life, and individualize it to each person:
    - ***Responsibility Sources***
    - ***Experiential Sources***
    - ***Attitudinal Sources***
    - ***Creative Sources***
    - ***Historical Sources***
- Facilitate a discussion on the phrase: ***"REACH into each source of meaningful opportunities, and dare to live beyond the limitations."***
- Ask clients how they have been able to or could try to: ***"Face life's challenges by turning tragedy into triumph."***

- PICTOGRAPH 18 -

Connect—Create—Convey: Living Life with Meaning and Purpose

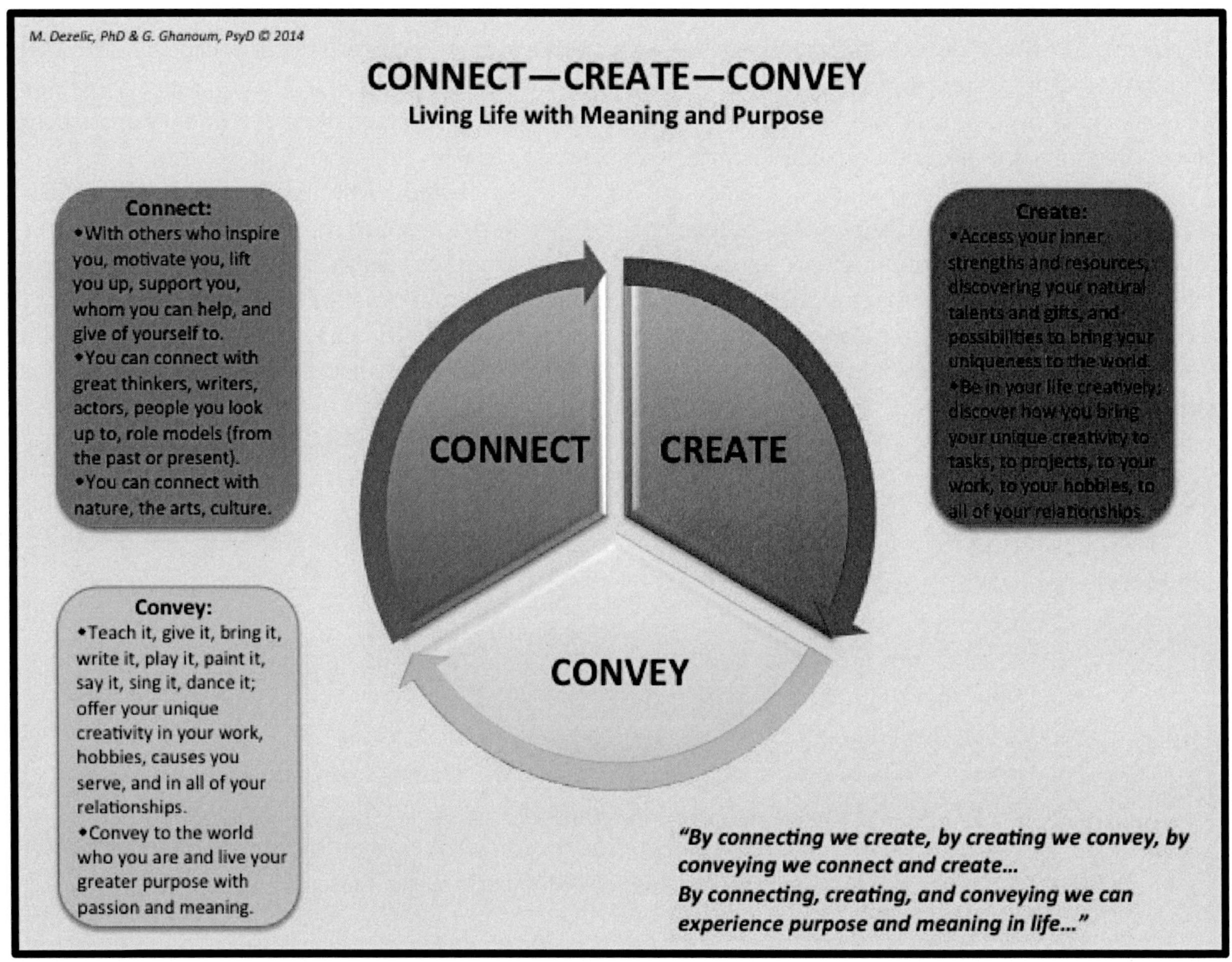

Black-and-White version available in the Appendix p.131

Pictograph 18: ***"Connect, Create, and Convey: Living Life with Meaning and Purpose"*** is the final *Conceptual Pictograph*—Client Handout based on the topics covered throughout this manual that can be used to help assist and inspire clients experiencing and discovering Meaning and purpose in life.

THERAPIST/ FACILITATOR CAN:

- Facilitate a discussion on the three aspects and how they relate to:
  (1) Their support network – those people, past or present, who promoted or are promoting positive growth, motivation and support.
  (2) Their particular resources, strengths, and talents or new areas of interests they can begin to cultivate.
  (3) Particular pathways that they can bring to the world in their own unique fashion.

- Facilitators or therapists can go over each aspect of the *Conceptual Pictograph* and discuss possibilities and ideas for the client or group members that will help them:

  Connect with:
  - Those who inspire, motivate and lift them up.
  - Those who may benefit from their help, love or support.
  - Those role models from the past or present, such as great thinkers, philosophers, authors, actors, leaders, or other people they look up to and admire.
  - The beauty of nature, the arts, culture.

  Create:
  - Access their inner strengths and resources; discover their natural talents and gifts, and possibilities to bring their uniqueness to the world.
  - Be in their life creatively; examine how they bring their unique creativity to tasks, to projects, to their work, to their hobbies, to all of their relationships.

  Convey:
  - Teach it, give it, bring it, write it, play it, paint it, say it, sing it, dance it; offer their unique creativity in their work, hobbies, causes they serve, and in all of their relationships.
  - Convey to the world who they are and live their greater purpose with passion and Meaning.

- The **Closing Discussion**: (You can read this text as written or adapt it in your own words)

  It is worthwhile to express and give in whatever way we can to humanity, and thereby experience self-transcendence. We can share our unique gifts and talents with others rather than keeping them inside and hidden from the world. This giving out helps us uncover meaning, and is a part of our experience with others; it can be the expression of our purpose or just of ourselves, as we discover Meaning in our life.

  One person's Purpose and Meaning may be to teach; another's to be an amazing friend, mother, father, partner, pillar in the community, etc. One person may be an inventor or innovator of some sort, and another may be someone who brings communities together, or a good assistant to someone who does something significant, thus being a part of a greater team. All are equally important and powerfully connecting roles.

  We have the freedom to be Response-able to life's demands, Responsible to transcend self and give to others and the world through our daily existence, and we are creative beings in simply our way of "being" in the world. We can connect with others, as we are biologically wired to do, and we can connect to life with our greater purpose. We can choose to connect with people who bring meaning in our lives and inspire us; and we can convey our uniqueness, give it out, share with others in a multitude of meaningful ways, and also discover personal Meaning through Self-Transcendence: the sharing of our gifts and talents with others and the world.

  "By connecting we create, by creating we convey, by conveying we connect and create...
  By connecting, creating, and conveying we can experience purpose and meaning in life..."

- **Final exercise:** Have clients describe one meaningful insight or lesson that they have learned throughout the 8 sessions that has impacted their life.
  - Write out the comments on a board.
  - If group therapy, have clients take notes of others' comments.
  - This can also be done in a group circle, where clients hold hands, and each make a statement about what they take away from the group and the experience.
- **Good-Byes: Allow clients some time to say their farewells to you and the other members of the group.**

III.
CONCLUSION

ACTIVATING POSSIBILITIES THROUGH LOGOTHERAPY

Summary

Activating Possibilities Through Logotherapy

Viktor Frankl's ***Meaning-Centered Logotherapy & Existential Analysis (LTEA),*** a theory, therapy, philosophy, and phenomenological approach to understanding human existence, offers an explanation for the specific quality of being human and calls on all of us to be "response-able" to the demands of Life. We are each unique individuals who discover meaning in life through engagement with creativity, experiences, nature, relationships, and self-transcendence—the giving of ourselves to others and the world. Meaning-Centered Logotherapy & Existential Analysis (LTEA) can be described as therapy and a process of healing through health, growth, and meaning (Barnes, 2005).

Meaning-Centered Logotherapy & Existential Analysis (LTEA) addresses the difficulties that we all experience in the existential realm, and explores our personal existence and sense of being alive. The teachings of Viktor Frankl guide us toward a meaningful and purposeful way of living, while helping us better understand that life inheritably contains difficult, and sometimes tragic or traumatic situations. At the epicenter of LTEA is *Logos*—Meaning, as well as the central theme of human existence—the *Search for Meaning*.

Viktor Frankl always stated that **life is potentially meaningful under any conditions, whether they are pleasurable or miserable and tragic situations** (Frankl, 1986). Meaning-Centered Logotherapy & Existential Analysis addresses meaning in life, suffering, and our attitudes in the face of unavoidable life conditions and situations. All human beings have the freedom to rise above and transcend beyond limitations and suffering, to discover and engage in their unique purpose in life.

Meaning-Centered Logotherapy & Existential Analysis (LTEA) illuminates our understanding of what it means to be human, and assists in uncovering our personal responsibility and our ability to respond to life. This therapeutic modality assists us to become conscious of ourselves through self-awareness and self-discovery of our overall existence and life experiences, and our inherent **Search for Meaning** through an ontological framework of mind, body, and spirit (the non-religious unique essence ever present in each individual). Meaning-focused interventions not only help us to activate and discover our unique meaning in life through our creative gifts and our experiences in the world and with others, nature, and the arts; they also lessen the impact of despair, hopelessness and meaninglessness by providing opportunities to modify our attitudes toward unavoidable pain, guilt or death. Meaning-Centered Logotherapy & Existential Analysis (LTEA) offers a pathway that encourages the discovery of the resources and creativity found within our spiritual dimension, and assists in our search for meaning through our uniquely human quality and ability to examine our life—our unique existence.

Through **Self-Awareness, Self-Reflection,** and **Self-Discovery,** we connect to our humanness, can engage in **Self-Compassion** and **Self-Transcendence,** and meaningfully connect with others and causes we serve. This manual and 8-session protocol is designed to enhance our **unique existential exploration** by providing the opportunity to discover and connect with what is meaningful in our lives and actualize our own unique purpose in the world by 1) Recognizing strengths and weaknesses, and utilizing both for growth; 2) Facilitating a greater understanding of the human experience as well as of our unique and personal journey within this condition of being human; 3) Uncovering and discovering inner strengths and resources to live passionate, fulfilling and meaningful lives; 4) Living authentically, healing traumas, and experiencing personal and relational growth.

"When we are no longer able to change a situation, we are challenged to change ourselves."

- (V. Frankl)

Epilogue ….. *By Lexie Brockway Potamkin*

Victor Frankl introduced into mainstream psychological practice the concept of having and maintaining a will to live in the face of suffering and adversity with his theory of Logotherapy & Existential Analysis. Dr. Marie Dezelic and Dr. Gabriel Ghanoum further translate his theories into an accessible existential atlas for both clinicians and clients to explore their own meaning and to rediscover meaning throughout life's trials and tribulations.

Our own consciousness has often been described as a conflicting element psychologically, a voice in our head with an ongoing inner dialogue. The tools in this manual are designed to focus and hone that dialogue into something useful and constructive. By asking and exploring existential questions, we can have access to unlocking our personal meaning and existence.

I ask some of the basic key questions to discovering our inner meaning and existence in my "What Is…" series: ***What is Spirit? What is Peace? What is Love? What is Laughter? What is Death?*** I posed these simple, yet existential questions to myself and people from all walks of life, and found from the responses that simply asking these questions can unlock deeply held sources to our own meaning, purpose and emotional chapters in life.

Finding value and meaning starts with asking the difficult and sometimes vague existential questions of our own existence. Seeking the meaning of life, death, spirit, peace, laughter and love can lead to new beginnings by rediscovering and reexamining our own previously held beliefs. This Meaning-Centered Therapy Manual is a guide to offset suffering, tragedy and despair by utilizing tools to recover and discover happiness, meaning and beauty in our lives.

We all crave the momentous discovery of that fabled "reason to live." We hear incredible stories of heroism, self-awakening, physical and mental triumph in the face of adversity. We fear suffering and therefore, also the process by which we are forced to deal with it. We may think that we do not possess the power needed to rise to the occasion if challenged in such a way in the course of our lives, but the human spirit innately wants to survive and will find a way to do so, described by Viktor Frankl as the Defiant Power of the Human Spirit.

The limits of our own individual mental and physical strengths may not be truly tested until we are confronted with adversity. This may be both fortunate and unfortunate in that we do not unlock this strength of spirit until it is in dire need. When called upon, we can tap into the spiritual reserve held specifically for our emotional and mental survival. The will to persevere and find meaning in our continued existence is innate, but can be trapped under the weight of guilt, sadness, suffering, loss, unknowing. How do we unlock the meaning in our own lives?

Frankl discovered that through darkness, suffering and brutality, we can still find meaning in existence—a gift of the human spirit to overcome even in the face of seemingly insurmountable odds.

Humans suffer for reasons of their own design as well as from the darkness of the human condition. Using Frankl's approach to overcoming our own dark moments can only serve to enrich and replenish our innate inner store of strength and resilience. Dr. Dezelic and Dr. Ghanoum have harnessed Frankl's theory and its clinical practices through their creative and systematic exercises that utilize visual cues to prompt the possibility of transformation through personal insights and new awareness.

This manual and workbook explores Frankl's methodology in an accessible way and within a modern context. The authors challenge the current roles of client and treatment provider by allowing individuals to become an active part of their own therapy or existential exploration. This process inspires an ongoing outcome and provides tools for continued success in overcoming the feeling of being overwhelmed by the power of our own spiritual indecision.

Using creativity both visually and mentally becomes the key to unlocking the existential and clinical experience. This manual provides an easy-to-navigate roadmap for exploring the meaning of our unique personal experience, meaning and the purpose of our individual existence.

The *Conceptual Pictographs*—Client Handouts provide simple visual cues to organize the disorganization of suffering, and discover new meaning and emotional growth. Visualization helps to light our path of self-exploration and categorize what we know from what remains unknown.

What do we know? We know that we are part of a vast universe filled with amazing and unexplainable things. We know that we ourselves are powerful beyond our own understanding. We know that some things are out of our control, but the ways we choose to deal with them are not necessarily beyond our control. We know that we are governors of our own happiness and keepers of our ability to choose, even if only by changing our attitudes in the face of unavoidable pain, guilt or death.

We are neither helpless nor hopeless. With the rise of self-help, support groups and a broader array of therapeutic and spirituality-based solutions, we all have a little more control than we may have previously given ourselves credit for. The emphasis, whether clinical or existential, is to keep on an intentional path toward a positive solution and productive way of being, by keeping in mind our own limitless power.

The focus is on progress and on persevering in a healthy way through negative experiences or occurrences using the tools we have learned in this book. We can then apply these tools to other situations in our lives in ways that empower us to come to terms with loss and transitions, and gain a new sense of ourselves in this new context.

This manual and workbook seeks to delve deep into not only the answers, but the inviting questions that are meaningful and significant to each of us, and teaches how to channel them into a more meaningful existence after loss, grief and suffering. Whether we are clinicians, support group facilitators, or simply curious seekers looking for ways to discover the meaning of our own experiences and existence, the beauty of this book is that it can serve as a meaningful psychological exercise and catalyst to self-discovery for anyone. Bravo Marie and Gabriel!

"As we drop deeper into our divine self, by letting go and finding who we really are, we discover our sacred strengths. The most important gift we can give one another is the pure transparency of our present. Our beauty lives in the quality of our aliveness" (Lexie Brockway Potamkin, *What is Death?* p.xlii).

Rev. Lexie Brockway Potamkin, MS
Inspirational Speaker, Human Rights Activist, Minister,
Counselor, Philanthropist, and former Miss America
Founding Member, *The Aspen Center for Living Peace,* Aspen, Colorado
Founding Member, *Fisher Island Day School,* Fisher Island, Florida
Founding Member, *Miami Children's Museum,* Watson Island, Miami, Florida
Author of ***What is Peace; What is Spirit; What is Love;***
What is Laughter; and ***What is Death***

APPENDIX

Black-and-White Version
Conceptual Pictographs—
Client Handouts
FOR PHOTOCOPYING

*** For downloadable, printable PDF versions of the Color and Black-and-White Conceptual Pictographs—Client Handouts to be used in sessions, please send an email request to: meaningcenteredtherapymanual@gmail.com

SECTION I

FIGURES 1 THROUGH 5

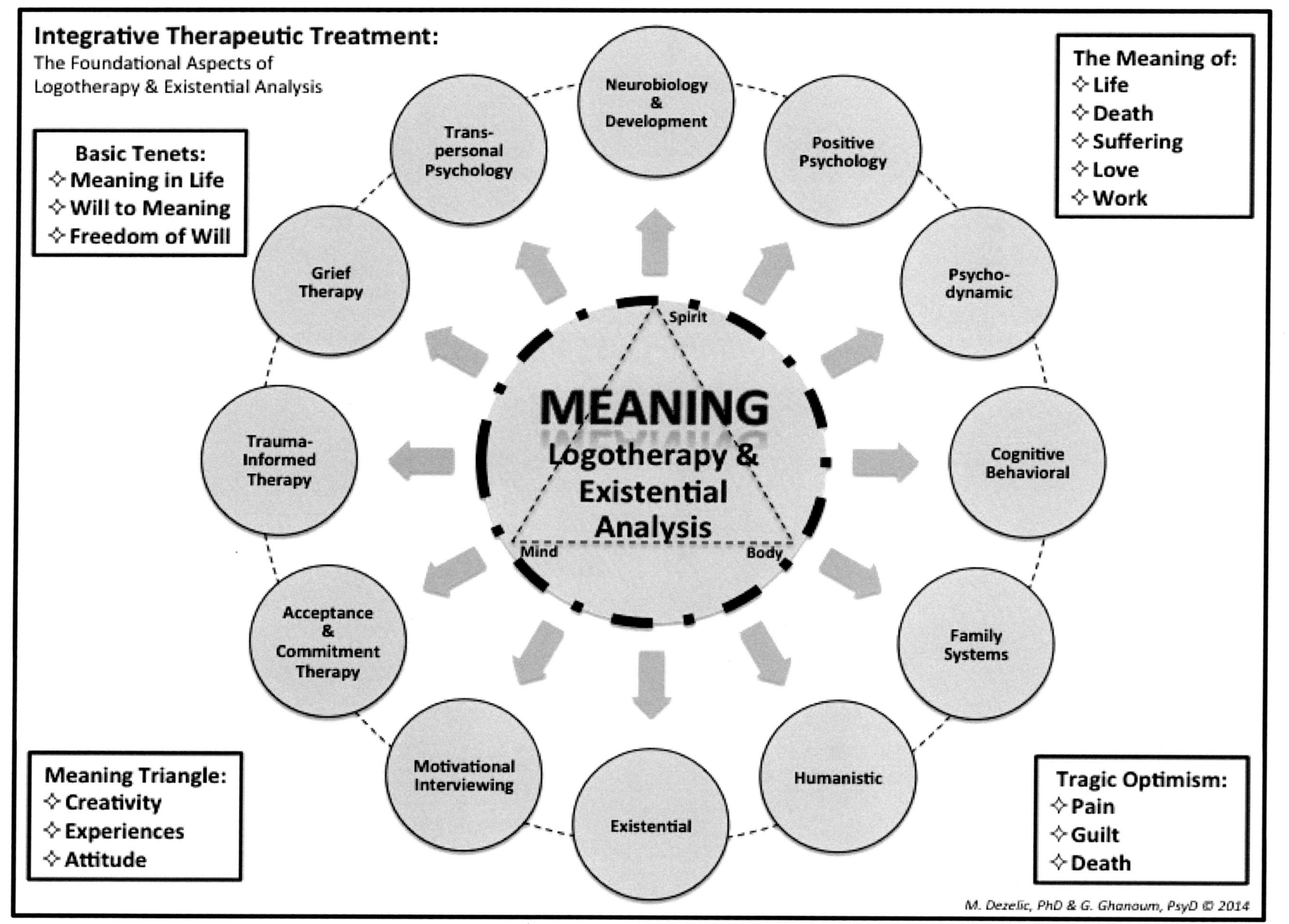

Integrative Therapeutic Treatment:
The Foundational Aspects of
Logotherapy & Existential Analysis
Basic Tenets:
✧ Meaning in Life
✧ Will to Meaning
✧ Freedom of Will
The Meaning of:
✧ Life
✧ Death
✧ Suffering
✧ Love
✧ Work
MEANING
Logotherapy &
Existential
Analysis
Spirit
Mind
Body
Neurobiology & Development
Positive Psychology
Psycho-dynamic
Cognitive Behavioral
Family Systems
Humanistic
Existential
Motivational Interviewing
Acceptance & Commitment Therapy
Trauma-Informed Therapy
Grief Therapy
Trans-personal Psychology
Meaning Triangle:
✧ Creativity
✧ Experiences
✧ Attitude
Tragic Optimism:
✧ Pain
✧ Guilt
✧ Death
M. Dezelic, PhD & G. Ghanoum, PsyD © 2014

Meaning Construct Model

BIOLOGICAL	PERSONAL
MEANING CONSTRUCT	
RELATIONAL-SOCIAL	CULTURAL

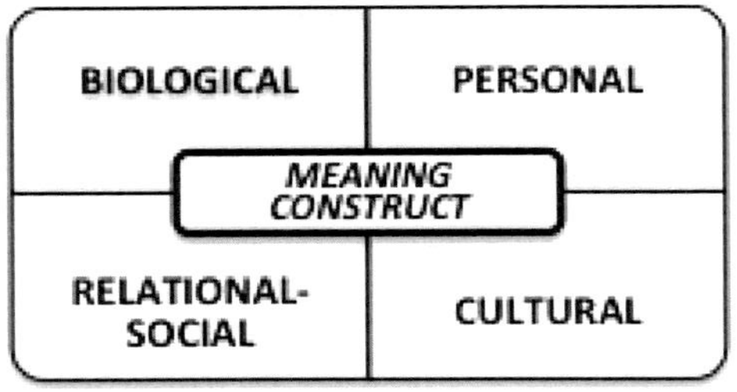

Meaning Construct
- *Central process of navigating through life*

Informed by the Specifics of
- ➢ *Biological: Age and brain development, genetic and physiological influences*
- ➢ *Personal: Temperament and personality characteristics*
- ➢ *Relational-Social: Attachment style, support, and mediating factors*
- ➢ *Cultural: Culture of the region and group, race, gender, rituals, religious/faith- based or spiritual beliefs*

New Meaning Construct

Experience ⇨ Meaning ⇨ Assimilate

3 Step Process: *Assimilating and integrating a new meaning construct*

1. Experience: The initial experience
   Actual sensory experience
2. Meaning: Discovering and making sense of it (significance)
   Through framework of Biological, Personal, Relational-Social, and Cultural factors
3. Assimilate: Integration of the experience
   Meaning (significance) discovered and synthesized into (1) self and (2) world views

Each Meaning Construct
- ➢ *Is a series of links to previous meaning constructs formed throughout life*
- ➢ *Is developing and changing as new experiences are introduced*

Meaning Construct Model:

Through a Bio-Psycho-Social-Spiritual Context

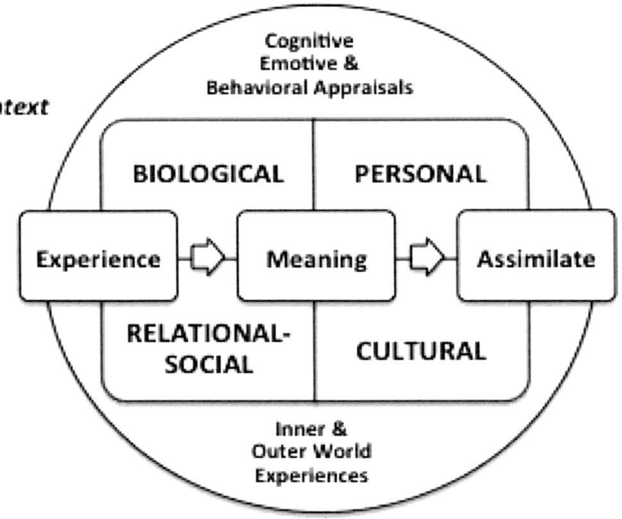

Cognitive Emotive & Behavioral Appraisals

BIOLOGICAL	PERSONAL
RELATIONAL-SOCIAL	CULTURAL

Experience ⇨ Meaning ⇨ Assimilate

Inner & Outer World Experiences

Understanding Meaning Constructs

- ➢ *Combination and interactional effect of 3 levels*
- *On the background of cognitive, emotive, and behavioral appraisals of inner & outer world experiences*
- *Through the framework of: Biological, Personal, Relational/Social, and Cultural factors*
- *The meaning construct is created by the 1-experience, 2-meaning, and 3-assimilation*

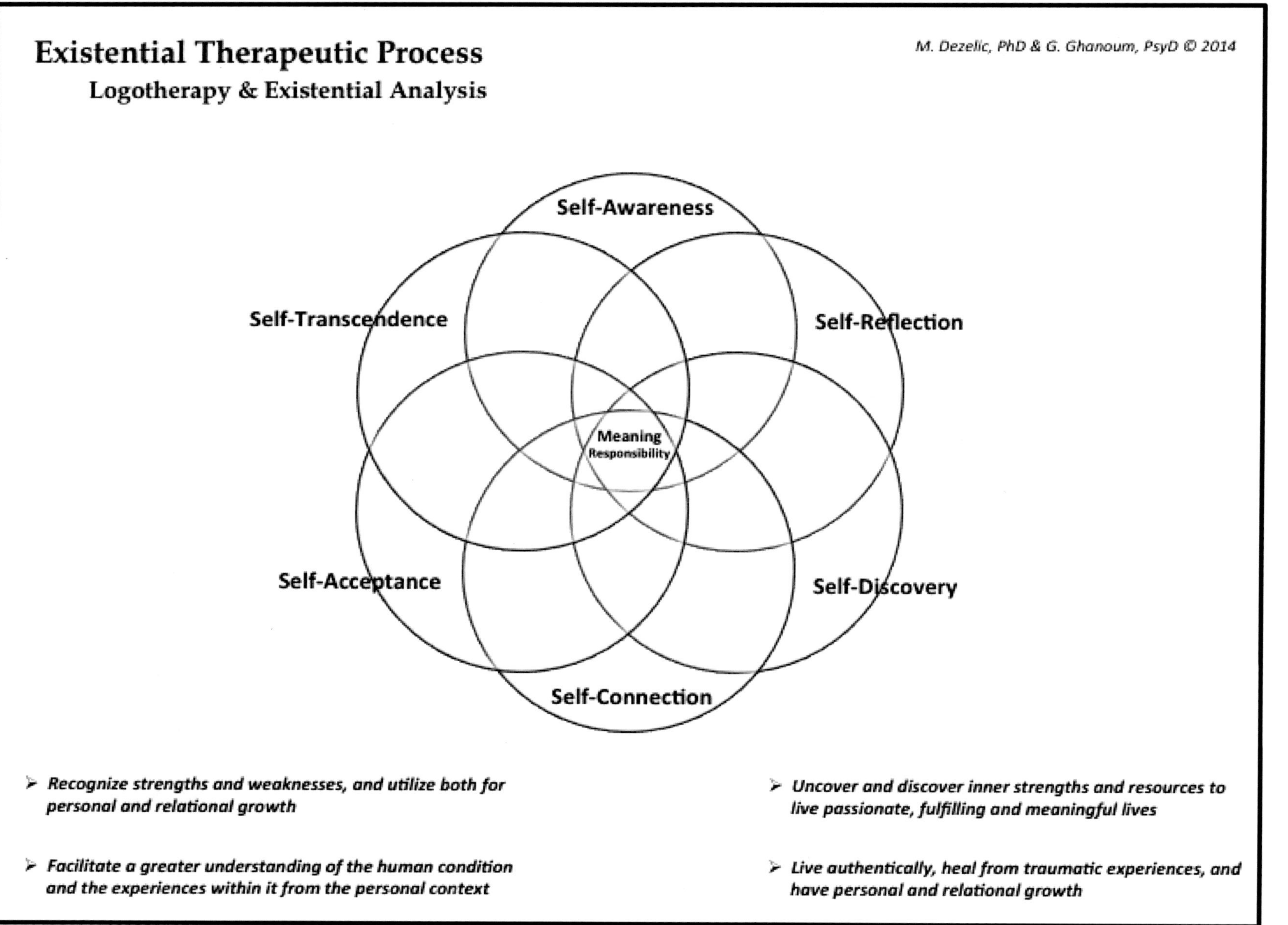
Existential Therapeutic Process
Logotherapy & Existential Analysis
M. Dezelic, PhD & G. Ghanoum, PsyD © 2014
Self-Awareness
Self-Transcendence
Self-Reflection
Meaning
Responsibility
Self-Acceptance
Self-Discovery
Self-Connection
➤ Recognize strengths and weaknesses, and utilize both for personal and relational growth
➤ Facilitate a greater understanding of the human condition and the experiences within it from the personal context
➤ Uncover and discover inner strengths and resources to live passionate, fulfilling and meaningful lives
➤ Live authentically, heal from traumatic experiences, and have personal and relational growth

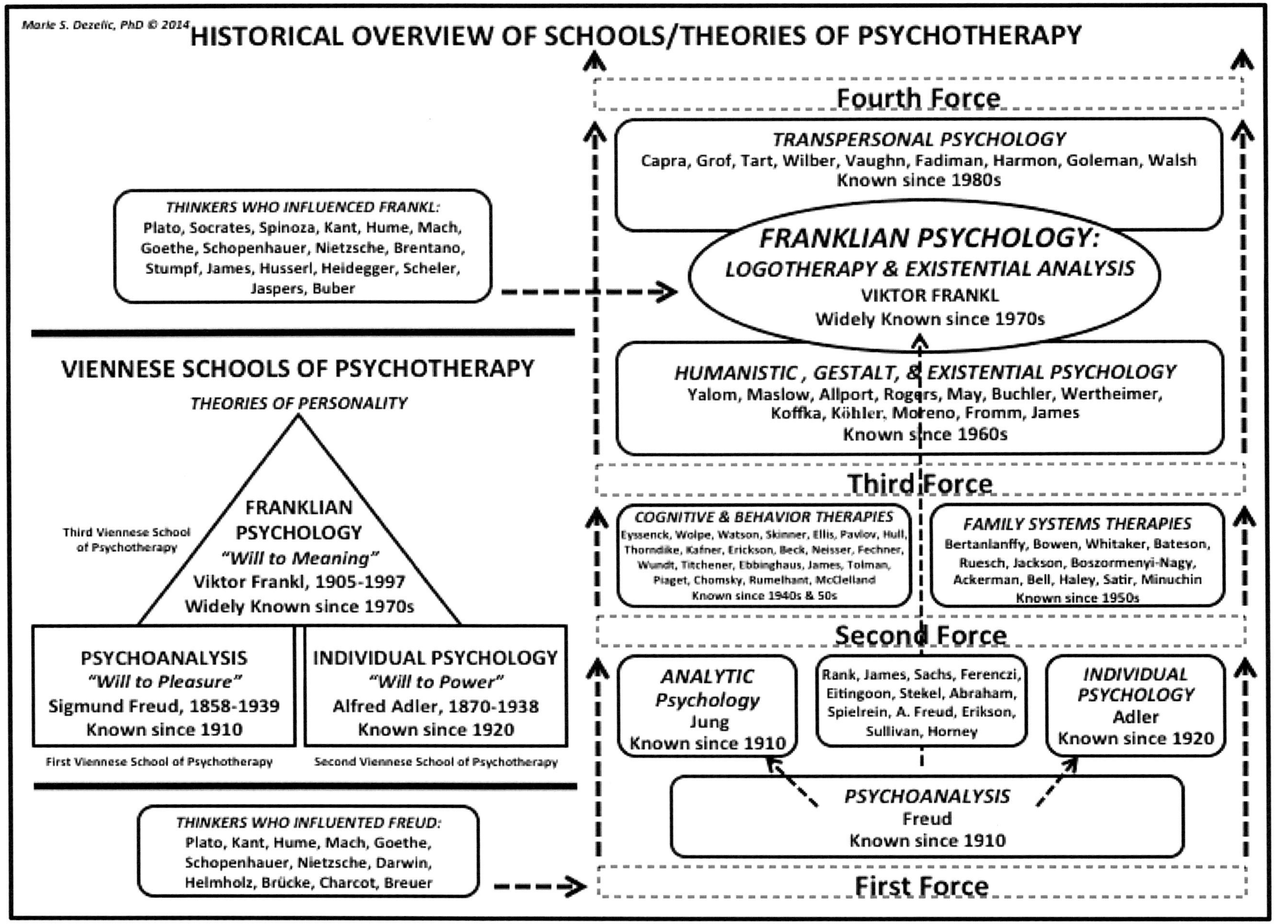
Marie S. Dezelic, PhD © 2014
HISTORICAL OVERVIEW OF SCHOOLS/THEORIES OF PSYCHOTHERAPY
THINKERS WHO INFLUENCED FRANKL:
Plato, Socrates, Spinoza, Kant, Hume, Mach, Goethe, Schopenhauer, Nietzsche, Brentano, Stumpf, James, Husserl, Heidegger, Scheler, Jaspers, Buber
VIENNESE SCHOOLS OF PSYCHOTHERAPY
THEORIES OF PERSONALITY
Third Viennese School of Psychotherapy
FRANKLIAN PSYCHOLOGY
"Will to Meaning"
Viktor Frankl, 1905-1997
Widely Known since 1970s
PSYCHOANALYSIS
"Will to Pleasure"
Sigmund Freud, 1858-1939
Known since 1910
First Viennese School of Psychotherapy
INDIVIDUAL PSYCHOLOGY
"Will to Power"
Alfred Adler, 1870-1938
Known since 1920
Second Viennese School of Psychotherapy
THINKERS WHO INFLUENTED FREUD:
Plato, Kant, Hume, Mach, Goethe, Schopenhauer, Nietzsche, Darwin, Helmholz, Brücke, Charcot, Breuer
Fourth Force
TRANSPERSONAL PSYCHOLOGY
Capra, Grof, Tart, Wilber, Vaughn, Fadiman, Harmon, Goleman, Walsh
Known since 1980s
FRANKLIAN PSYCHOLOGY:
LOGOTHERAPY & EXISTENTIAL ANALYSIS
VIKTOR FRANKL
Widely Known since 1970s
HUMANISTIC, GESTALT, & EXISTENTIAL PSYCHOLOGY
Yalom, Maslow, Allport, Rogers, May, Buchler, Wertheimer, Koffka, Köhler, Moreno, Fromm, James
Known since 1960s
Third Force
COGNITIVE & BEHAVIOR THERAPIES
Eyssenck, Wolpe, Watson, Skinner, Ellis, Pavlov, Hull, Thorndike, Kafner, Erickson, Beck, Neisser, Fechner, Wundt, Titchener, Ebbinghaus, James, Tolman, Piaget, Chomsky, Rumelhant, McClelland
Known since 1940s & 50s
FAMILY SYSTEMS THERAPIES
Bertanlanffy, Bowen, Whitaker, Bateson, Ruesch, Jackson, Boszormenyi-Nagy, Ackerman, Bell, Haley, Satir, Minuchin
Known since 1950s
Second Force
ANALYTIC Psychology
Jung
Known since 1910
Rank, James, Sachs, Ferenczi, Eitingoon, Stekel, Abraham, Spielrein, A. Freud, Erikson, Sullivan, Horney
INDIVIDUAL PSYCHOLOGY
Adler
Known since 1920
PSYCHOANALYSIS
Freud
Known since 1910
First Force

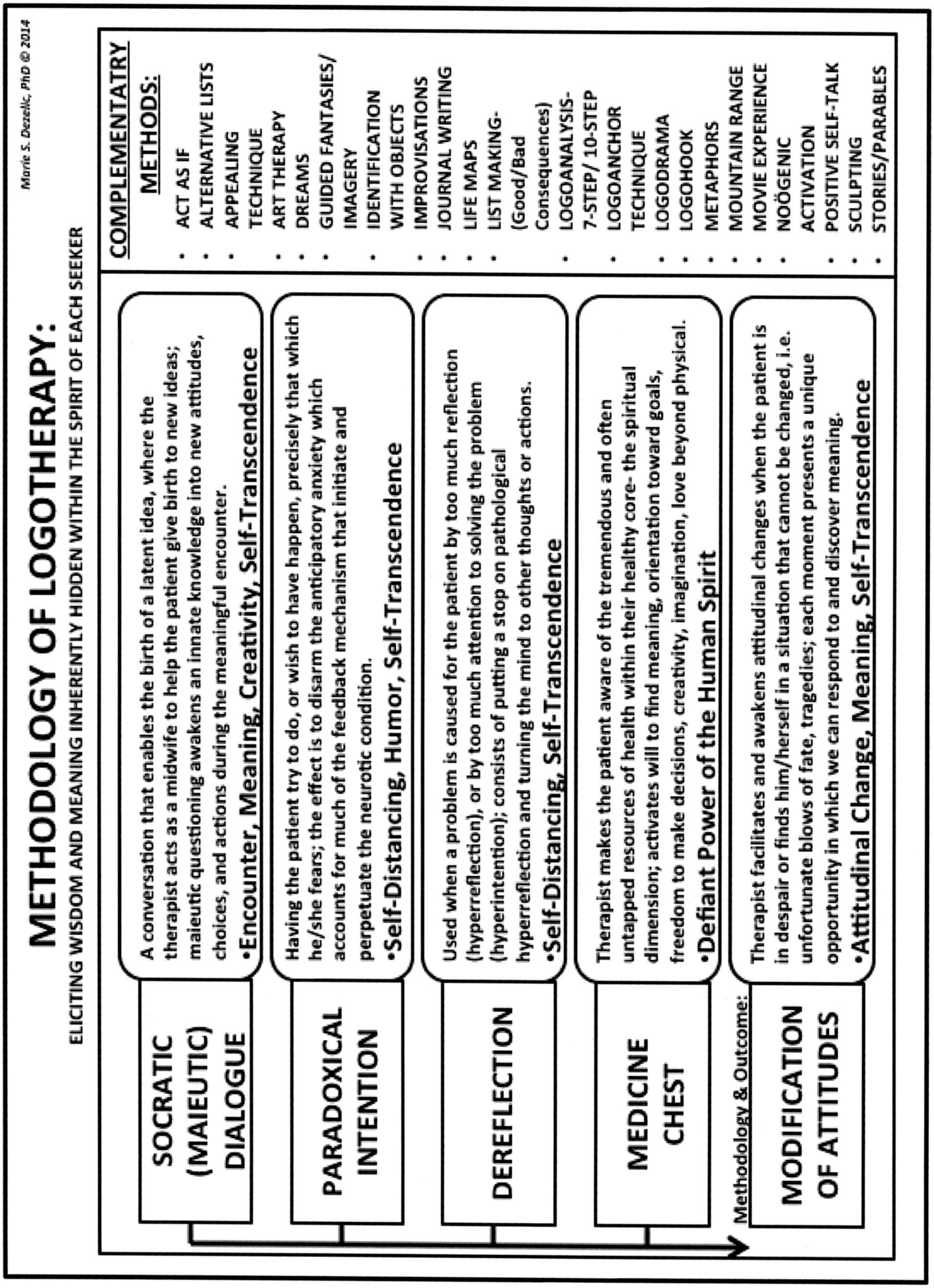

METHODOLOGY OF LOGOTHERAPY:

ELICITING WISDOM AND MEANING INHERENTLY HIDDEN WITHIN THE SPIRIT OF EACH SEEKER

SOCRATIC (MAIEUTIC) DIALOGUE	A conversation that enables the birth of a latent idea, where the therapist acts as a midwife to help the patient give birth to new ideas; maieutic questioning awakens an innate knowledge into new attitudes, choices, and actions during the meaningful encounter. •Encounter, Meaning, Creativity, Self-Transcendence
PARADOXICAL INTENTION	Having the patient try to do, or wish to have happen, precisely that which he/she fears; the effect is to disarm the anticipatory anxiety which accounts for much of the feedback mechanism that initiate and perpetuate the neurotic condition. •Self-Distancing, Humor, Self-Transcendence
DEREFLECTION	Used when a problem is caused for the patient by too much reflection (hyperreflection), or by too much attention to solving the problem (hyperintention); consists of putting a stop on pathological hyperreflection and turning the mind to other thoughts or actions. •Self-Distancing, Self-Transcendence
MEDICINE CHEST	Therapist makes the patient aware of the tremendous and often untapped resources of health within their healthy core- the spiritual dimension; activates will to find meaning, orientation toward goals, freedom to make decisions, creativity, imagination, love beyond physical. •Defiant Power of the Human Spirit
Methodology & Outcome: MODIFICATION OF ATTITUDES	Therapist facilitates and awakens attitudinal changes when the patient is in despair or finds him/herself in a situation that cannot be changed, i.e. unfortunate blows of fate, tragedies; each moment presents a unique opportunity in which we can respond to and discover meaning. •Attitudinal Change, Meaning, Self-Transcendence

COMPLEMENTATRY METHODS:

- ACT AS IF
- ALTERNATIVE LISTS
- APPEALING TECHNIQUE
- ART THERAPY
- DREAMS
- GUIDED FANTASIES/ IMAGERY
- IDENTIFICATION WITH OBJECTS
- IMPROVISATIONS
- JOURNAL WRITING
- LIFE MAPS
- LIST MAKING- (Good/Bad Consequences)
- LOGOANALYSIS- 7-STEP/ 10-STEP
- LOGOANCHOR TECHNIQUE
- LOGODRAMA
- LOGOHOOK
- METAPHORS
- MOUNTAIN RANGE
- MOVIE EXPERIENCE
- NOÖGENIC ACTIVATION
- POSITIVE SELF-TALK
- SCULPTING
- STORIES/PARABLES

SECTION II

8-SESSION GROUP & INDIVIDUAL THERAPY PROTOCOL

CONCEPTUAL PICTOGRAPHS—CLIENT HANDOUTS 1 THROUGH 18

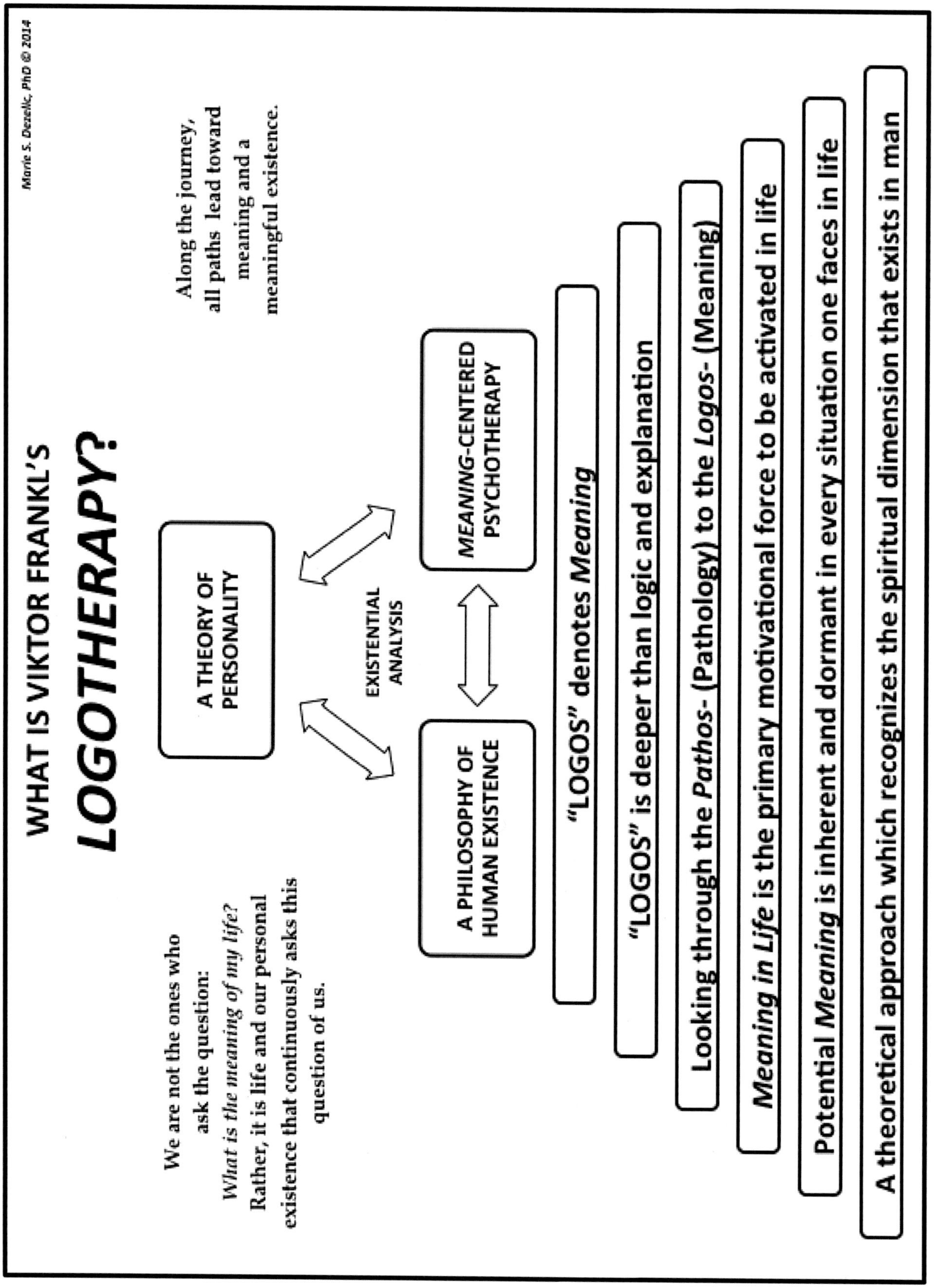

Marie S. Dezelic, PhD © 2014

WHAT IS VIKTOR FRANKL'S

LOGOTHERAPY?

We are not the ones who ask the question: *What is the meaning of my life?* Rather, it is life and our personal existence that continuously asks this question of us.

Along the journey, all paths lead toward meaning and a meaningful existence.

A THEORY OF PERSONALITY

EXISTENTIAL ANALYSIS

A PHILOSOPHY OF HUMAN EXISTENCE

MEANING-CENTERED PSYCHOTHERAPY

"LOGOS" denotes *Meaning*

"LOGOS" is deeper than logic and explanation

Looking through the *Pathos*- (Pathology) to the *Logos*- (Meaning)

Meaning in Life is the primary motivational force to be activated in life

Potential *Meaning* is inherent and dormant in every situation one faces in life

A theoretical approach which recognizes the spiritual dimension that exists in man

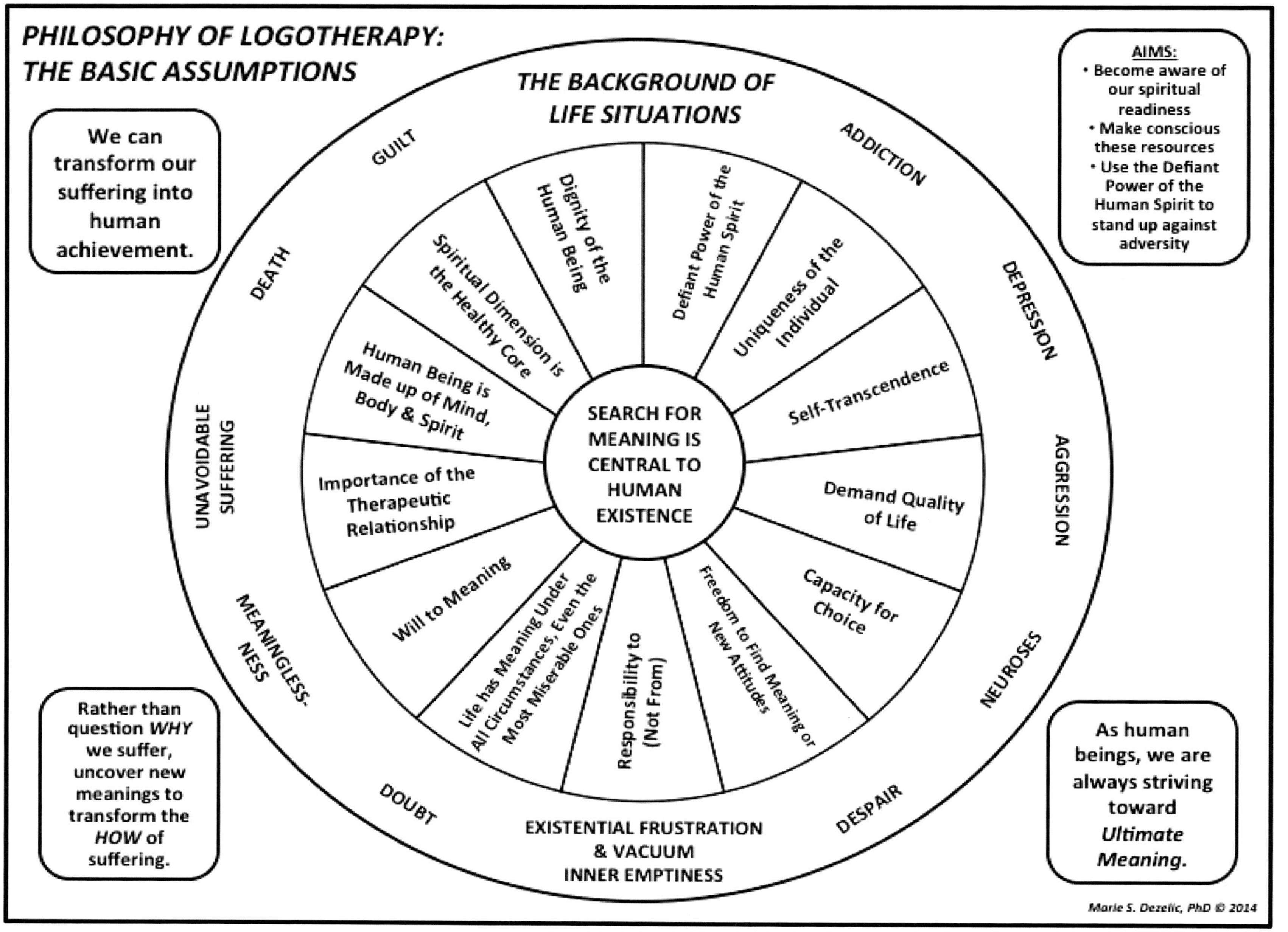
PHILOSOPHY OF LOGOTHERAPY:
THE BASIC ASSUMPTIONS
We can transform our suffering into human achievement.
THE BACKGROUND OF
LIFE SITUATIONS
AIMS:
• Become aware of our spiritual readiness
• Make conscious these resources
• Use the Defiant Power of the Human Spirit to stand up against adversity
GUILT
ADDICTION
DEATH
DEPRESSION
UNAVOIDABLE SUFFERING
AGGRESSION
MEANINGLESS-NESS
NEUROSES
DOUBT
DESPAIR
EXISTENTIAL FRUSTRATION
& VACUUM
INNER EMPTINESS
SEARCH FOR MEANING IS CENTRAL TO HUMAN EXISTENCE
Dignity of the Human Being
Defiant Power of the Human Spirit
Uniqueness of the Individual
Self-Transcendence
Demand Quality of Life
Capacity for Choice
Freedom to Find Meaning or New Attitudes
Responsibility to (Not From)
Life has Meaning Under All Circumstances, Even the Most Miserable Ones
Will to Meaning
Importance of the Therapeutic Relationship
Human Being is Made up of Mind, Body & Spirit
Spiritual Dimension is the Healthy Core
Rather than question *WHY* we suffer, uncover new meanings to transform the *HOW* of suffering.
As human beings, we are always striving toward *Ultimate Meaning.*
Marie S. Dezelic, PhD © 2014

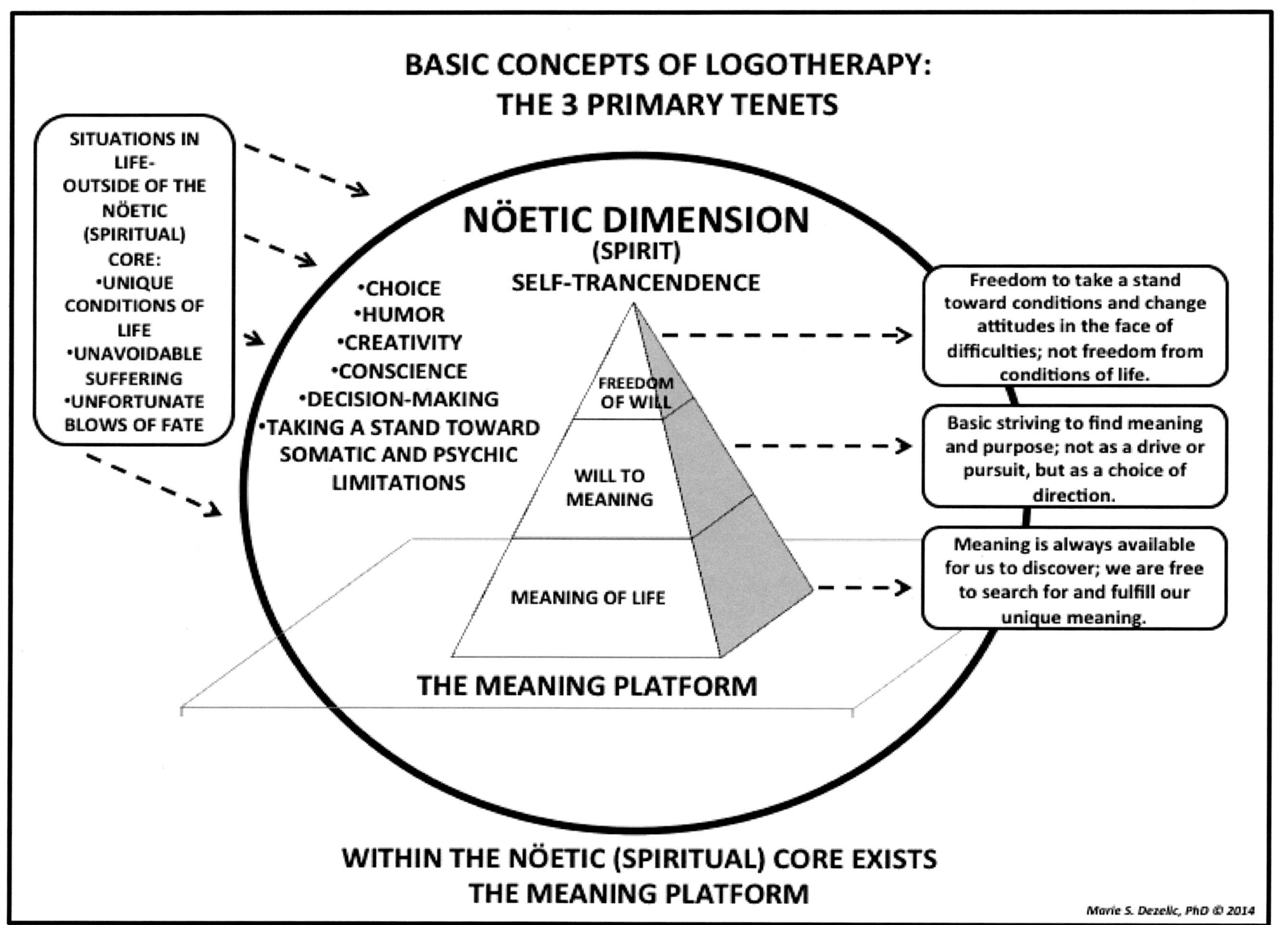
BASIC CONCEPTS OF LOGOTHERAPY:
THE 3 PRIMARY TENETS
SITUATIONS IN LIFE- OUTSIDE OF THE NÖETIC (SPIRITUAL) CORE:
•UNIQUE CONDITIONS OF LIFE
•UNAVOIDABLE SUFFERING
•UNFORTUNATE BLOWS OF FATE
NÖETIC DIMENSION
(SPIRIT)
SELF-TRANCENDENCE
•CHOICE
•HUMOR
•CREATIVITY
•CONSCIENCE
•DECISION-MAKING
•TAKING A STAND TOWARD SOMATIC AND PSYCHIC LIMITATIONS
FREEDOM OF WILL
WILL TO MEANING
MEANING OF LIFE
THE MEANING PLATFORM
Freedom to take a stand toward conditions and change attitudes in the face of difficulties; not freedom from conditions of life.
Basic striving to find meaning and purpose; not as a drive or pursuit, but as a choice of direction.
Meaning is always available for us to discover; we are free to search for and fulfill our unique meaning.
WITHIN THE NÖETIC (SPIRITUAL) CORE EXISTS
THE MEANING PLATFORM
Marie S. Dezelic, PhD © 2014

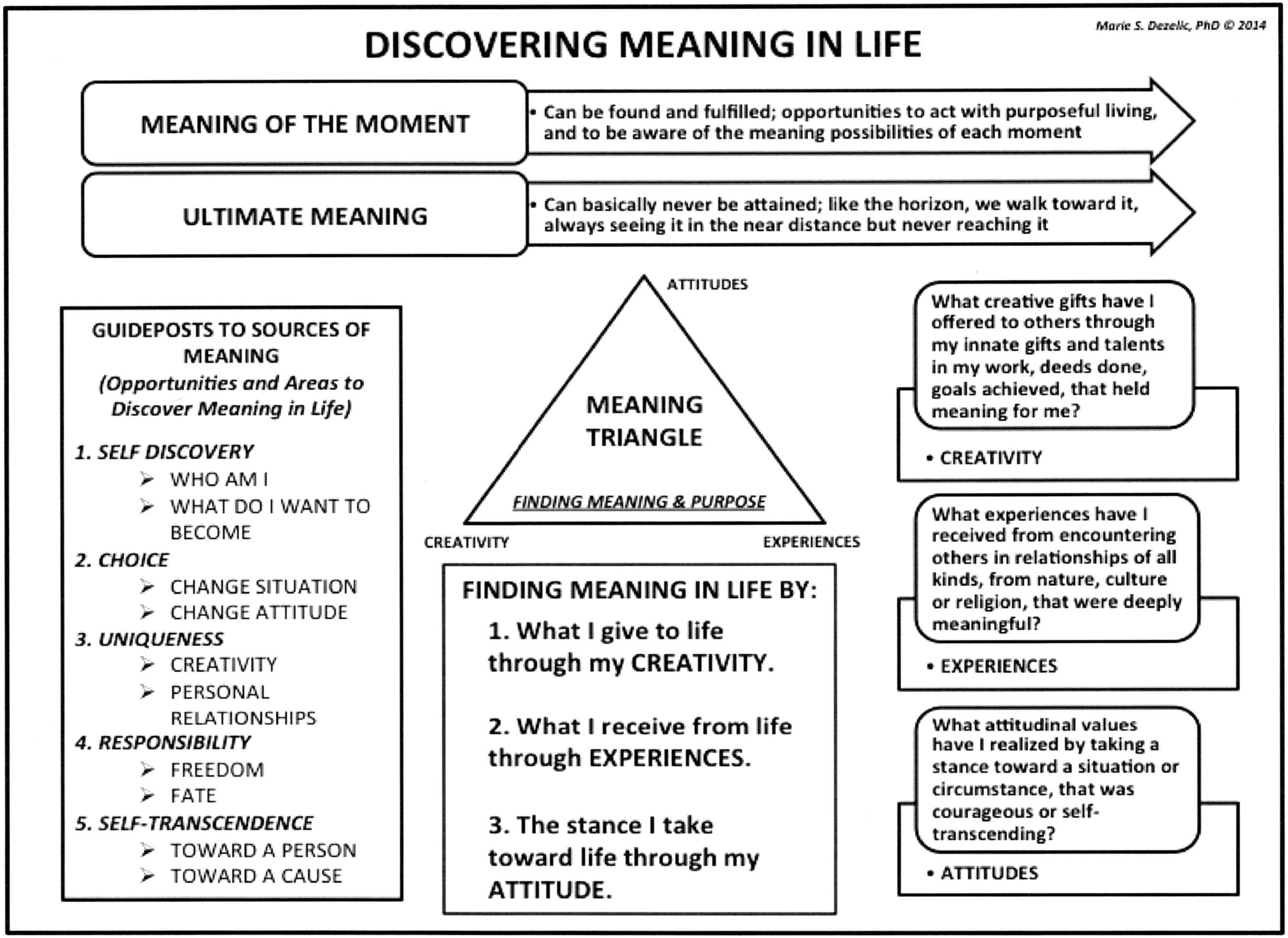

DISCOVERING MEANING IN LIFE

Marie S. Dezelic, PhD © 2014

MEANING OF THE MOMENT
- Can be found and fulfilled; opportunities to act with purposeful living, and to be aware of the meaning possibilities of each moment

ULTIMATE MEANING
- Can basically never be attained; like the horizon, we walk toward it, always seeing it in the near distance but never reaching it

GUIDEPOSTS TO SOURCES OF MEANING

(Opportunities and Areas to Discover Meaning in Life)

1. ***SELF DISCOVERY***
   - WHO AM I
   - WHAT DO I WANT TO BECOME
2. ***CHOICE***
   - CHANGE SITUATION
   - CHANGE ATTITUDE
3. ***UNIQUENESS***
   - CREATIVITY
   - PERSONAL RELATIONSHIPS
4. ***RESPONSIBILITY***
   - FREEDOM
   - FATE
5. ***SELF-TRANSCENDENCE***
   - TOWARD A PERSON
   - TOWARD A CAUSE

MEANING TRIANGLE

ATTITUDES

CREATIVITY

EXPERIENCES

FINDING MEANING & PURPOSE

FINDING MEANING IN LIFE BY:

1. What I give to life through my CREATIVITY.

2. What I receive from life through EXPERIENCES.

3. The stance I take toward life through my ATTITUDE.

What creative gifts have I offered to others through my innate gifts and talents in my work, deeds done, goals achieved, that held meaning for me?

- CREATIVITY

What experiences have I received from encountering others in relationships of all kinds, from nature, culture or religion, that were deeply meaningful?

- EXPERIENCES

What attitudinal values have I realized by taking a stance toward a situation or circumstance, that was courageous or self-transcending?

- ATTITUDES

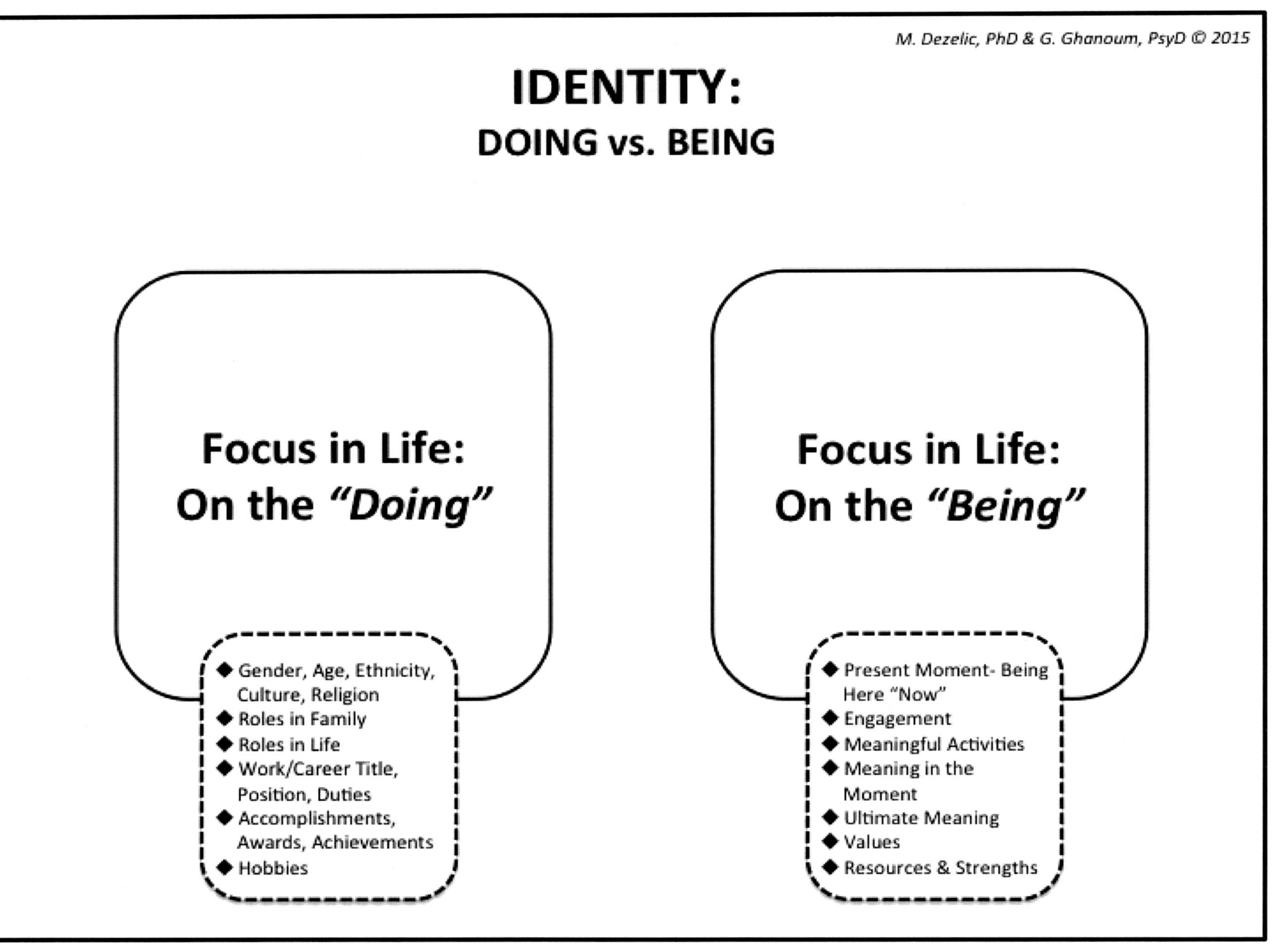
M. Dezelic, PhD & G. Ghanoum, PsyD © 2015
IDENTITY:
DOING vs. BEING
Focus in Life:
On the "Doing"
◆ Gender, Age, Ethnicity, Culture, Religion
◆ Roles in Family
◆ Roles in Life
◆ Work/Career Title, Position, Duties
◆ Accomplishments, Awards, Achievements
◆ Hobbies
Focus in Life:
On the "Being"
◆ Present Moment- Being Here "Now"
◆ Engagement
◆ Meaningful Activities
◆ Meaning in the Moment
◆ Ultimate Meaning
◆ Values
◆ Resources & Strengths

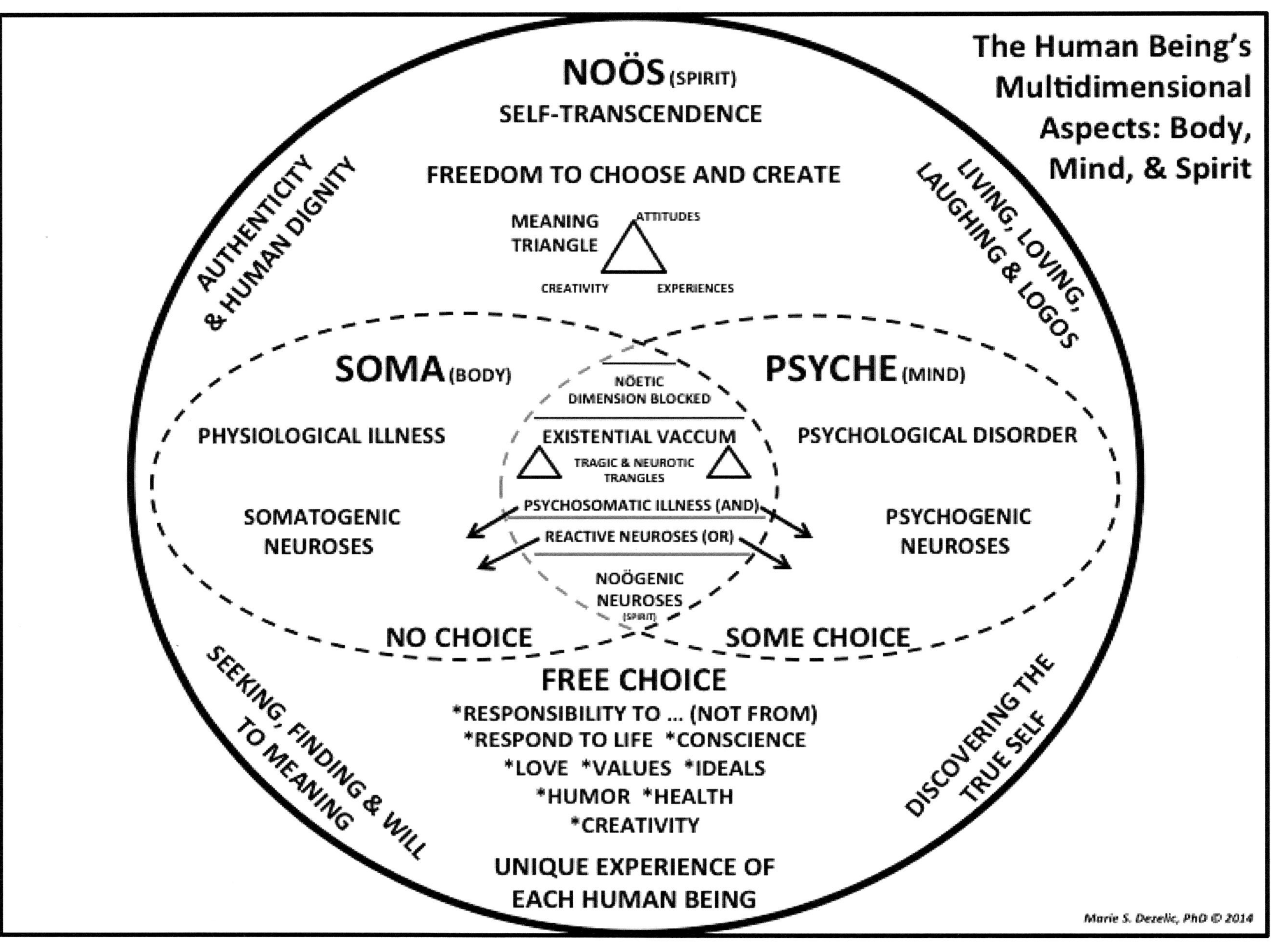
The Human Being's
Multidimensional
Aspects: Body,
Mind, & Spirit
NOÖS (SPIRIT)
SELF-TRANSCENDENCE
FREEDOM TO CHOOSE AND CREATE
MEANING
TRIANGLE
ATTITUDES
CREATIVITY
EXPERIENCES
AUTHENTICITY
& HUMAN DIGNITY
LIVING, LOVING,
LAUGHING & LOGOS
SOMA (BODY)
PHYSIOLOGICAL ILLNESS
SOMATOGENIC
NEUROSES
NÖETIC
DIMENSION BLOCKED
EXISTENTIAL VACCUM
TRAGIC & NEUROTIC
TRANGLES
PSYCHOSOMATIC ILLNESS (AND)
REACTIVE NEUROSES (OR)
NOÖGENIC
NEUROSES
(SPIRIT)
PSYCHE (MIND)
PSYCHOLOGICAL DISORDER
PSYCHOGENIC
NEUROSES
NO CHOICE
SOME CHOICE
FREE CHOICE
*RESPONSIBILITY TO ... (NOT FROM)
*RESPOND TO LIFE *CONSCIENCE
*LOVE *VALUES *IDEALS
*HUMOR *HEALTH
*CREATIVITY
SEEKING, FINDING & WILL
TO MEANING
DISCOVERING THE
TRUE SELF
UNIQUE EXPERIENCE OF
EACH HUMAN BEING
Marie S. Dezelic, PhD © 2014

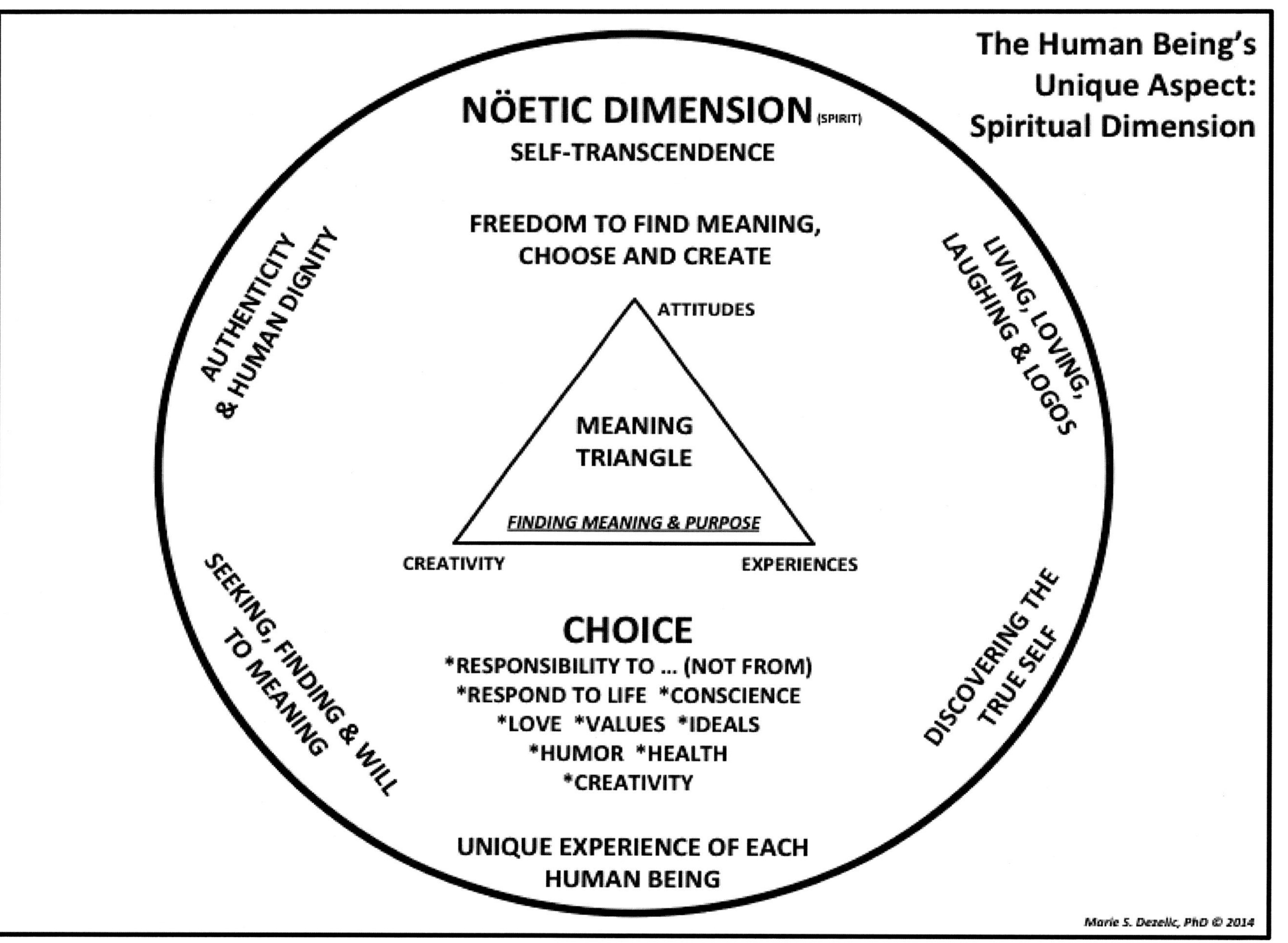
The Human Being's
Unique Aspect:
Spiritual Dimension
NÖETIC DIMENSION (SPIRIT)
SELF-TRANSCENDENCE
FREEDOM TO FIND MEANING,
CHOOSE AND CREATE
AUTHENTICITY
& HUMAN DIGNITY
LIVING, LOVING,
LAUGHING & LOGOS
ATTITUDES
MEANING
TRIANGLE
FINDING MEANING & PURPOSE
CREATIVITY
EXPERIENCES
SEEKING, FINDING & WILL
TO MEANING
DISCOVERING THE
TRUE SELF
CHOICE
*RESPONSIBILITY TO ... (NOT FROM)
*RESPOND TO LIFE *CONSCIENCE
*LOVE *VALUES *IDEALS
*HUMOR *HEALTH
*CREATIVITY
UNIQUE EXPERIENCE OF EACH
HUMAN BEING
Marie S. Dezelic, PhD © 2014

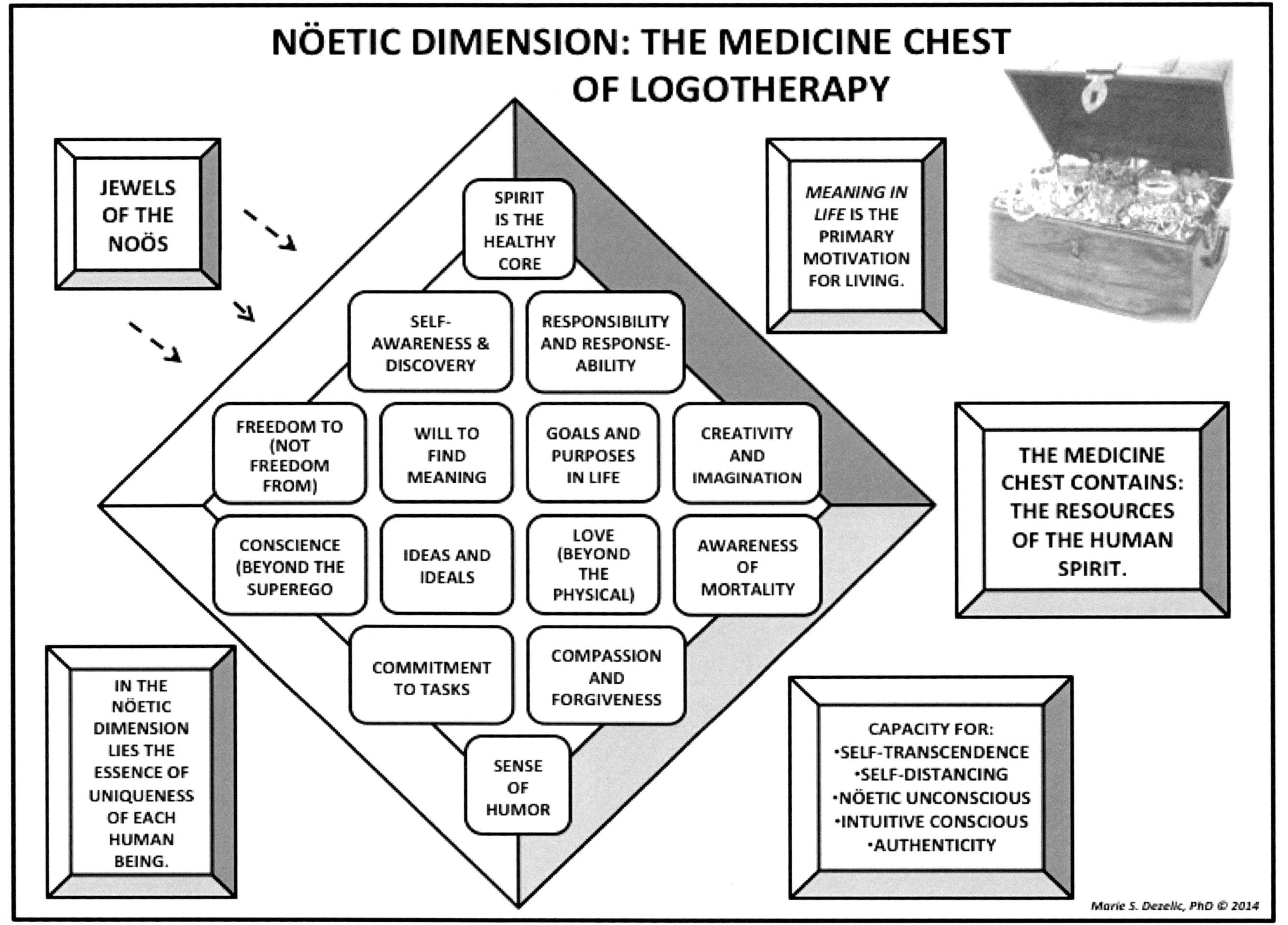

NÖETIC DIMENSION: THE MEDICINE CHEST OF LOGOTHERAPY
JEWELS OF THE NOÖS
SPIRIT IS THE HEALTHY CORE
MEANING IN LIFE IS THE PRIMARY MOTIVATION FOR LIVING.
SELF-AWARENESS & DISCOVERY
RESPONSIBILITY AND RESPONSE-ABILITY
FREEDOM TO (NOT FREEDOM FROM)
WILL TO FIND MEANING
GOALS AND PURPOSES IN LIFE
CREATIVITY AND IMAGINATION
THE MEDICINE CHEST CONTAINS: THE RESOURCES OF THE HUMAN SPIRIT.
CONSCIENCE (BEYOND THE SUPEREGO
IDEAS AND IDEALS
LOVE (BEYOND THE PHYSICAL)
AWARENESS OF MORTALITY
COMMITMENT TO TASKS
COMPASSION AND FORGIVENESS
SENSE OF HUMOR
IN THE NÖETIC DIMENSION LIES THE ESSENCE OF UNIQUENESS OF EACH HUMAN BEING.
CAPACITY FOR:
•SELF-TRANSCENDENCE
•SELF-DISTANCING
•NÖETIC UNCONSCIOUS
•INTUITIVE CONSCIOUS
•AUTHENTICITY
Marie S. Dezelic, PhD © 2014

MIND-BODY-SPIRIT REJUVENATION METHOD

SIMPLE TECHNIQUES FOR STRESS REDUCTION & HEALTHY LIVING

- CONNECTING WITH GOD/ UNIVERSE OR A HIGHER POWER
- DAILY SPIRITUAL MEDITATION OR CENTERING PRAYER
- CONNECTING WITH NATURE
- HEALTHY RELATIONSHIPS
- YOGA PRACTICE
- BEING CREATIVE
- BEING INSPIRED
- BEING PASSIONATE

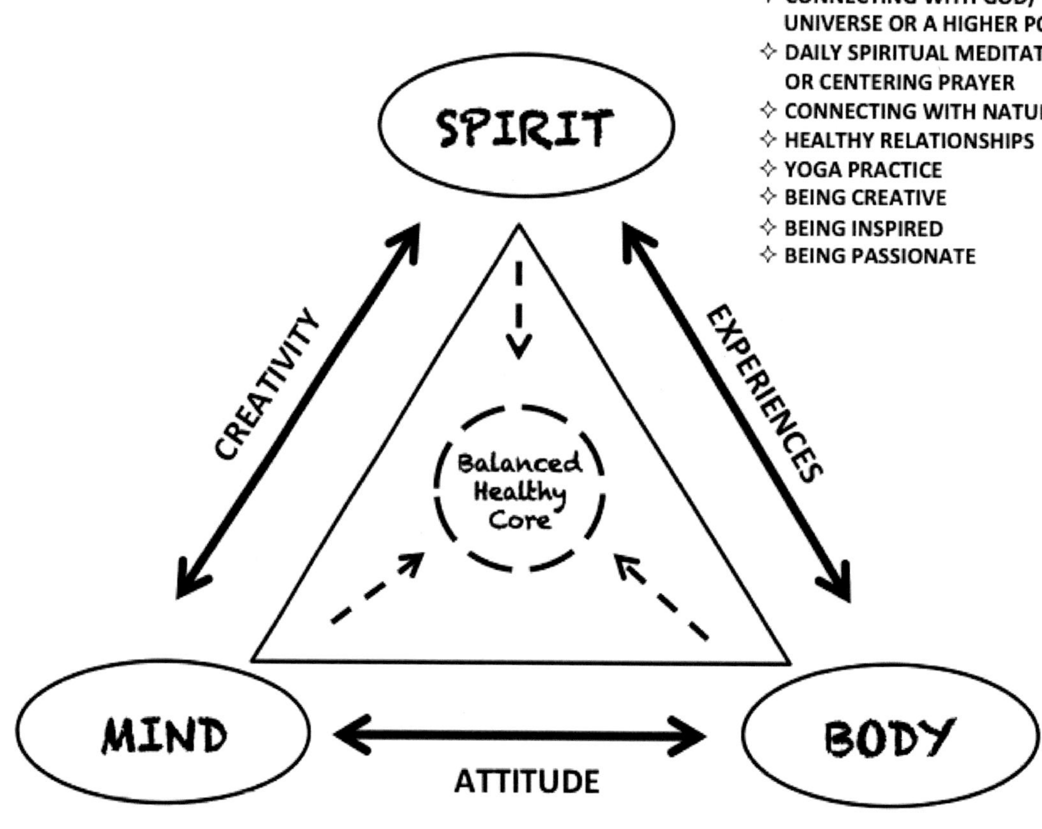

- INCREASING POSITIVE THOUGHTS, RELEASING NEGATIVE THOUGHTS
- SETTING AN INTENTION FOR THE DAY
- 1 DAILY POSITIVE SELF-AFFIRMATION
- CURRENT GOALS & FUTURE GOALS
- CREATING A GRATITUDE JOURNAL
- WORKING ON FORGIVENESS
- DAILY MINDFULNESS PRACTICE
- MANTRA/SAYING FOR THE DAY

- TAKING CARE OF MY BODY
- REGULAR PHYSICAL EXAMS
- NUTRITION & HEALTHY EATING
- VITAMINS/SUPPLEMENTS/MEDS
- ADEQUATE SLEEP/REST
- PHYSICAL EXERCISE
- ACTIVITIES & HOBBIES
- STRETCHING DURING THE DAY
- DAILY BREATHING PRACTICE

FINDING A HEALTHY BALANCE

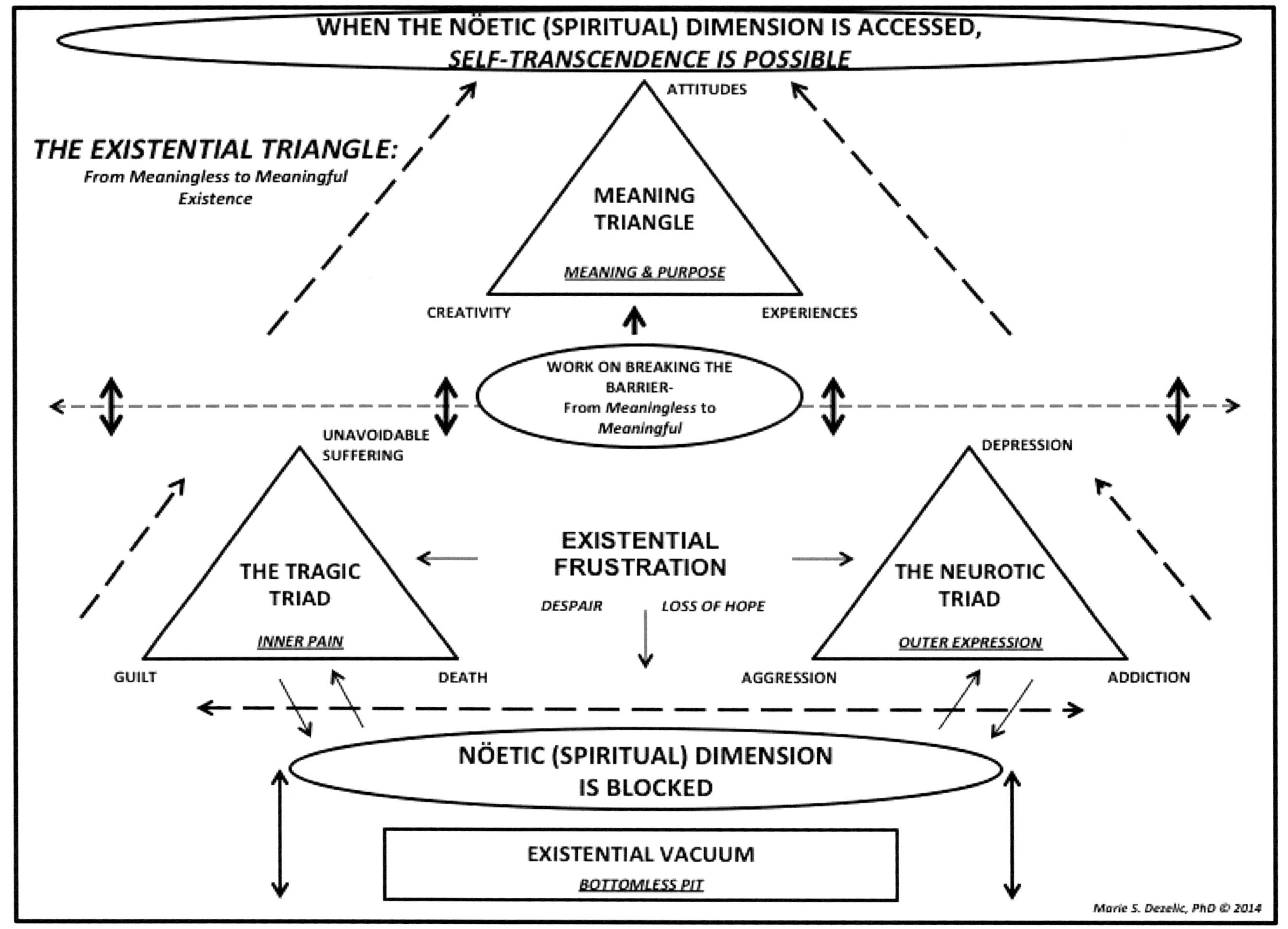
WHEN THE NÖETIC (SPIRITUAL) DIMENSION IS ACCESSED,
SELF-TRANSCENDENCE IS POSSIBLE
THE EXISTENTIAL TRIANGLE:
From Meaningless to Meaningful Existence
ATTITUDES
MEANING TRIANGLE
MEANING & PURPOSE
CREATIVITY
EXPERIENCES
WORK ON BREAKING THE BARRIER-
From Meaningless to Meaningful
UNAVOIDABLE SUFFERING
DEPRESSION
EXISTENTIAL FRUSTRATION
DESPAIR
LOSS OF HOPE
THE TRAGIC TRIAD
INNER PAIN
GUILT
DEATH
THE NEUROTIC TRIAD
OUTER EXPRESSION
AGGRESSION
ADDICTION
NÖETIC (SPIRITUAL) DIMENSION IS BLOCKED
EXISTENTIAL VACUUM
BOTTOMLESS PIT
Marie S. Dezelic, PhD © 2014

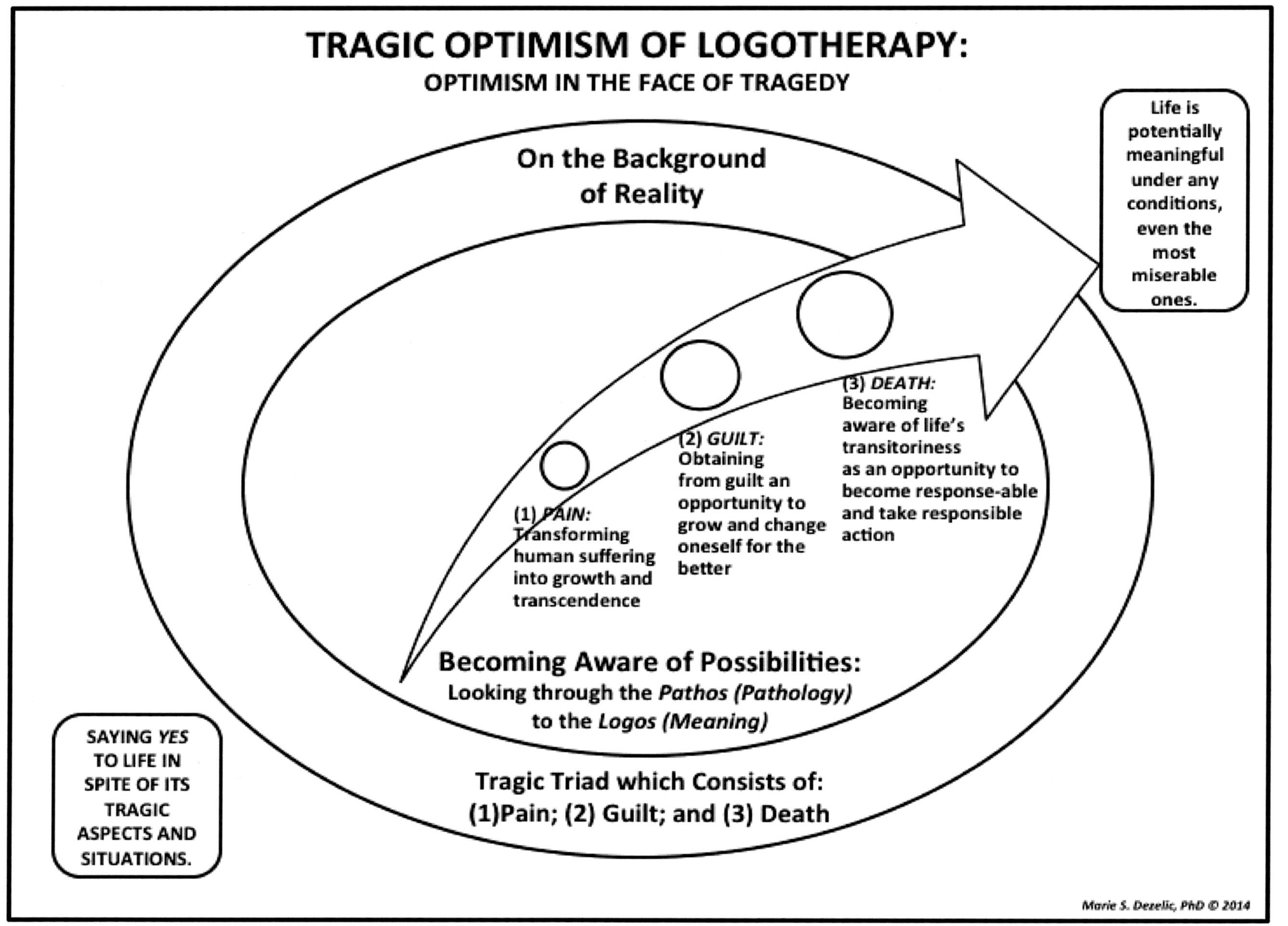
TRAGIC OPTIMISM OF LOGOTHERAPY:
OPTIMISM IN THE FACE OF TRAGEDY
Life is potentially meaningful under any conditions, even the most miserable ones.
On the Background of Reality
(1) PAIN: Transforming human suffering into growth and transcendence
(2) GUILT: Obtaining from guilt an opportunity to grow and change oneself for the better
(3) DEATH: Becoming aware of life's transitoriness as an opportunity to become response-able and take responsible action
Becoming Aware of Possibilities:
Looking through the Pathos (Pathology) to the Logos (Meaning)
SAYING YES TO LIFE IN SPITE OF ITS TRAGIC ASPECTS AND SITUATIONS.
Tragic Triad which Consists of:
(1)Pain; (2) Guilt; and (3) Death
Marie S. Dezelic, PhD © 2014

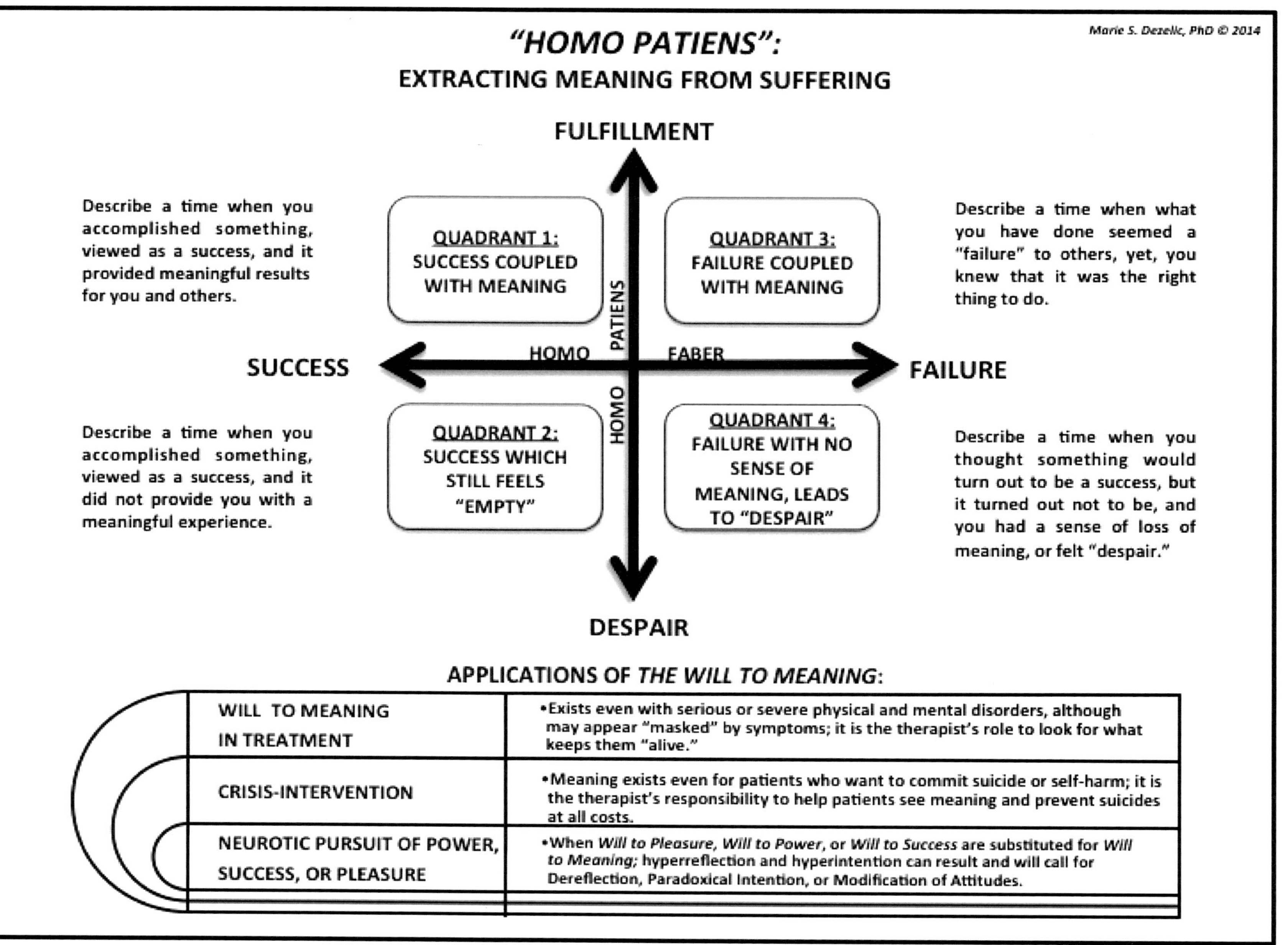
Marie S. Dezelic, PhD © 2014
"HOMO PATIENS":
EXTRACTING MEANING FROM SUFFERING
FULFILLMENT
Describe a time when you accomplished something, viewed as a success, and it provided meaningful results for you and others.
QUADRANT 1:
SUCCESS COUPLED WITH MEANING
QUADRANT 3:
FAILURE COUPLED WITH MEANING
Describe a time when what you have done seemed a "failure" to others, yet, you knew that it was the right thing to do.
PATIENS
SUCCESS
HOMO
FABER
FAILURE
HOMO
Describe a time when you accomplished something, viewed as a success, and it did not provide you with a meaningful experience.
QUADRANT 2:
SUCCESS WHICH STILL FEELS "EMPTY"
QUADRANT 4:
FAILURE WITH NO SENSE OF MEANING, LEADS TO "DESPAIR"
Describe a time when you thought something would turn out to be a success, but it turned out not to be, and you had a sense of loss of meaning, or felt "despair."
DESPAIR
APPLICATIONS OF THE WILL TO MEANING:
WILL TO MEANING IN TREATMENT
•Exists even with serious or severe physical and mental disorders, although may appear "masked" by symptoms; it is the therapist's role to look for what keeps them "alive."
CRISIS-INTERVENTION
•Meaning exists even for patients who want to commit suicide or self-harm; it is the therapist's responsibility to help patients see meaning and prevent suicides at all costs.
NEUROTIC PURSUIT OF POWER, SUCCESS, OR PLEASURE
•When Will to Pleasure, Will to Power, or Will to Success are substituted for Will to Meaning; hyperreflection and hyperintention can result and will call for Dereflection, Paradoxical Intention, or Modification of Attitudes.

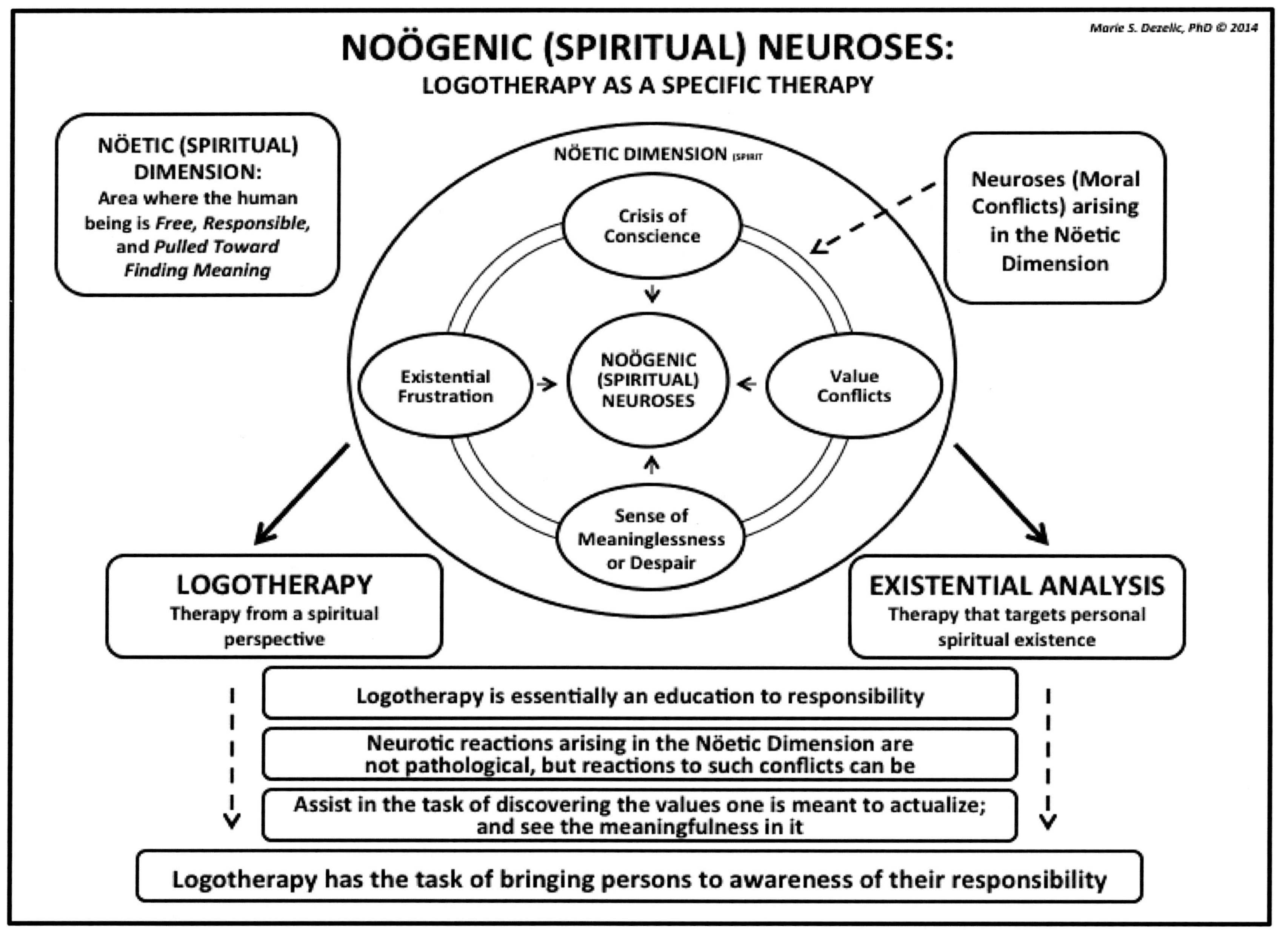
Marie S. Dezelic, PhD © 2014
NOÖGENIC (SPIRITUAL) NEUROSES:
LOGOTHERAPY AS A SPECIFIC THERAPY
NÖETIC (SPIRITUAL) DIMENSION: Area where the human being is *Free, Responsible,* and *Pulled Toward Finding Meaning*
NÖETIC DIMENSION (SPIRIT
Neuroses (Moral Conflicts) arising in the Nöetic Dimension
Crisis of Conscience
Existential Frustration
NOÖGENIC (SPIRITUAL) NEUROSES
Value Conflicts
Sense of Meaninglessness or Despair
LOGOTHERAPY
Therapy from a spiritual perspective
EXISTENTIAL ANALYSIS
Therapy that targets personal spiritual existence
Logotherapy is essentially an education to responsibility
Neurotic reactions arising in the Nöetic Dimension are not pathological, but reactions to such conflicts can be
Assist in the task of discovering the values one is meant to actualize; and see the meaningfulness in it
Logotherapy has the task of bringing persons to awareness of their responsibility

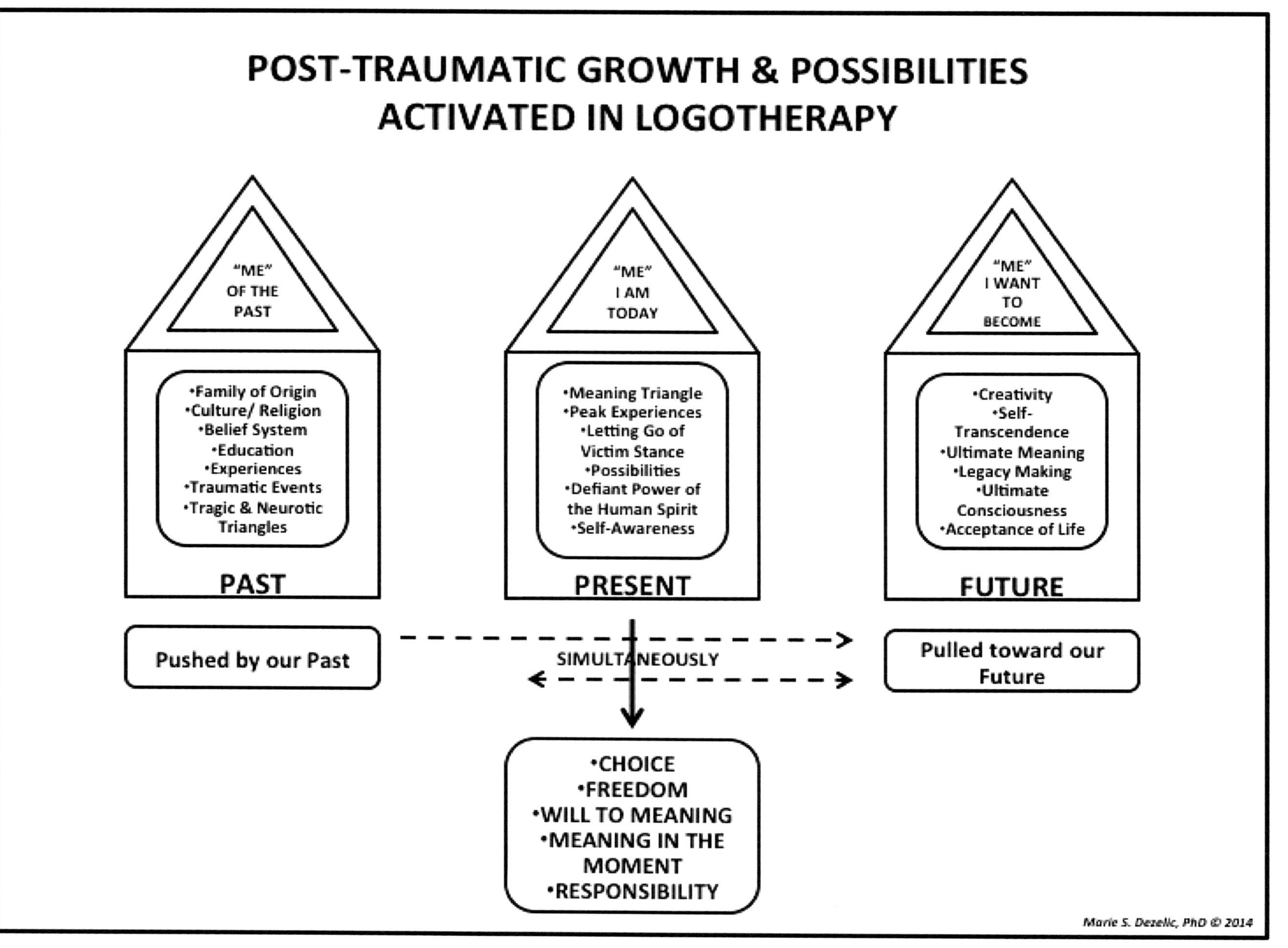
POST-TRAUMATIC GROWTH & POSSIBILITIES
ACTIVATED IN LOGOTHERAPY
"ME" OF THE PAST
•Family of Origin
•Culture/ Religion
•Belief System
•Education
•Experiences
•Traumatic Events
•Tragic & Neurotic Triangles
PAST
"ME" I AM TODAY
•Meaning Triangle
•Peak Experiences
•Letting Go of Victim Stance
•Possibilities
•Defiant Power of the Human Spirit
•Self-Awareness
PRESENT
"ME" I WANT TO BECOME
•Creativity
•Self-Transcendence
•Ultimate Meaning
•Legacy Making
•Ultimate Consciousness
•Acceptance of Life
FUTURE
Pushed by our Past
SIMULTANEOUSLY
Pulled toward our Future
•CHOICE
•FREEDOM
•WILL TO MEANING
•MEANING IN THE MOMENT
•RESPONSIBILITY
Marie S. Dezelic, PhD © 2014

THE MEANING-ACTION TRIANGLE:

Becoming Existentially Aware

(1.) NOTICE *-CONSCIOUS-*

- Awareness
- Notice without judgment
- Recognize old patterns
- Become conscious of self-defeating behaviors/cycles
- Acknowledge victim role stance
- Recognize unhealthy relationship interactions
- Be fully present and conscious of self
- Acknowledge one's own existence

(2.) RESPONSIBILITY *-TO SELF-*

- Awareness, Self-Transcendence
- Responsible to self, to one's meaning in life, to the ultimate meaning of life
- Own one's feelings, actions and behaviors
- Acknowledge wanting to choose to change past self-limiting patterns
- Recognize one's healthy core—Spiritual Nöetic Dimension

(3.) TAKE ACTION *-CHOICE-*

- Awareness
- Freedom to act
- Choose to be conscious of self-improving behaviors
- Choose not to be a victim
- Decision to have healthy relationship interactions
- Be fully present to and conscious of one's actions
- Acknowledge one's own existence in the present
- Meaning in the moment
- Ultimate meaning

Taking Flight from your PAST, While Being Pulled to your FUTURE

M. Dezelic, PhD, J. Rogina, PhD, G. Ghanoum, PsyD ©2014

7-Step Noögenic Activation Method:

Igniting the ***Defiant Power of the Spirit*** and Activating Resources of the ***Nöetic Dimension***
For ***Transformation*** and ***Self-Transcendence***

1	**~ ACCESS ~** ***Access to the Nöetic Dimension***	• **"As I take a few deep breaths... I become aware of the healthy core within me (my human spirit)."**
2	**~ UNIQUENESS ~** ***Recognize the Uniqueness of the individual***	• **"I affirm the uniqueness that I am in this particular moment of my life with all my experiences, needs, wants and aspirations."**
3	**~ CHOICES ~** ***Evaluating and Making Choices***	• **"I affirm the reality of having choices: I choose flexibility over rigidity; I choose to tolerate uncertainty and resolve ambiguity; I choose to reduce my tendency to form self-harming interpretations about the meaning of my experiences; I choose to reduce emotional referencing and increase reality skills."**
4	**~ RESPONSIBILITY ~** ***Responsibility to... not from***	• **"I am gradually making experiential shifts from passivity and/or excessive stimulation with increased referencing of my personal responsibility to myself and to others."**
5	**~ WILL ~** ***Will to Meaning***	• **"I continue to listen for meaningful possibilities with attentiveness for contextual cues, which are inviting me to appropriate action that will guide me into a hopeful future."**
6	**~ FREEDOM ~** ***Freedom of Will***	• **"I choose specific actions, made in harmony with nöetic referencing and my personal values."**
7	**~ MEANING ~** ***Meaning in Life, Meaning in the Moment, Ultimate Meaning***	• **"I remind myself that my thoughts, my feelings or my sensations, do not decide any action I take, I do! I experience meaning in every action I choose to take and I walk toward my ultimate meaning in life everyday!"**

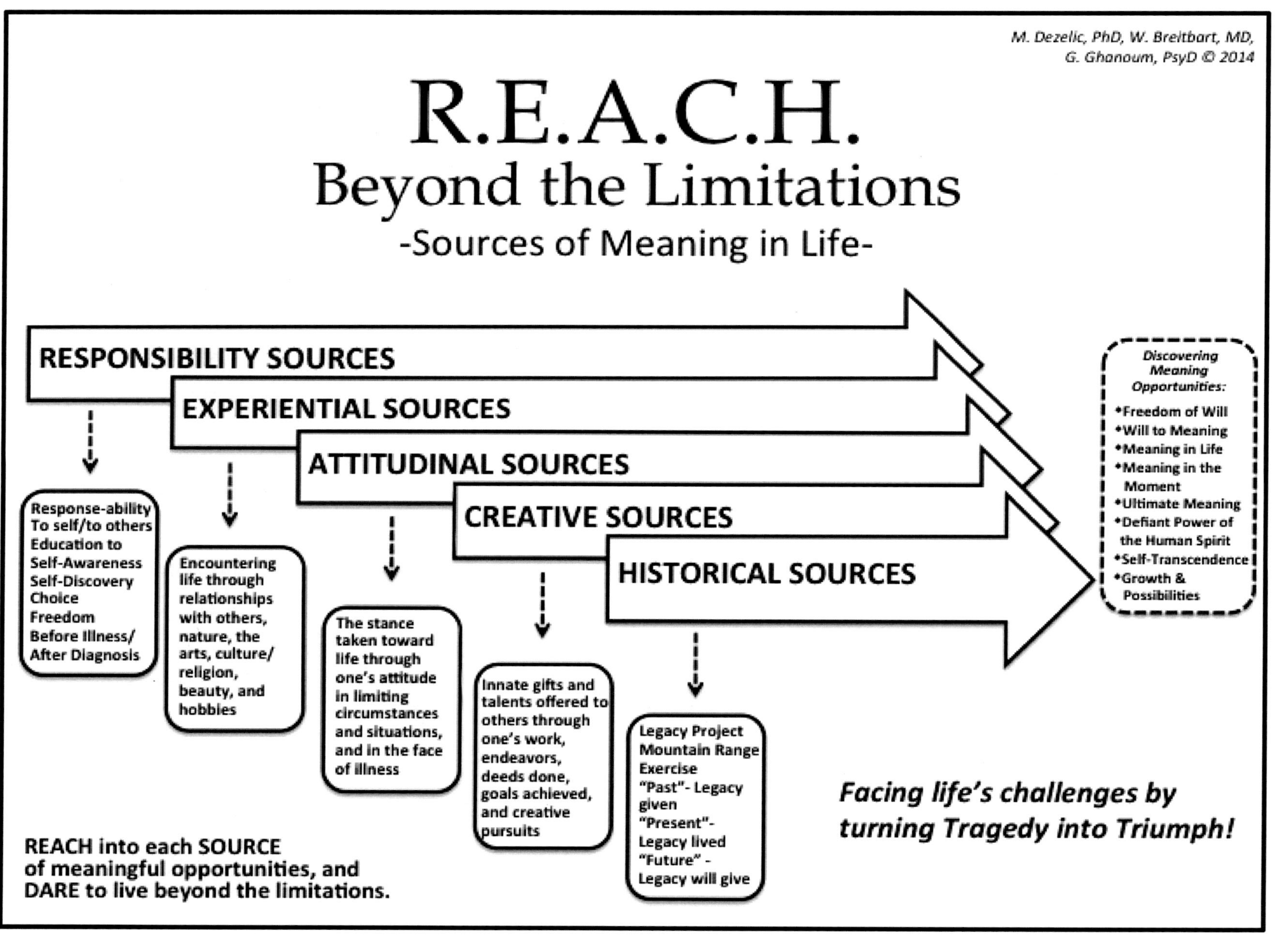
M. Dezelic, PhD, W. Breitbart, MD,
G. Ghanoum, PsyD © 2014
R.E.A.C.H.
Beyond the Limitations
-Sources of Meaning in Life-
RESPONSIBILITY SOURCES
EXPERIENTIAL SOURCES
ATTITUDINAL SOURCES
CREATIVE SOURCES
HISTORICAL SOURCES
Discovering Meaning Opportunities:
•Freedom of Will
•Will to Meaning
•Meaning in Life
•Meaning in the Moment
•Ultimate Meaning
•Defiant Power of the Human Spirit
•Self-Transcendence
•Growth & Possibilities
Response-ability To self/to others Education to Self-Awareness Self-Discovery Choice Freedom Before Illness/ After Diagnosis
Encountering life through relationships with others, nature, the arts, culture/ religion, beauty, and hobbies
The stance taken toward life through one's attitude in limiting circumstances and situations, and in the face of illness
Innate gifts and talents offered to others through one's work, endeavors, deeds done, goals achieved, and creative pursuits
Legacy Project Mountain Range Exercise "Past"- Legacy given "Present"- Legacy lived "Future" - Legacy will give
Facing life's challenges by turning Tragedy into Triumph!
REACH into each SOURCE of meaningful opportunities, and DARE to live beyond the limitations.

CONNECT—CREATE—CONVEY

Living Life with Meaning and Purpose

Connect:

- With others who inspire you, motivate you, lift you up, support you, whom you can help, and give of yourself to.
- You can connect with great thinkers, writers, actors, people you look up to, role models (from the past or present).
- You can connect with nature, the arts, culture.

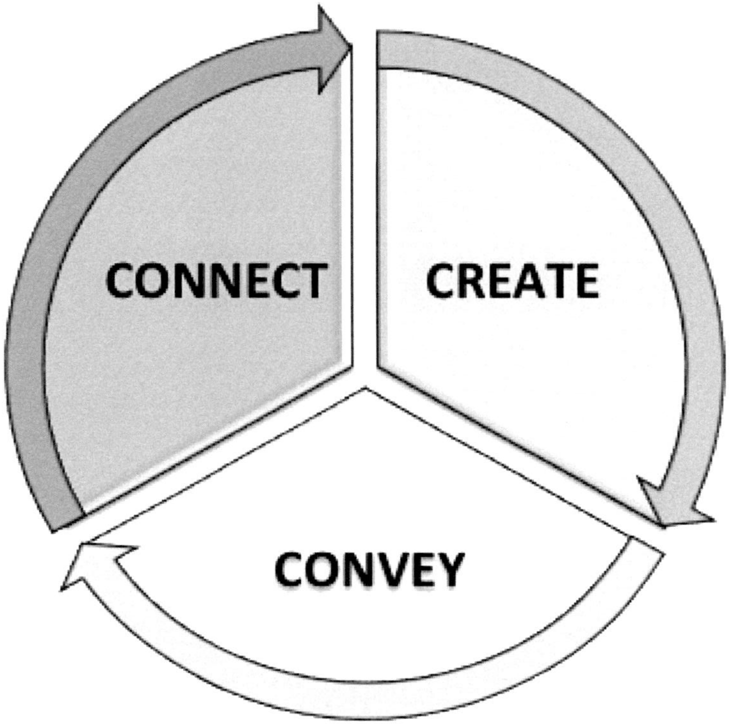

Create:

- Access your inner strengths and resources, discovering your natural talents and gifts, and possibilities to bring your uniqueness to the world.
- Be in your life creatively; discover how you bring your unique creativity to tasks, to projects, to your work, to your hobbies, to all of your relationships.

CONNECT

CREATE

CONVEY

Convey:

- Teach it, give it, bring it, write it, play it, paint it, say it, sing it, dance it; offer your unique creativity in your work, hobbies, causes you serve, and in all of your relationships.
- Convey to the world who you are and live your greater purpose with passion and meaning.

"By connecting we create, by creating we convey, by conveying we connect and create…
By connecting, creating, and conveying we can experience purpose and meaning in life…"

GLOSSARY OF TERMS
Encountered in Logotherapy & Existential Analysis

The terms listed here are key to understanding *Frankl's philosophy, which, in turn, offers the tools for his therapy. It is hoped that an understanding of these terms will help you in your pursuit of meaning. The terms marked with an asterisk* are those coined by Frankl.*

Anthropology— The study of human beings and their ancestors through time and space and in relation to physical character, environmental and social relations, and culture. Theological definition: dealing with the origin, nature, and destiny of human beings.

Attitudinal Values— Values of acceptance of life's vicissitudes and of irreversible suffering, trying to transcend them and search for a meaning in them.

Authenticity— All that a person has not yet become but could be, through active use of powers of awareness and decision making; that human ability to surpass or transcend limitations which mitigates or seeks alternatives to the specific facticity of each person's life.

Boredom— Extreme boredom is a critical indication of a beginning existential frustration. It is an increasing symptom in an affluent, industrial society, not to be neglected by the psychologist, and can lead to severe psychological illness (Sunday neuroses, loss of meaning in retirement, and the tendency to drift in people who have everything and find no satisfaction in anything).

Cartesian— Pertaining to doctrines and methods of Rene Descartes, a French philosopher and mathematician of the 17th century, whose thinking greatly influenced Western scientific postulates.

Catharsis— A state often experienced in psychotherapy by patients who uncover their deepest feelings and emotions. Doing this, they may find psychological relief.

Collective Neuroses— Franklian psychosocial entities of meaninglessness and meaning frustration that lead to collective actions such as collectivism, fanaticism, provisional and fatalist actions.

Comprehension— A psychological method of captivating the patient's meaning through emphatic approach and through intuition. It is different from explication, where the therapist uses reason to captivate patient's meanings and logic.

Conceptual Pictograph— A term coined by co-author Marie Dezelic; images that illustrate and convey theoretical concepts through pictures, objects, text and graphic systems. These *Conceptual Pictographs* depict the principles and techniques of Meaning-Centered Logotherapy & Existential Analysis (LTEA) and are applicable across many clinical populations and settings.

Conscience— A specifically human organ to detect the meaning potentials offered by life. Franklian Psychology sees conscience as more than the product of the superego. Beyond the outside influences, powerful as they may be, the conscience contains a personal voice, faint and prone to error, which can advise us to take a stand beside and even against the dictates of the superego. Our capacity to hear the voice of our conscience and respond to it to the best of our abilities is strengthened.

Dasein— (German) A term that comes from the existential theories of Martin Heidegger and Ludwig Binswanger that signifies a "being in the world" as it is and the way the individual experiences it.

***Defiant Power of the Human Spirit**— The conscience resistance against biological, psychological, or sociological limitations, the human capacity to take a stand against our fate. Franklian Psychology helps us become aware and develop the defiant power of his spirit to overcome our existential frustration. Anything that reduces our will to defy our unhappy fate (such as unhappy childhood, negative influences in one's upbringing, poor health, poverty) will only strengthen the effect of such a fate.

***Dereflection**— A "logotherapeutic technique" that resorts to self-distancing ability and attitudinal decision of the human being to counteract obsessive preoccupations with psychological conflicts or symptoms, through finding meaning in some other feelings, thoughts or actions.

Determinism— A philosophical doctrine that our choices, decisions and actions are decided by antecedent causes, inherited or environmental, acting upon our character: opposed to free will.

Dialogue, Socratic— It is both an educational and a psychotherapeutic method. By asking maieutic (midwifing) questions, the client's own inner knowing is brought to light (birthed). Thus, insights gained from the spiritual or psychological dimension can be implemented for best therapeutic results.

***Dimensional Ontology**— The human being is seen as a totality in three dimensions: the biological-physiological (the *body*), the socio-psychological (the *psyche*), and the spiritual-*nöetic* (the *spirit*). Just as a drinking glass, when projected from its three dimensional reality onto a two-dimensional plane appears in the ground plan only as a circle, and in the side view as a rectangle, so the human being can be reduced to a mere projection when only one dimension is considered. The human being is not a body plus a spirit, just as a glass is not a circle plus a rectangle.

Dialogic Duality— A term coined by Martin Buber, that shows individuals as being in relation with other human beings, constituting a unity. Dialogue is the essential meaning link.

Ecclesiogenic Distress— Caused by clergy, often inadvertently by inducing excessive fear and guilt.

Empirical— Relating to or based on experience or observation; given to experiments.

Epistemology— That department of Philosophy which investigates critically the nature, grounds, limits and criteria, or validity of human knowledge.

Existential— Pertaining to existence. Coming from existentialism, a movement in 20th Century Philosophy, influenced in its development by Kierkegaard and Nietzsche and popularized in France by Sartre, emphasizing the active participation of the will rather than the reason in confronting life situations.

***Existential Analysis**— Frankl's initial term for his psychotherapy was intended to distinguish his treatment model from Freud's psychoanalysis. Frankl's existential analysis focuses on the "here and now" of existence and looks to the future with hope, instead of being retrospective like Freudian psychoanalysis. Later, Frankl's theory became better known as Logotherapy or Franklian Psychology.

***Existential Neurosis**— As opposed to clinical neurosis, it is characterized by a sense of despair over the meaning of life.

***Existential Frustration**— Frustration in our search for meaning, caused by affluence, homeostasis, elimination of stress, release from commitments and responsibility. Symptoms are boredom, discontent, feeling of meaningless, lack of interest, and a frantic desire to fill our emptiness leading to an overemphasis on sexual pleasure seeking, drug addiction or violence. Possible therapy: challenges to assume tasks, expansion of a personal value system, orientation toward meaning and toward the partner as a human being rather than a mere tool for the satisfaction of the sexual drive.

***Existential Vacuum**— A term introduced by Frankl in 1955 to denote the feeling of inner emptiness. Symptoms: increasing idleness, tendency toward aggression, drug addiction, over emphasis on fashionable "games," increase of criminal acts, solvency, excess sexuality and seeking of pleasure, discontent, and increasing doubts about the world, society, and life.

Facticity— The given facts of a person's existence over which he/she cannot have total control; physical statue, environmental resources, demands made by employers or teachers, and inevitability of death.

Fate— All that lies beyond our power and responsibility to control. Fate is the totality of all determining factors. It can also become the springboard for our freedom of will to be exercised —the challenge to respond to fate in various ways, and be response-able for our choices. It serves as the crucible of our becoming more fully human.

***Franklian Psychology**— A method of psychology founded in Vienna by the Austrian psychiatrist Viktor Emil Frankl, after the Second World War and, today, named the "Third Viennese School of Psychotherapy." It postulates that meaning is the main motivation for living. A therapy that maintains or restores mental health by helping patients find meaning. It goes beyond other psychologies and psychotherapies by including the *nöetic*, a uniquely human dimension of the spirit; thus rehumanizing psychotherapy. Specifically indicated for *noögenic neuroses*, has supplementary uses for psychogenic and somatogenic neuroses, for despair in situation of unalterable fate such as incurable illness (medical ministry), as well as preventive uses for people tending toward existential frustration.

***Freedom of Will**— One of the three main tenets of Franklian Psychology. "Freedom" is understood not as "freedom from something," but as "freedom to something." The human being is considered free, under all circumstances, to choose his attitude toward conditions he cannot change. Without this freedom of choice, there is no responsibility, no guilt, no evaluation of human behavior, and no meaning of human existence.

Frustration— State of keeping plans, schemes, purposes or aims from being fulfilled.

Heuristic— Human knowledge which aids or guides in discovery, inciting to find out new ways, methods or theories of investigation.

***Hyperintention**— Excessive striving for a goal such as pleasure, happiness, potency, orgasm, sleep, relaxation. We thereby transfer our intention form, our principal goal (finding meaning) such mere side effects such as pleasure. As a consequence, the side effect—if directly intended—is missing resulting in a neurotic pattern of behavior. Symptoms are sexual dysfunction if sexual pleasure, rather than the sexual partner, is made the focal point of intention. Sexual pleasure, hyper intended, slips away. Dereflection from the side effect (pleasure) to the main goal (partners or meaning) is used as therapy.

***Hyperreflection**— Twin condition to hyperintention implies excessive attention to an unwanted condition and its symptoms, causing a worsening of the condition and increasing of the symptoms. For instance, if a stutterer, instead of thinking of the content of his speaking, hyperreflects on the speaking itself, his stuttering becomes intensified. A state of emotional tension due to extreme preoccupation with some psychological disturbances. symptoms, conflicts, illnesses, etc. Hyperreflection is a term often used in Logotherapy to show its influence in reinforcing such disturbances.

Iatrogenic Damage— Induced inadvertently by a therapist or any helper or by their treatment.

I and You Buberian approach— ["I – Thou" relationship] Is a way of relating between two persons that entails a direct and authentic feeling one to the other and vice versa. Martin Buber calls it the "between," a mysterious relationship not explainable either by reason or by comprehension. Buber states this relationship as a transcendent divine attribute of man and characterizes it as a duality and a fundamental of human life. Logotherapy recognizes this approach as authentic.

Intuition— Quick perception of truth without either conscious attention or reasoning. Knowledge from within. Direct perception or knowledge of an object, truth, or principle. Immediate apprehension of reality, through feelings and emotions, without using reason.

Logos— In Greek "word" that denotes "spirit" and "meaning." ["Word of God" is often used as the theological definition of *Logos*]. Frankl preferred "meaning" [that which gives reason for being].

***Logotherapy**— Treatment through finding meaning. See Franklian Psychology.

Meaning— According to Franklian Psychology, the essence of existence, and the main motivation for living. Our realizations of values, in a spiritually transcendent way, freely and responsibly intentioned, are inherent in searching for meaning. Meaningful and purposeful human actions constitute the main postulate of Logotherapy.

***Meaning of Life**— One of three tenets of Franklian Psychology. Life has meaning under all circumstances because meaning can be found not only through actions and experiences, but also through attitudes in situation of unavoidable suffering which in themselves are meaningless. An ultimate meaning is postulated as an awareness of an existing order in which we can take part and which is gradually elucidated by our responding to the best of our abilities, to the meaning potentials life offers from moment to moment.

Metaphysical— Pertaining to metaphysics. Beyond or above the physical or experiential; pertaining to or being of the essential nature of reality; transcendental.

Methodology— The science of method or of arranging investigations and studies in due order.

Monanthropism— Oneness of humankind.

Moral Conflicts— Conflicts, which come from the spiritual intuition that some acts, feelings, or thoughts are not in conformity with the internal and the external personal ethics.

Neurosis— The term designates a mild personality disorder, thought to be acquired, such as: anxiety, phobias, obsessive-compulsive reactions, chronic fatigue, hypochondria, situational depressive reactions.

Nihilism— The doctrine that affirms that nothing exists and can be known. That rejects, also, religious and moral creeds.

Nöetic— Pertaining to the ***noös*** or spiritual dimension of man, beyond the biological, psychological, and social.

***Nöetic Dimension**— Dimension of the human spirit containing our healthy core whose ingredients the Logotherapist mobilizes so that we can tap our own spiritual resources. Among the contents of the *nöetic* dimension are such uniquely human capacities as the will to meaning, ideas and ideals, creativity, imagination, faith, love, his conscience, self-detachment, self-transcendence, humor, a learning from past experiences, a striving toward goals, the taking on of commitments, and responsibility.

***Noödynamisms**— A composed term that comes from "noös"—spiritual, ethereal, abstract—and from "dynamic"—transit, movement, motion. Noodynamisms, then, signify movement of the spirit toward a meaning fulfillment in life.

Noögenic— Originating in the *noös* or the *nöetic* dimension.

***Noögenic Neurosis**— Neurosis caused by value collisions between our *nöetic* (spiritual, inner) knowing and outer mandates, resulting in conflicts of conscience, existential frustration, or the existential vacuum. Statistical evidence indicates that some 20 percent of all neuroses are *noögenic.*

Noös— From the Greek language, means **spirit**. Our *noetic* dimension lifts us above the somatic and psychic dimension. This is the dimension of our being that sets us apart from other animals and makes us specifically human. *Noös*—the spirit—is not a substance. It is beyond time and space. Only that which is matter (material) can become sick, old, and die. The spirit, being outside of time and space, can never become sick nor can it die.

***Medical Ministry**— Helps patients where actual cures are impossible (incurable disease, death of a loved one, loss of sight or limb). Here "therapy" aims at changing the patients' attitudes toward their unalterable fate.

Ontological— Pertaining to ontology—the science of being; the doctrine of the universe and necessary characteristics of all existence; including the physiologic, psychosocial, as well as the noetic or spiritual.

Pan-determinism— The view that human beings are fully conditioned and determined. Frankl strongly opposed this view as "a dangerous assumption" that disregards our capacity to take a stand toward conditions and robs us of self-determination.

Paradigm— Any pattern or example of things or actions existent in the world.

***Paradoxical Intention**— Logotherapeutic technique, first presented by Frankl in 1939, using the human quality of self-detachment to help patients step away from themselves and their symptoms and to break the vicious circle caused by anticipatory anxiety in psychogenic neurosis, especially phobias and obsessive-compulsive neurosis. Paradoxical intention encourages us to do, or wish to happen, the very things we fear, making use of our sense of humor and our defiant power of human spirit.

Pastoral Logotherapy— Is the application of logotherapeutic analysis and treatment within the context of a spiritual understanding of the human situation and its relevance to mental health. Though not specifically faith-based, pastoral logotherapy is practiced within the context of a spiritual awareness of self-transcendent reality. [The term was developed by the Graduate Theological Foundation, Mishawaka, Indiana.]

Philosophical Anthropology— Max Scheler's theory of humanity, which considers the human being's transcendent, existential, and spiritual dimensions as a reality.

Phenomenology— Scientific investigation and description of all life phenomena or experiences. General doctrine of phenomena, distinguished from ontology.

Phenomenological Methodology— A method that uses phenomenology to captivate or describe phenomena. Logotherapy takes individual experiences of phenomena seriously.

Phenomenon— Something visible or directly observable, as an appearance, action, change, or occurrence of any kind.

Positivism— A system of philosophy elaborated by Auguste Comte holding that human beings can have no knowledge of anything but actual phenomena and facts, rejecting all speculations regarding ultimate origin or causes.

Pragmatic Realism— Frankl's treatment approach is characteristically pragmatic or practical. The insights gained need to be implemented in life to change a situation; when the outer circumstances cannot be changed, a change in attitude toward "fate" may be called for.

Psychologism— Reduction of the human being onto the merely psychological plane. Truly human phenomena are seen as nothing but "masks" hiding primitive and neurotic motivation-love is seen as sublimation of the sexual drive, friendship as a form of narcissism, religious faith as an expression of the father image. Everything is demasked even where there is nothing to demask. Psychologism denies us our freedom to make decisions and devalues genuine human phenomena.

Psychogenic Neurosis— The traditional denomination of mental disorders in psychodynamic psychiatry, which are considered to originate in the psychological dimension.

Psychopathology— Is the study of illnesses and symptoms of the mind.

Psychosis— Severe mental health disorders that seriously impair usual life functions. Unlike neuroses, which are acquired mild mental health disorders, psychoses include organic brain dysfunctions and functional impairments.

Psychotherapy— Treatment of mental disorders.

Realism— The doctrine which establishes that things have reality apart from the conscious perception of them.

Reductionism— Seeing only the physical and psychological aspects of the human being without acknowledging the spiritual dimension, a sub-human "image of man."

Responsibility— Literally "response-ability," the ability to respond to the meaning potentials offered by life. Logotherapy is education to responsibility because it challenges us to take on concrete tasks, to accomplish human achievements. The tasks must be self-chosen, regardless of whether they are suggested by others or society ("responsibility" proper) or assumed by ourselves ("responsibleness"). Without response-ability, freedom brings not meaning but meaningless chaos.

Self-Detachment— Also referred to as Self-distancing, the ability to detach from a situation or from oneself in order to expand one's view.

Self-Distancing— The human capacity to step away from one's self and look at one's self from the "outside," possibly with a sense of humor.

Self-Realization— The striving toward the actualization of our potentials presupposes freedom of will. However, Logotherapy sees self-realization never as the ultimate goal, but only as a side-effect of meaning fulfillment. Only to the extent that we fulfill our meanings and realize ourselves. On the other hand, indiscriminate self-realization, not directed toward meaning, may lead to the realization of negative, even criminal qualities.

***Self-Transcendence**— The human capacity to "reach out beyond oneself, toward meanings to fulfill, people to love, causes to serve." The human being is not considered a closed system, but as being directed and pointing to something or someone other than self. Self-transcendence is the basis for the technique of dereflection.

Spiritual— Pertaining to spirit. It is a non-corporeal content of human existence, pertaining to or affecting the immaterial nature of man's soul. It is a dimension that transcends the biological, psychological or social conditions of life.

Spiritual-Person Nucleus— A term from Max Scheler's Philosophical Anthropology, which designates the spiritual dimension of human beings that orients life, through which they decide intentionally their meaning of life and assume their place in the Universe.

Spiritual Thought— Max Scheler's denomination of intuition, especially when human beings deal with their spiritual values.

Subjectivism— The doctrine that knowledge is merely subjective and relative and is derived from one's own consciousness. Subjectivism leads to "Psychologism" a term used by Viktor Frankl to describe the tendency of traditional psychology to appraise and reduce all of man's behavior as psychological reactions and causes.

***Super-Meaning**— "*Logos* is deeper than logic."

Teleology— Philosophical view of vitalism inclusive of reason, experience and intuition; in the healing arts it reaches beyond the biochemistry of an organism to find purpose and meaning.

Therapy— Treatment; also, having curative or healing properties.

***Tragic Optimism**— The ability to remain optimistic in spite of unavoidable suffering by turning suffering into a human achievement' by deriving from guilt the opportunity to change oneself for the better; and deriving from life's transitoriness the incentive to take responsible action.

***Tragic Triad**— Comprised of unavoidable suffering, inerasable guilt, and death -- three inescapable predicaments of human life which can cause pathologic conditions, mostly depressions. Logotherapy offers aid through medical ministry, by helping find meaning through changed attitudes in unchangeable situations (see "tragic optimism"). Confrontation with death is termed "last-aid" and is considered an important part of the psychotherapeutic task.

Transcendence— The act of rising above a condition or limit; excelling or surpassing in excellence or degree. In Kantianism, lying beyond the bounds of all human experience and knowledge.

Transitoriness of Life— State of existing for a short time only; temporary passage through time.

Uniqueness— "One of a kind." Logotherapy maintains that every person is unique, totally new and unrepeatable.

Value— Desirability or worth of a thing. This work follows postulates of Viktor Frankl's and Max Scheler's theories of values which have a concept on the "material contents" of existence in a spiritual dimension as ethics, religiousness, esthetics, etc. Max Scheler approaches values in their content, as transcendent and metaphysical. Viktor Frankl adds his contribution disclosing the dynamics of values, their "transit" to Transcendence through searching for their meanings and value realizations.

Value Systems— A pyramidal value system places one value on top, while all others are regressively subordinated. In contrast, a parallel value system places several values at more or less the same level. Psychologically, the pyramid arrangement is more dangerous because meaning is lost when the value on top is removed. This arrangement also causes intolerance *vis-à-vis* other people who have different values on top of their pyramid. The parallel value system is a better guarantee for a healthy psycho-hygiene.

Weltanschauung— **(German)** Worldview, a vision, a theory or assumption about the way things appear to be in the world.

***Will to Meaning**— One of three main tenets of Franklian Psychology. In contrast to Freud who considered the "will to pleasure" the principal human motivation, and Adler who emphasized the "will to power," Frankl sees the "will to meaning" as the central force of human motivation. We human beings are seen as creatures in search for meaning and mental health is dependent on the extent to which we are able to find it.

Zeitgeist— (German) The prevailing spirit at a given time; the intellectual and moral tendencies that characterize any given age or epoch.

The Glossary of Terms was prepared and provided by
Dr. Ann V. Graber
for the
Pastoral Logotherapy Curriculum at
The Graduate Theological Foundation
(Used with Expressed Permission)

"Conceptual Pictograph" was added to the original Glossary of Terms.

REFERENCES

American Psychiatric Association. (2013). *Diagnostic and statistical manual of mental disorders (5th Ed.).* Washington, DC: Author.

Auhagen, A. E. (2000). On the psychology of meaning of life. *Swiss Journal of Psychology,* 59, 34-48.

Barnes, R. C. (1989). Finding meaning in suffering: A personal account. *The International Forum for Logotherapy,* 12(2), 82-88.

Barnes, R. C. (1994). Finding meaning in unavoidable suffering. *The International Forum for Logotherapy,* 1(2), 20-26.

Barnes, R. C. (2005). *Franklian psychology: An introduction to logotherapy.* Abilene, Texas: Viktor Frankl Institute of Logotherapy.

Batthyany, A. & Levinson, J., (Eds.). (2009). *Existential psychotherapy of meaning.* Phoenix, AZ: Zeig, Tucker & Theisen, Inc.

Batthyany, A., (Ed.). (2010). *Viktor Frankl, the feeling of meaninglessness: A challenge to psychotherapy and philosophy.* Milwaukee, WI: Marquette University Press.

Breitbart, W., Rosenfeld, B., Gibson, C., Pessin, H., Poppito, S., Nelson, C., Tomarken, A., et al. (2010). Meaning-centered group psychotherapy for patients with advanced cancer: a randomized controlled trial. *Psycho-Oncology, 19,* 21-28.

Breitbart, W., Poppito, S., Rosenfeld, B., Vickers, A. J., Li, Y. Abbey, J., Olden, M., et al. (2012). Pilot randomized controlled trial of individual meaning-centered psychotherapy for patients with advanced cancer. *Journal of Clinical Oncology, 30,* 1304-1309.

Breitbart, W. S. & Poppito, S. R. (2014a). *Meaning-centered group psychotherapy for patients with advanced cancer, a treatment manual.* NY: Oxford University Press.

Breitbart, W. S. & Poppito, S. R. (2014b). *Meaning-centered individual psychotherapy for patients with advanced cancer, a treatment manual.* NY: Oxford University Press.

Breitbart, W., Rosenfeld, B., Pessin, H., Applebaum, A., Kulikowski, J., & Lichtenthal, W. G. (2015). Meaning-centered group psychotherapy: An effective intervention for improving psychological well-being in patients with advanced cancer. *Journal of Clinical Oncology, 33,* 749-754. doi: 10.1200/JCO.2014.57.2198.

Borysenko, J. (1988). *Minding the body, mending the mind.* NY: Bantam.

Crumbaugh, J. C., & Maholick, L. T. (1964). An experimental study in existentialism: The psychometric approach to Frankl's concept of noogenic neurosis. *Journal of Clinical Psychology,* 20, 200-207.

Crumbaugh, J. C. (1971). Frankl's logotherapy: A new orientation in counseling. *Journal of Religion and Health,* 10, 373-386.

Crumbaugh, J. C. (1977). The seeking of noetic goals test (SONG): A complementary scale to the Purpose in Life test (PIL). *Journal of Clinical Psychology,* 33, 900-907.

Crumbaugh, J. C. & Henrion R. (1994). The ecce homo technique: A special case of dereflection. *The International Forum for Logotherapy,* 17, 1-7.

Dezelic, M. S. (2014a). Logotherapy & existential analysis: A meaning-centered and spiritually integrated psychotherapy, applicable across clinical settings. *Foundation Theology, 2014,* 93-121.

Dezelic, M. S. (2014b). *Meaning-centered therapy workbook: Based on Viktor Frankl's logotherapy and existential analysis.* San Rafael, CA: Palace Printing and Design.

Dezelic, M. S. (2014c). Meaning constructions model: Through a bio-psycho-social-spiritual context. *Dezelic & Associates, Inc.* Retrieved from http://www.drmariedezelic.com/#!meaning-constructions-model/c1oe6.

Ernzen, F. (1990). Frankl's mountain range exercise: A Logotherapy activity for small groups. *International Forum for Logotherapy,* 13(2), 133-134.

Fabry, J. (1988). *Guideposts to meaning: Discovering what really matters.* Oakland, CA: New Harbinger Publications, Inc.

Fabry, J. B. (2013). *The pursuit of meaning: Viktor Frankl, logotherapy, and life.* Birmingham, AL: Purpose Research.

Fehr, S. S. (2003). *Introduction to group therapy: A practical guide (2nd Ed.).* New York: The Haworth Press, Inc.

Frankl, V. E. (1978). *The unheard cry for meaning: Psychotherapy and humanism.* New York: Simon and Schuster, Inc.

Frankl, V. E. (1986). *The doctor and the soul: From psychotherapy to logotherapy (2nd Vintage Books Ed.).* New York: Random House, Inc.

Frankl, V. E. (1988). *The will to meaning: Foundations and applications of logotherapy (Expanded Ed.).* New York: Penguin Books USA Inc.

Frankl, V. E. (2000). *Man's search for ultimate meaning.* New York: Perseus Publishing.

Frankl, V. E. (2004). *On the theory and therapy of mental disorders: An introduction to logotherapy and existential analysis (James M. Dubois, Translation).* New York: Brunner-Routledge.

Frankl, V. E. (2006). *Man's search for meaning.* Boston, Massachusetts: Beacon Press.

Gomez de Perez Underzo, L. (1990). An example of a logotherapuetic doctor-patient relationship. *The International Forum for Logotherapy,* 8, 112-114.

Gould, W. B. (1987). Scheler's 'philosophy of the heart' and Frankl's understanding of the self. *The International Forum for Logotherapy,* 10(2), 118-123.

Graber, A. V. (2004). *Viktor Frankl's logotherapy: Method of choice in ecumenical pastoral psychology (2nd Ed.).* Lima, Ohio: Wyndham Hall Press.

Graber, A. V. (2009). *The journey home: Preparing for life's ultimate adventure.* Birmingham, Alabama: LogoLife Press.

Graber, A. V. & Madsen, M. (2010). *Journey to your interior castle (recording).* St. Louis, Missouri: Midnight Sunburst Music and Recording Studio.

Hablas, R., & Hutzell, R. (1982). The Life Purpose Questionnaire: An alternative to the Purpose-in-Life test for geriatric, neuropsychiatric patients. *In S. A. Wawrytko (Ed.), Analecta Frankliana: The proceedings of the First World Congress of Logotherapy,* 211-215. Berkeley, CA: Strawberry Hill.

Halama, P. (2009). Research instruments for investigating meaning of life and other logotherapuetic constructs. In A. Batthyany & J. Levinson, (Eds.), *Existential psychotherapy of meaning,* 415-444. Phoenix, AZ: Zeig, Tucker & Theisen, Inc.

Henrion, R. (1987). Making Logotherapy a reality in treating alcoholics. *The International Forum for Logotherapy,* 10(2), 112-117.

Henrion, R. (2002). Alcohol use disorders: Alcohol dependence. *The International Forum for Logotherapy,* 25, 30-38.

Henrion, R., Stephanies C., & Hutzell, R R. (2006). *Franklian psychology: Theory and therapy of mental disorders.* Abilene, Texas: Viktor Frankl Institute of Logotherapy.

Hutzell, R. R. (1986). Meaning and purpose in life: Assessment techniques of logotherapy. *The Hospice Journal,* 2, 37-50.

Hutzell, R. R. & Peterson, T. J. (1986). Use of the life purpose questionnaire with an alcoholic population. *International Journal of Addiction,* 21(1), 51-57.

Hutzell, R. R. (1988). A review of the Purpose in Life test. *The International Forum for Logotherapy,* 11, 89-101.

Hutzell, R. R. (1989). *Life Purpose Questionnaire overview sheet.* Berkeley, CA: Institute of Logotherapy Press.

Hutzell, R. R. (2002). A general course of group logoanalysis. *Journal: Viktor Frankl Foundation of South Africa,* 7, 15-26.

Hutzell, R. R. & Eggert, M. D. (2009). *A workbook to increase your meaningful and purposeful goals (MPGs).* PDF Edition. Retrieved from http://www.viktorfrankl.org/source/hutzell_workbook_2009.pdf

Kimble, M. A., (Ed.). (2007). *Viktor Frankl's contribution to spirituality and aging.* Binghamton, New York: The Haworth Press, Inc.

Kish, G. B., & Moody, D. R. (1989). Psychopathology and life purpose. *The International Forum for Logotherapy,* 12, 40-45.

Lukas, E. (1979). The 'ideal' logotherapist—three contradictions. *The International Forum for Logotherapy,* 3, 3-7.

Lukas, E. (1982). The 'birthmarks' of paradoxical intention. *The International Forum for Logotherapy,* 15, 20-25.

Lukas, E. (1990). Overcoming the 'tragic triad.' *The International Forum for Logotherapy,* 2, 89-96.

Lukas, E. (2000). *Logotherapy textbook: Meaning-centered psychotherapy consistent with the principles outlined by Viktor E. Frankl, MD, Concept of human beings and methods in logotherapy (Theodor Brugger, Translation).* Toronto, Canada: Liberty Press.

Lukas, E. (2014). *Meaning in suffering: Comfort in crisis through Logotherapy (Joseph Fabry, Translation).* Birmingham, AL: Purpose Research.

Merriam-Webster (2005). *Merriam-Webster's Collegiate Dictionary.* Springfield, MA: Merriam-Webster Inc.

Marshall, M. & Marshall, E. (2012). *Logotherapy revisited: Review of the tenets of Viktor E. Frankl's logotherapy.* Ottawa: Ottawa Institute of Logotherapy.

May, R. (1994). *The courage to create.* New York: W. W. Norton & Company Ltd.

May, R., Angel, E. & Ellenberger, H. F. (Eds). 1958. *Existence.* New York: Rowman & Littlefield Publishers, Inc.

Melton, A. M. A., & Schulenberg, S. E. (2007). On the relationship between meaning in life and boredom proneness: Examining a logotherapy postulate. *Psychology Reports,* 101, 1016-1022.

Moomal, Z. (1999). The relationship between meaning in life and mental well-being. *South African Journal of Psychology,* 29, 36-41.

Moore, C. (1989). The use of visible metaphor in logotherapy. *International Forum for Logotherapy,* 21(2), 85-90.

Phillips, W. M. (1980). Purpose in life, depression, and locus of control. *Journal of Clinical Psychology,* 36, 661-667.

Prochaska, J., Norcross, J. and DiClemente, C. (1994). *Changing for Good.* New York, NY: Harper Collins Publishers.

Prochaska, J. O., DiClemente, C. C., & Norcross, J. C. (1992). In search of how people change: Applications to addictive behaviors. *American Psychologist, 47*(9), 1102-1114.

Reker, G. T. (1992). *Manual of the Life Attitude Profile-Revised.* Peterborough, Ontario: Student Psychologists Press.

Reker, G. T., & Cousins, J. B. (1979). Factor structure, construct validity and reliability of the Seeking of Noetic Goals (SONG) and Purpose in Life (PIL) tests. *Journal of Clinical Psychology,* 35, 85-91.

Reker, G. T., & Fry, P. S. (2003). Factor structure and invariance of personal meaning measures in cohorts of younger and older adults. *Personality and Individual Differences,* 35, 977-993.

Reker, G. T., Peacock, E. J., & Wong, P. T. P. (1987). Meaning and purpose in life and well-being: A life-span perspective. *Journal of Gerontology,* 42, 44-49.

Rice, G. E., Graber, A. V., Sjolie I., Pitts, M. A., & Rogina, J. M. (2004). Franklian psychology: Meaning-centered interventions. Abilene, Texas: Viktor Frankl Institute of Logotherapy.

Robak, R. W., & Griffin, P. W. (2000). Purpose in life: What is its relationship to happiness, depression, and grieving? *North American Journal of Psychology,* 2, 113-120.

Rodrigues, R. (2004). Borderline personality disturbances and logotherapeutic treatment approaches. *The International Forum for Logotherapy,* 27, 21-27.

Rogina, J. M. (2013, June). Importance of second-order change in clinical practice of logotherapy and existential analysis (LTEA), Presentation, *XIX World Congress V. Frankl's Logotherapy,* Dallas, TX. jmrogina@sbcglobal.net.

Rogina, J. M. (2002). Logotherapeutic mastery of generalized anxiety disorder. *The International Forum for Logotherapy,* 25, 60-67.

Rogina, J. M. (2004). Treatment and interventions for narcissistic personality disorder. *The International Forum for Logotherapy,* 27, 28-33.

Rogina, J. M., & Quilitch, H. R. (2006). Treating dependent personality disorders with logotherapy: A case study. *The International Forum for Logotherapy,* 29, 54-61.

Sappington, A. A., Bryant, J., & Oden, C. (1990). An experimental investigation of Viktor Frankl's theory of meaningfulness in life. *The International Forum for Logotherapy,* 13, 125-130.

Scannell, E. D., Allen, F. C. L., & Burton, J. (2002). Meaning in life and positive and negative well-being. *North American Journal of Psychology,* 4, 93-112.

Schopenhauer, A. (1969). *The world as will and representation (E. F. J. Payne, Translation).* New York: Dover Publications, Inc.

Schulenberg, S. E. (2003). Empirical research and logotherapy. *Psychological Reports,* 93, 307-319.

Schulenberg, S. E. (2004). A psychometric investigation of logotherapy measures and the Outcome Questionnaire (OQ–45.2). *North American Journal of Psychology,* 6, 477-492.

Schulenberg, S. E., Gohm, C. L., & Anderson, C. (2006). The Meaning in Suffering Test (MIST): A unitary or multidimensional measure? *The International Forum for Logotherapy,* 29, 103-106.

Schulenberg, S. E., Melton, A. M. A., & Foote, H. L. (2006). College students with ADHD: A role for logotherapy in treatment. *The International Forum for Logotherapy,* 29, 37-45.

Shapiro, D. (1999). *Neurotic Styles.* New York: Basic Books.

Siegel, R. D. (2010). *The mindfulness solution.* New York: The Guildford Press.

Starck, P. L. (1983). Patients' perceptions of the meaning of suffering. *The International Forum for Logotherapy,* 6, 110-116.

Starck, P. L. (2008) The human spirit: The search for meaning and purpose through suffering. *Journal of the Art and Science of Medicine,* 8(2). Retrieved April 11, 2013 from http://www.humanehealthcare.com/Article.asp

Van Deurzen-Smith, E. (1997). *Everyday mysteries: Existential dimensions of psychotherapy.* New York: Routledge.

Welter, P. R. (2005). *Franklian psychology: Attitudinal change.* Abilene, Texas: Viktor Frankl Institute of Logotherapy.

Yalom, I. D. (1980). *Existential Psychotherapy.* New York: Basic Books.

Yalom, I. D. (2008). *Staring at the sun: Overcoming the terror of death.* San Francisco, CA: Jossey-Bass.

Yalom, I. D. & Leszcz, M. (2005). *Theory and practice of group psychotherapy, (5th Ed.).* New York: Basic Books.

Zika, S., & Chamberlain, K. (1992). On the relation between meaning in life and psychological well-being. *British Journal of Clinical Psychology,* 83, 133-145.

SPECIAL RECOGNITION

Information adapted from and embodied within this Workbook from:

V. E. Frankl's key works:

The Doctor and the Soul, (1986/1955)
Man's Search for Meaning, (2006/1959)
The Will to Meaning, (1988/1969)
Man's Search for Ultimate Meaning, (2000/1975)
The Unheard Cry for Meaning, (1978)
On the Theory and Therapy of Mental Disorders, (2004)

Meaning-Centered Therapy Workbook:
Based on Viktor Frankl's Logotherapy &
Existential Analysis
Marie S. Dezelic (2014)

Viktor Frankl's Logotherapy:
Method of Choice in Ecumenical
Pastoral Psychology (2nd Ed.)
Ann V. Graber (2004)

Viktor Frankl Institute of Logotherapy
Abilene, Texas, USA
www.viktorfranklinstitute.org

Viktor Frankl Institute Vienna, Austria
Scientific Society for Logotherapy & Existential Analysis
www.viktorfrankl.org

Marie S. Dezelic, PhD, MS, CCTP, NCLC, CFRC, NCAIP, Diplomate in Logotherapy, is an author, workshop presenter and educator, and has a private psychotherapy practice in South Florida. Dr. Dezelic sees adolescents, adults, couples, and families, and travels nationally and internationally for crisis intervention. Her clinical research and work focuses on trauma, grief, spirituality, and psycho-oncology through an integrative Existential framework. In addition to her Diplomate in Logotherapy credential from the Viktor Frankl Institute of Logotherapy in the USA, Dr. Dezelic is an accredited member of the International Association of Logotherapy and Existential Analysis at the Viktor Frankl Institute Vienna, Austria, and holds several advanced certifications in trauma treatment, grief, spirituality, couples and family therapy, and several other treatment modalities. She designs and offers healthcare presentations on implementing programs and support teams using the holistic patient-centered approach to patient care, with an emphasis on discovering Meaning within Illness, Palliative Care, Psycho-Spiritual Oncology Treatment, Trauma Treatment, Grief Support, Pastoral Care, Spirituality, Compassion Fatigue and Stress Reduction. Dr. Dezelic has published *Meaning-Centered Therapy Workbook: Based on Viktor Frankl's Logotherapy & Existential Analysis,* writes extensively and presents nationally and internationally in various venues.

Visit:

www.DrMarieDezelic.com

Gabriel Ghanoum, PsyD, MDiv, GCC, BCC, CFRC, NCAIP, Diplomate in Logotherapy, is a workshop presenter, educator and the Director of Pastoral Care Services for a network of hospitals in South Eastern Florida. He holds various degrees in Psychology, Theology, and Business, is a certified grief therapist, holds a Diplomate credential from the Viktor Frankl Institute in the USA, and is an accredited member of the International Association of Logotherapy and Existential Analysis at the Viktor Frankl Institute Vienna, Austria. Dr. Ghanoum is passionate about bringing spiritual and psychological awareness through his national and international lectures and retreats on relationships, spirituality, positive psychology, and the psycho-spiritual approach to oncology and healing. He offers health-care staff psycho-educational seminars on various topics, such as Implementing Palliative Care Programs, Pastoral Care, Psycho-Spiritual Approach to Oncology, Spiritual Well-Being, Compassion Fatigue, Staff Satisfaction and Motivation in Healthcare, Trauma and Grief Support. Dr. Ghanoum is a member on various non-profit boards, and is deeply involved in promoting the mental health perspective within several charity programs, including aiding the homeless of South Florida through bio- psycho- social-spiritual care.

Made in the USA
San Bernardino, CA
07 October 2016